Movement Research

Performance Journal

#60

Gender Disarray

Movement Research
Performance Journal
#60, Spring/Summer 2024

Published twice annually
By Movement Research, Inc.
150 First Avenue
New York, NY 10009
212.598.0551
www.movementresearch.org
info@movementresearch.org

The Movement Research Performance Journal is deeply grateful for the visionary support from our LEGACY PARTNERS:
Artists Space
Center for the Art of Performance UCLA
The Chocolate Factory
Danspace Project
The Kitchen
Lili Chopra
Lower Manhattan Cultural Council
Performance Space New York
Walker Art Center
The Whitney Museum of American Art

MRPJ #60 EDITORIAL TEAM:
Contributing Editors: Amalle Dublon, Kay Gabriel, Keioui Keijaun Thomas, Anh Vo
Editor in Chief: Joshua Lubin-Levy
Managing Editor: John Arthur Peetz
Editorial Assistant: Nicole Bradbury
Copy Editor: Elaine Carberry
Design: spreeeng (John Philip Sage and Carlos Romo-Melgar)

MRPJ #60 COVER IMAGE:
Keioui Keijaun Thomas, *COME HELL OR HIGH FEMMES: ACT 2. THE LAST TRANS FEMMES ON EARTH: DRIPPING DOLL ENERGY*, 2021.
Photo by Hannah Patterson. Image courtesy of the artist.

ABOUT MOVEMENT RESEARCH
Movement Research is one of the world's leading laboratories for the investigation of dance and movement-based forms. Valuing the individual artist, their creative process and their vital role within society, Movement Research is dedicated to the creation and implementation of free and low-cost programs that nurture and instigate discourse and experimentation. Movement Research strives to reflect the cultural, political and economic diversity of its moving community, including artists and audiences alike.

Movement Research accomplishes its mission through a range of programs including ongoing classes and workshops taught by artist educators and innovators; creative residencies offered for choreographers and movement-based artists; festivals bringing together leaders in the field; and publications and public events providing artists with forums for discourse on a broad range of issues. For more information, please visit www.movementresearch.org.

ACKNOWLEDGEMENTS
Movement Research gratefully acknowledges public support from the New York City Department of Cultural Affairs in partnership with the City Council; City Council Member Carlina Rivera; Manhattan Borough President Gale Brewer's Manhattan Community Award Program; Materials for the Arts (a program of NYC Department of Cultural Affairs, NYC Department of Sanitation, and NYC Department of Education); The New York State Council on the Arts with the support of the Office of the Governor and the New York State Legislature; and the National Endowment for the Arts (a federal agency).

Movement Research gratefully acknowledges the generous contributions of private support from The Andrew W. Mellon Foundation; Dance/NYC's New York City Dance Rehearsal Space Subsidy Program, an initiative made possible by The Mellon Foundation; Davis Dauray Family Fund; Harkness Foundation for Dance; Howard Gilman Foundation; James E. Robison Foundation; Jerome Foundation; Marta Heflin Foundation; Mertz Gilmore Foundation; Mid Atlantic Arts Foundation Regional Resilience Fund; NYU Community Fund; Robert Rauschenberg Foundation; Ruth Foundation for the Arts; and Trust for Mutual Understanding. Movement Research is a member of Coalition of Small Arts NYC. Movement Research also acknowledges the individual donors and dear Friends of Movement Research, who contribute financial, support, labor, and love.

Thanks always to the clergy and staff of Judson Memorial Church. Judson Memorial Church continues to be a beacon for free spirits in the arts and politics, and a leader among progressive faith communities in the city and nation for over 100 years. Enormous gratitude to Frances Alenikoff (1920-2012), founder of Eden's Expressway, and to her daughter Francesca Rheannon and family, for their continuing belief in the mission of Movement Research and for keeping alive Frances' spirited example of what lifelong artistry is.

SUBSCRIBE
Receive MRPJ in the mail!
Distribute MRPJ to your Community!
MOVEMENT RESEARCH PERFORMANCE JOURNAL is available for domestic and international subscriptions for individuals as well as non-profit organizations and educational institutions. We also offer back issue orders and bulk orders.
Individual subscription rates:
2-issue: $24 plus shipping
4-issue: $42 plus shipping
Institutional subscription rates:
USA: 2-issue: $124 / 4-issue: 218
Canada: 2-issue: $218 / 4-issue: $148
Int'l: 2-issue: $240 / 4-issue: $450
Back issue and bulk order pricing available upon request.

For more information or to subscribe online visit:
www.movementresearch.org/publications/performance-journal/or mail a check to: Movement Research, 150 First Ave, New York, NY 10009

CONTRIBUTE
Movement Research, Inc. is a not-for-profit 501(c)3 tax-exempt organization. Tax deductible donations are greatly appreciated and can be made Online at www.movementresearch.org;
or by Texting "GIVE2MR" to 44-321; or by Mailing a check to Movement Research, 150 First Ave, New York, NY 10009.

MOVEMENT RESEARCH PERFORMANCE JOURNAL is made possible through the generous support of MRPJ donors, advertisers and subscribers. To advertise in the MRPJ, email performancejournal@movementresearch.org

Upcoming Movement Research Performance Journals seeking dance and performance-related topics and guest co-editors for future issues. Stay tuned for details, or contact: mrpjeditors@movementresearch.org

To contact Journal Contributors, please contact the Movement Research office or email mrpjeditors@movementresearch.org

ISSN 1077-0933
ISBN 979-8-9906299-0-5

A guide, a warning, a trigger

On page 50 of this issue you will find a reproduction of an image that was first printed in the *MOVEMENT RESEARCH PERFORMANCE JOURNAL*, Issue #3, 1991. The image is of a poster created by the artist collective GANG titled, "Read My Lips." It includes a closely cropped and detailed image of a vulva, along with text and graphics related to the ongoing battle over reproductive rights and women's bodily autonomy. Consider this your invitation, dear reader, to navigate that page in whatever way you must and by marshaling all the creativity that goes into the way you, like so many of us, guide yourself through the potentially injurious landscape of a world that is still so structured around gender norms and gender-based violence every level.

"Read My Lips" will be familiar to some—so infamous that the mere citation will be enough to call it to mind for many longtime readers of the *MRPJ*. Published amid the Culture Wars, a scandal centered on "Read My Lips" when the NEA threatened to withdraw funding from Movement Research for using government money for "lobbying." The direct link between aesthetics and politics instigated government backlash. But that same link also drew outrage from many members of the performance community who considered Issue #3 to be deliberately provoking the so-called "war," intentionally taking a political position that some worried might comprise future funding of the field. Several editors associated with the production of Issue #3 recall only Bill T. Jones and Arthur Aviles publicly coming to the journal's defense. The mere fear of retaliation and its easy mutation into a pressure to remain silent remains all too relatable today in what feels like an increasingly regressive and conservative cultural sphere.

In the thirty-three years since its publication, Issue #3 has developed a patina familiar to many artist-activist histories that are looked upon with romance and nostalgia, often by those for whom that history is only a fantasy (rather than a lived experience). For the current issue, Issue #60, we revisit Issue #3 attempting to move beyond this idealization by engaging critically with the original content. Under the direction of four contributing editors—Amalle Dublon, Kay Gabriel, Keioui Keijaun Thomas, and Anh Vo—we've assembled a new body of work by mostly trans and queer artists reflecting on the keyword "gender" and its relation to contemporary performance. Their work moves across multiple genres of writing—from analytic essays to poetry to performance scripts. While gender is a central topic for some, many more of the pieces in Issue #60 approach this keyword obliquely, almost evasively. Overseeing the editorial process, I can't help but feel this is somehow connected to the punitive relation one seems to expect will result from direct political speech today—as though it were just common sense, as though expecting anything but backlash would be hopelessly naïve.

Then again, there are more ways to understand what might at first glance seem like a refusal to speak to gender directly and discretely. Perhaps gender as a concept can only be approached indirectly and in relation to other ways of knowing one's own body, identity, and their relation to social life. Perhaps it's a way of defending against the demand to explain *AGAIN AND AGAIN* the fallacy of gender as a biological binary, which is its own kind of political sabotage, a tactical exhaustion of momentum towards liberation through weaponized ignorance. Certainly, the need to explain how things are can get in the way of imagining how they could be. The works assembled in Issue #60 do both—explicating a contemporary impasse while also theorizing alternatives, opening up to other ways of rehearsing a relationship between gender and contemporary performance of all kinds.

In that sense, I hope the following triggers something for the reader. Not in the way that word is often associated with a warning but rather with a release, the unleashing of an energy in its full force that exists in the field of contemporary performance and in the fabric of the world around all of us, that existed thirty-three years ago, and has existed and will exist long before/after now. This issue doesn't follow the line of history: it is not an attempt to ask what has changed, to compare then and now, to comment on the way things have progressed or regressed. Issue #3 and Issue #60 fold into one another, part of an ongoing body of work that is bigger than any one image, contribution, or issue could possibly hold.

JOSHUA LUBIN-LEVY

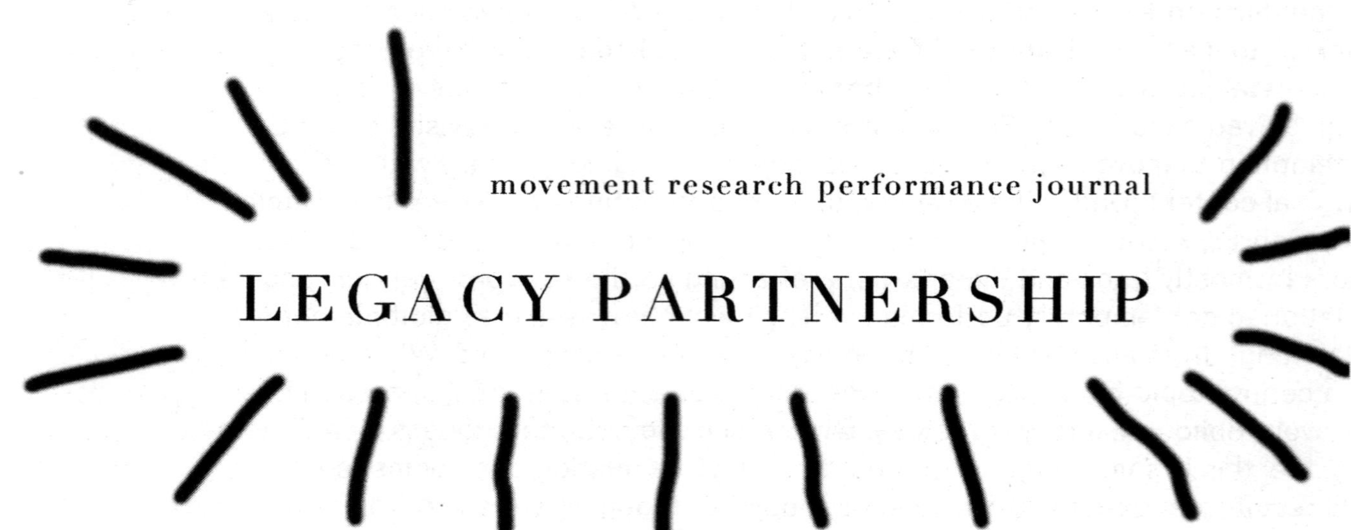
movement research performance journal
LEGACY PARTNERSHIP

Artists Space
Center for the Art of Performance UCLA
The Chocolate Factory
Danspace Project
The Kitchen
Lili Chopra
Lower Manhattan Cultural Council
Performance Space New York
Walker Art Center
The Whitney Museum of American Art

“Legacy Partners” are arts organizations that have committed to offering long term financial support to the *MOVEMENT RESEARCH PERFORMANCE JOURNAL* (MRPJ), a publication run by and for artists who work in dance and performance. These partnership suggest the fluid relation between the stage and the page (so to speak) as both should exist as venues guided by and in support of artists as they experiment with their practices.

Design Notes of Issue #60

In the design of this issue we begin to explore the relationship between the shape of these pages with the way you will *ENUNCIATE* – in your head or out loud – the words and images your eyes may come across. If the *MRPJ* is a conceptual space for rehearsal akin to the literal rehearsal space Movement Research provides, we want to contribute to it with an attempt to choreograph reading with the placement of, and relations between, objects featured in the pages, which create sequences of temporal and spatial change. Our approach is choreographic, seeing these objects – *PARATEXTS* – as devices that move the reader through the publication and orchestrate the interpretation of meaning.

While the drops of ink may have dried static on the paper, the act of reading will always include a degree of improvisation, a "set of vectorial forces in play."[1] This relational system, in the words of Johanna Drucker, "is always emergent and conditional, its values relative, its production of effects inexhaustibly variable and specific."[2] Designing with this consideration requires us to find what are the questions that will shape an answer we expect, a printed publication. In the words of João Fiadeiro, "[w]e know that looking at the world again as if it was the first time is an impossibility. But if we resort to the capacity we have to fictionalize the real, it is possible to look at ourselves looking at the world for the first time. And that is where we can put ourselves at the 'other's place', a necessary condition for us to be surprised anew."[3]

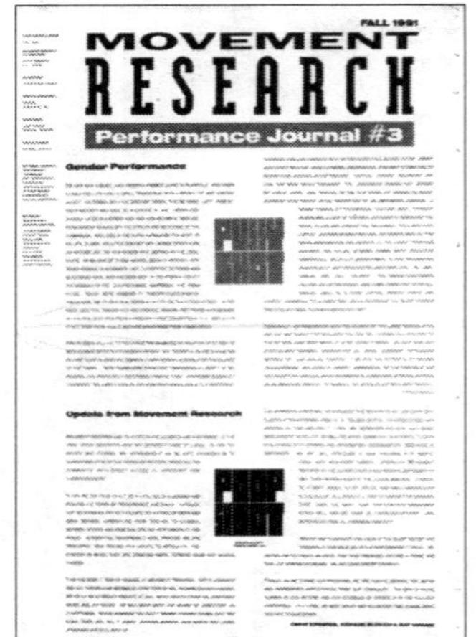
MOVEMENT RESEARCH
Performance Journal #3
FALL 1991

GENDER DISARRAY looks into issue #3, the *GENDER ISSUE*, choosing to explore transtextuality as the primary gesture featured in the design of the issue. Transtextuality, according to Gérard Genette, transtextuality is "everything that brings a text into relation (manifest or hidden) with other texts".[4] For Issue #60, we retrofit formal elements and design decisions from issue #3, creating meaningful collisions with the current contents. We have collected elements ranging from details like folios and signatures, to structural devices like the use of marginalia, carousel image sequences, and the development of a typeface aiming to resurface the heat transfer lettering works of Marlene McCarthy.

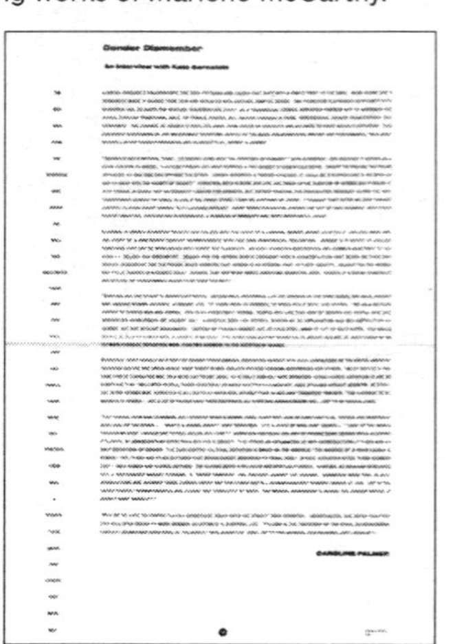

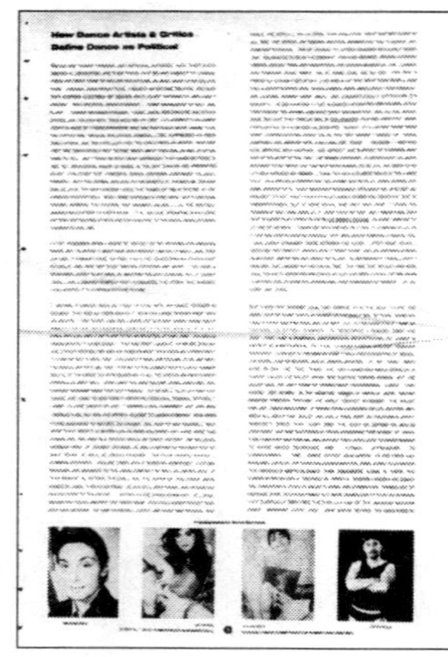

1 Johanna Drucker, *DIAGRAMMATIC WRITING.* (The Netherlands: Onomatopee, 2013), 29.
2 Ibid.
3 João Fiadeiro, *"PRESENTATION," REAL TIME COMPOSITION.* https://atelierealtextoctrgb.blogspot.com/2010/05/presentation.html
4 Gerard Génette, *PARATEXTS: THRESHOLDS OF INTERPRETATION,* trans. Jane E. Lewin (Cambridge, UK: Cambridge University Press, 1997), xv.

Amalle Dublon

Issue 60
Spring/Summer 2024

Untimely Transmissions

I am late turning in this letter because I started watching porn. Actually, I was already very late, and kind of stuck, and then the porn helped get me going. I needed to spend time with Annie Sprinkle, whose interview with Amelia Groom appears in this issue of the *MRPJ*. Amelia described to me a feeling of being in the presence of "a legendary slut," with fifty years of service — community and sexual service, as well as service in the religious sense, stretching back from Annie's present-day ecosexual performance and film work all the way to *TEENAGE DEVIATE* (1975), her first porn. I needed to feel Annie's presence too, and some time travel was involved.

The works in my contributing editor section — performance texts by S*an D. Henry-Smith and Geo Wyex, an essay by Zoey Lubitz, and the conversation between Amelia and Annie — each concern a delayed message from another time in one way or another. "The past inside the present" is how my friend Park described it, or the future inside the past and present. The contributing editors for this issue were invited to loosely revisit the third-ever issue of *MRPJ,* published thirty-three years ago, in 1991. Theme: "Gender Disarray." This visitation is both pleasurable and discomfiting.

When I first heard about Annie it was the late 1990s. I was having a little gender disarray of my own and earnestly studying what I thought she represented. Annie had been making performance art for a decade, and I was newly co-president of my high school's Gay/Straight Alliance, my highest-ranking office to date. I was also running a photocopied feminist magazine with two friends. The three of us wrote most of the articles, on topics like how it was okay to do whatever you wanted with your body hair, pro-porn feminism, and *THELMA AND LOUISE*. On St. Mark's Place, I bought an issue of *ON OUR BACKS*, the lesbian-run sex mag whose title spoofed *OFF OUR BACKS*, an older, anti-porn feminist periodical. I inspected it carefully, trying to get my cultural bearings. It didn't turn me on, which worried me: was I "really" gay? No matter how kinky the content, a certain edge of shame, fear, or vulnerability essential to my own fantasy life was blunted by the very mechanism that made sex "positive." Bringing sex under the redemptive halo of queer belonging somehow both neutralized it and made it anxiety-producing in a different way.

Inwardly, I was beset by bad faith: virginal, but ambushing high school health classes to protest the lack of adequate information about dental dams. How had I arrived at this delicate predicament? When Justin P. called me an ugly dyke in eighth grade, was the main point that I was a dyke, or that I was ugly? Which of these conditions had caused the other?

"Ugly" felt painfully final, "dyke" vertiginously confusing, an abyssal, scary little void of non-meaning, which I abruptly leapt into a few years later, without exactly knowing why. It wasn't because I was *GAY* gay: I had scientifically tested this by carefully examining my half-dressed peers in the locker room for a fixed count and assessing my inner state, which under inspection remained tensely neutral. Girls could be very pleasurable to be around, but this was an impersonal empirical fact around which all of society was plainly organized, evident on any tv show or billboard. I regarded their beauty, the skill and substance of it, with the kind of wistful respect I might accord an Olympic athlete, or a very tall tree. I had long hoped to be impossibly beautiful and powerfully seductive myself, but I was a tiny, aggressive person wearing a sweatsuit my mom had bought me. I went super hard in class and then ate lunch by myself behind the gym. Attempts to act on or reveal my aspirations (for example, by applying makeup) were generally mortifying.

If anything, I knew my feelings about boys and men to be somewhat closer to the compelling toxic stew of my sexual imagination. I wanted to be better than them at everything, I wanted them to want me, and I wanted to win. Whether Justin P. was beautiful was immaterial, since his judgments mattered, and his desire too. If I could be someone whose desire and judgments mattered, perhaps I too could circumvent being judged.

Thus I embarked upon the fairly short path to who I am today: a guy who has, broadly speaking, parlayed the reframing of judgments about value, beauty, and desire into the dubious pursuit of queer academia. I'm watching vintage Annie Sprinkle porn for work, and re-reading old issues of *MRPJ*, and having feelings about the 1990s.

In particular, I'm reading *MRPJ* Issue #3, the 1991 "Gender Disarray" issue, in which Annie's work also appears. It's nice to see Annie there, in boy and girl drag, along with Les Nichols, her co-star in possibly the first post-phallo transmasc porn, *LINDA/LES AND ANNIE* (1989). Annie also has photo credits on some beautiful portraits that invoke a web of relationships. Other highlights include a gemlike short story by poet Cheryl Clarke. Among the lowlights is a Jill Johnston essay that compares her feelings about modern dance to "how Native Americans feel about *US*" on the possible basis that the former was created by women and then 'taken over' by other dance forms. Interviews with two different trans guys, Danny and Vern, supply occasionally heartwarming answers to dubious questions in the name of "research into the gender community."

In short, the 1991 "Gender Disarray" issue is an emotional rollercoaster of continuities and discontinuities with the present — some pleasurable, some uncomfortable, and some a heady mix of both that is the special gift of being gay in the flux of time. Watching *DEEP INSIDE ANNIE SPRINKLE* (1981), by contrast, is more of an emotional Ferris wheel, an exalted, wholesome sweep above whatever angsty identificatory tangles might melt away below. As it opens, we find Annie playing a piano. She rises to show us her baby photos and divulges her given name (Ellen!), before the camera pivots to reveal two muscled nudes with silky bowl cuts who have been arm-wrestling forehead-to-forehead by the fireplace this whole time. There are orgies, another piano break, and a masturbation scene that, despite Annie relentlessly breaking the fourth wall to address the viewer, feels so genuine that for several minutes I really thought she just got carried away and was talking dirty to the camera operator. About an hour in, Annie appears on a midtown street at dawn, walks into a porn theater where she herself is also on screen, finds a seat, and begins consorting with the audience, like Athena arriving to encourage the Greeks in *THE ILIAD*. I love these men, my fellow fans, and can't help but feel that our common delight is at least a little bit about the sheer giddy wholesomeness of this plot twist.

The ecosexual turn in Annie's work, which arrived some decades later, bears out this unabashedly wholesome magic. When Annie and her partner-collaborator Beth Stephens perform an ecosexual wedding, "all the wedding guests can join us in the vows to 'love, honor and cherish' the mountains or the water or rocks or the snow." The sublimely mismatched scale of this union is a kind of inversion of the monumental sublime of Land Art. Maybe there are problems of scale at any wedding — the compression of various boggling incommensurables into the contractual vow — and that's why people cry.

I'm not sure if ecosexual weddings include the traditional acknowledgment that you're both going to die and you don't know when. The mortality, or aliveness, of the earth nonetheless coexists with the ways that mountains, water, rocks, snow, and sex all express forms of mind-bendingly dilatory time. Amelia Groom is an especially good interlocutor for Annie because of her own love of rocks and minerals and the ways they render time. She has written a book on Beverly Buchanan's *MARSH RUINS*[1] — barely-marked concrete-and-cement mounds perpetually eroding into Georgia's coastal wetlands — and with M. Ty, an essay on rust in art.[2] Time appears in these texts as simultaneous accumulation and loss, among other forms: rust, for example, indexing and ensuring a tool's removal from the rhythms of use.

Although I would love to be a diminutive bridegroom with an incalculably bigger, sexier body of water on my arm, the scale comedy runs alongside another version in which the ecosexual celebrants are understood not as individuals entering a contract but as entangled substances the vow invokes, as in a spell. Annie defines ecosex as the expansion of sexual love to an ecosystem beyond the imagined boundaries of the physical body. Sex fucks with scale, both spatial and

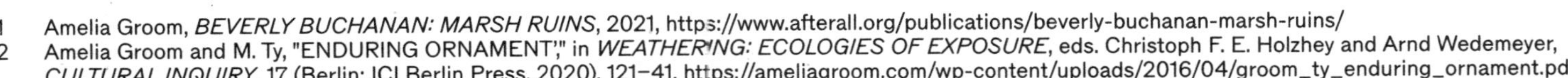
1 Amelia Groom, *BEVERLY BUCHANAN: MARSH RUINS*, 2021, https://www.afterall.org/publications/beverly-buchanan-marsh-ruins/
2 Amelia Groom and M. Ty, "ENDURING ORNAMENT," in *WEATHERING: ECOLOGIES OF EXPOSURE*, eds. Christoph F. E. Holzhey and Arnd Wedemeyer, *CULTURAL INQUIRY*, 17 (Berlin: ICI Berlin Press, 2020), 121–41, https://ameliagroom.com/wp-content/uploads/2016/04/groom_ty_enduring_ornament.pdf

temporal, as anyone knows who has found themselves enveloped mid-act by a colorful auratic mist or errant historical grief, not to mention the ways that bodies reliably morph, big people turning small and small people big, imaginary-real genitals becoming undeniably palpable to all parties, etc.

In their performance text, "astringency principle of the looking drum," S*an D. Henry-Smith shares and enacts these metamorphic powers with the camera and its tempos. Of all media, photography has been perhaps most captured by the framework of capture and fixity. S*an, which you can pronounce "swan," among other possibilities, manages a release from this bind. As they perform the text included here, their hands work the swish of flash and shutter, trigger the film winder's dizzy ribbon/snap, thump the chamber. Fitted with vocal, instrument, and contact mics, the camera resonates as it's played like a drum kit. Its breath or interiority fills the room, the way a drum does.

Watching this performance a year ago relieved me of a discourse on the camera as (masculinized) eye or weapon. Anatomies of its violent histories often understand the camera as phallic, when it's more readily a chamber or a sticky trap, its violations taking the form of capture as much as penetration or rupture. In any case, genital morphology as metaphor for violence is itself violent. Here is hope of another inside-outside arrangement — maybe camera as lung, with all that implies about respiratory exchange, rhythm, even wind instruments: "Akin to its operator, [the camera] must be treated as porous." The eroto-ethical question is how to play with oneself and one's instruments, or with what comes through them.

Unworking the camera as instrument of capture entails a kind of timing that is not conventionally photographic, but musical, respiratory, choreographic, and echoic, offering untimely constellations "conscious and unconscious to [the camera's] user at the time of exposure." It also invokes a different historical temporality. S*an sketches a glossary for "a language of proto-photography" which precedes and conditions the camera's invention -- "precedes colonialism, catalog, capture, surveillance," and survives it too, into an ongoing "creolization of photo-speak," a "burning latency" that remains to be practiced. At stake here is language's porosity as well — its mutations and its tendency to preserve and replicate unanticipated roots.

Strains of linguistic mutation and replication move through Zoey Lubitz's essay, "Language Analog for Trans." She follows Jules Gill-Peterson's argument in *HISTORIES OF THE TRANSGENDER CHILD* (2018) that the concept of gender plasticity found scientific and cultural legitimacy by way of a persistent analogy to childhood language learning. In both cases, the analogy goes, we come to fluency in a grammar that no one is born speaking.

Although it's come to be a familiar feature of how both the structure and experience of gender are narrated, the language analogy for gender plasticity has a longer history reaching back to sexologists like John Money and his eugenicist predecessors, who argued for the malleability of sex and gender, albeit within a limited developmental window and under interventionist medical oversight. Money's falsified research and grotesque abuse of children yielded an ongoing legacy of surgeries on intersex infants. It also helped establish and legitimize the idea that sex and gender are learned.

The language analogy pervades academic, political, clinical, and personal accounts of sex. A Hegelian like Judith Butler in *GENDER TROUBLE* (1990) but even more so in the sequel, *BODIES THAT MATTER* (1993), drawing on the same bedrock of signification, finds sex less open to voluntary determination, whether by terrifying psychologists or actual trans and intersex people. That's because the production of sex, for them, is much more widely distributed and ongoing, fractaling into endless little shards of signification, each a brief opening for slippage or aspirational obedience. The cumulative effect of these fragments is like a magic-eye picture: a wobbly illusion of coherence, that, for all its obvious fragility, nonetheless can't be willfully formed into a different image.

Ample personal experience of the willful forming of sex contradicts this idea. Still, it's always a satisfying topographical twist when one's "insides" turn out, yet again, to be an enfolded alien "outside." If we follow the language analogy, having a sex or a gender is an instance of what Walter Benjamin called "the foreignness of languages." Languages, plural. What Zoey Lubitz points out (and I initially decided to write this essay primarily so I could repeat it) is that the language analogy for transness contains a universalist account of "native language":

> The language analogy also relies on an unquestioned idea of the native language, discounting bilingualism, aphasia, indeed the arbitrariness of language understood through multilingual experience, through learning a new language, through translation. What makes a language native? The unquestioned performance of mastery in a language? Or the way one feels about the shape of language, not needing to know the rules and conventions, but feeling them? And then what becomes of this analogy if the primacy of a native language is really an affective structure, both a product of, and displaced by, historical and political exigencies or dalliance?

Zoey draws on Samuel Delany's novel *BABEL-17*, which takes as its central plot device and thought experiment an alien grammar that reorganizes the sensoria of its learners and eventually the form of the book itself. Perhaps we don't acquire languages so much as become infected and altered by them over time. I'm in agreement with Zoey (and to be honest, with some terrible people) that transness is plainly contagious. Sometimes it's in the air, to follow the logic of S*an's porous, respiring camera, and sometimes it's like anything good and delicious your friend is eating that you need to try, and then keep eating. Sometimes the incubation period is long and unpredictable, a small dormant germ that gradually reorganizes sense itself.

Zoey's essay is bookended by a series of car accidents, or near collisions — the kind where meaning is slow to form, and the world glitches and malfunctions as the grammar that holds things in place warps. What is that animal form, bleached by headlights, hurtling toward my windshield? Is that blood and hair on my front fender? What did that driver see when he swerved and yelled "hey lady" at me, a teenage boy? Is that radiating heat my own pee?

That which seemed impossible according to one grammar comes to have been inevitable. Should we understand trans experience as full of messages from other space-times, slips of the tongue that call something into being, linguistic seeds that grow wild and unpredictable? The call is coming from the future, or the past, or from inside the house; the inside of the house is an alien galaxy.

Geo Wyex introduces a further polyvocal variation on the sci-fi thought experiment. "D.O.U.B.T., a density" takes up the *BACK TO THE FUTURE* paradox of traveling back in time to find and alter a seed of the present. In this case, the mission is to cast a spell on a white ancestor who receives a visitation, a message piped into his timeline as if through a portal. He is to be infused with perpetual unrest, with doubt, "tiny stars to maul you for all of eternity. Doubt thine hands, thine eyes, ears, mind, thine mouth."

The spell is cast in a graveyard, the message delivered in the white ancestor's language, a kind of half-decayed "Shakespearean" English, larded generously with festering organic matter, fragments of baseball radio, and other lost transmissions, "a woven curtain of words and references." There's a lot happening linguistically, but it could be summarized as sportscasting performed by warlocks with community theater energy and Yonkers bagel store accents. In this confusion of tongues is a profusion of balls and fields — sporty, salty, slapping, aching, lumpy, galactic:

> The baseball field, the plantation field, the field of stars, the art field, the field work, the fielding of eyes or feelings. The balls on a body, the balls in a body, the balls of stars or planets, the balls to hit hard.

The long trajectories and high-impact collisions of these fields produce space dust of a particularly stinky variety: skin flakes, teeth, eyeballs, stage blood, splintered bats, intestinal gas. Geo's general insistence on flotsam and dreck is characteristic of Muck Studies Dept., the open-ended dramatic verse work of which "D.O.U.B.T." is a part. The rivers are dirty on both sides of the Atlantic, their churn unsettling the muck. The stage directions are very difficult to stage:

> *(SOUND OF A SUCK, SOMETHING THAT REALLY HAS JUST SUCKED, FOR A VERY LONG TIME, AND CONTINUES TO SUCK)*
>
> *(RELENTLESS ONCOMING RIVER CURRENTS, THE SOUND OF WHAT'S NAUGHTY, COVERED IN MUD, COVERED IN ECZEMA, A VERY BAD DOG, WHAT STINKS, AND CAN'T STOP)*
>
> *(ONCOMING RIVER CURRENTS, BRINGING RELIEF TO CENTURIES OF RAGE AND ABUSE, THE HOME RUN STUNNER, WIELDING THE SLUGGER)*

The particulars of rage and abuse are not recounted, a decision not to translate black suffering for white audiences. Neither is repair to be had. ("Repair! Repair? With my grandmother's hair???") Instead, the restless stirring of muck yields a strange refreshment. The oncoming river of muck might be time, both its accumulated sediments and the churning together of "multiple timelines in one scene" that Geo admires in the plays of Adrienne Kennedy. Since his earliest work in cabaret, Geo has shown a loving regard for theater — its people, its conventions, and the way it can hold in tandem "so many worlds in ways that feel less possible in daily life." Here, the deliberately impossible-to-execute stage directions stretch this capacity to hold multiple worlds and timelines past its limits, into another dimension: a fifth wall, a ceiling, a basement, a science fictional thought experiment. How to stage "*THE SOUND OF WHAT STINKS, STANK, HAS STUNK FOR A LONG TIME, LOUD SNIFF FOR EFFECT*"?

I admit to a bit of loud sniffing at the 1991 *MRPJ* issue. A sniff can be dismissive or investigative — hesitantly checking for appetite and/or revulsion, where they lead or come from, pursuing an ephemeral trail, following your nose. My friend Tina said the sniff is a fold. It's not just that you're tracing what was, "you smell your own nose a bit too. You can't pick up a scent without leaving one. Since everyone on the trail is doing this, one person's past is another's future." When I asked Amelia about it, she texted back to say she wondered what our present will look like from the perspective of the near future. You smelt it, you dealt it. I like how Annie handles it:

> we had a lot of fun. We made mistakes too. When *LINDA/LES & ANNIE* shows these days, I make sure to use a disclaimer. Same with my other videos; I need to apologize. People still sometimes want to screen those old films, like *SLUTS & GODDESSES VIDEO WORKSHOP* (1992), which is full of what I thought was respecting and honoring some other cultures but is actually cultural appropriation. In *LINDA/LES & ANNIE*, the information is way out of date. Rather than try to erase these works, I say, ok, these are historical documents, and I wouldn't do it the same way now, obviously.

Anh Vo

In 2021, my body collapsed from a severe episode of Graves' Disease, an autoimmune disorder that causes hyperthyroidism. I vividly remember the terror setting in one night when I could not stand up from the couch, having only enough strength to crawl into the bathroom, to haul myself into the bathtub to pee, and then slither my way into bed. Among all the thoughts racing in my head that night, I prayed that I would keep on dancing, no matter what; that if my limp paralysis happened to be permanent, I would not waver in my dancerly devotion to the body and its visceral unknowability. I needed that existential comfort to distract myself from the waves of shock unleashed by the sudden loss of movement control. Sure, the body is never under our control anyway and the body/mind split is always fictional. But when my legs gave out and my illusion of bodily autonomy was shattered, it was apparent that the fiction of control was more important to me than I'd realized. It is difficult to contend with the fact that, a lot of times, things happen to us. There is not much we can do, other than to surrender.

The bouts of paralysis in my limbs ended up being temporary, though my body continued slipping away from my grasp. One year later, I had a total thyroidectomy because my Graves' Disease was too aggressive and did not respond well to the first lines of treatment. As I was spiraling out of control trying to find oneness with my new post-op body, an existential sense of peace crept in. The thyroidec- tomy unexpectedly initi- ated a new chapter in my gender transition. I was on the operating table. I now self-administer hormone every day, just like other dolls out there. I joined the rank of mothers, aunties, and sisters who struggle with thyroid problems and hormonal turbulence. The surgery released me from the compulsive de- sire to prove my femininity to the world and to myself — even though I did not become a woman, per se, I was not so haunted by my own manhood and its ghostlike emptiness, passed down from generations of Vietnamese men who emerged from wartime so lifeless that they do not feel like real people in my psyche. By undergoing a ritual of organ sacrifice, I let go of the rigid need to reject masculinity and welcome into my life the expansive horizon of transness. The surgical cut into my throat paradoxically helped heal the penetrative wound of manhood. If gender is something that happens to me and punctures my being, the ritual of being opened up allowed for more improvisational dialogue, more alignment between what presses in from the outside and what I am willing and able to receive. Gender and I, we are dancing more with each other.

THE SURGICAL CUT INTO MY THROAT PARADOXICALLY HELPED HEAL THE PENETRATIVE WOUND OF MANHOOD

I am taking up this cue from Avgi Saketopoulou and Ann Pellegrini to think through gender allocentrically, not as a given interiorized truth within the self, but as a painful unending process of making meaning in response to the invasive penetration from the outside world. In their book, *GENDER WITHOUT IDENTITY*, when Saketopoulou and Pellegrini describe this process as "wildly improvisational," it also helps me circumvent the autocentric mode of improvisation that revolves around the individualized subject and its capacity to do things (e.g., with words, with the body, with gender). There is something wild and out of control about gender, which, if surrendered to, can bring forth waves of pain, confusion, and helplessness. For my guest editorial contribution, I wanted to stay with this existential pain of letting in what happens to us. My invitation is extended mostly to artists and writers in the Vietnamese diaspora, who bear the historical burden of wars and displacements. Maybe the fact of being born into the apocalypse of postwar devastation humbles us, crushing any feeble attempts to do away our existential fragility. It is impossible to do anything with this weight. Making do will have to be enough.

Kay Gabriel

WE'RE IN A DIFFERENT PERIOD OF PROFOUND POLITICAL REACTION IN WHICH THERE ARE ALSO, EMPIRICALLY, MANY MORE PEOPLE ALIVE WHO UNDERSTAND THAT THEY HAVE A STAKE IN THE THRIVING OF TRANS PEOPLE

The third issue of *MOVEMENT RESEARCH PERFORMANCE JOURNAL*, to which the *PJ* editors requested we respond, is comfortingly of its (1991) moment: an interview with auntie Kate Bornstein; research into the "gender community (transvestites, cross-dressers, transgenderists and transsexuals);" a strong and somewhat stick-bending emphasis on how drag isn't about sex change. What's changed and what hasn't? We're in a different period of profound political reaction in which there are also, empirically, many more people alive who understand that they have a stake in the thriving of trans people, which both centers on and means more than the ability of people to change sex.

In this section, I invited a roster of primarily trans writers and performers to reflect on social encounters and cultural forms that make life worth living, even as they also freight it with stress and challenge. More frequently than not, nightlife sets the stage for the encounter — Josie Bettman asks if "the nightclub is a theatre"— though the reason for this has less to do with the power of a particular space or musical genre than the fact that party culture, like church, brings people into contact in such a way that they can become something else through each other. The LEGACY Black Queer Production Collective (Kyle Carrero Lopez, Garrett Allen, Arewà Basit) reflects on "learning, growing, and building new modes of being" through the scenario of dance music, which reverberates well after the lights go up and the fog clears. Rayna Russom examines the longest interval of that reverberation — across life and death — observing that whenever anybody dances, they move as others have taught them to move, only some of whom are currently alive. The process of how people at any point come to understand themselves as a single political constituency is obscure, but not unclear. Aaina Amin insists: "later there is a we and it's waiting."

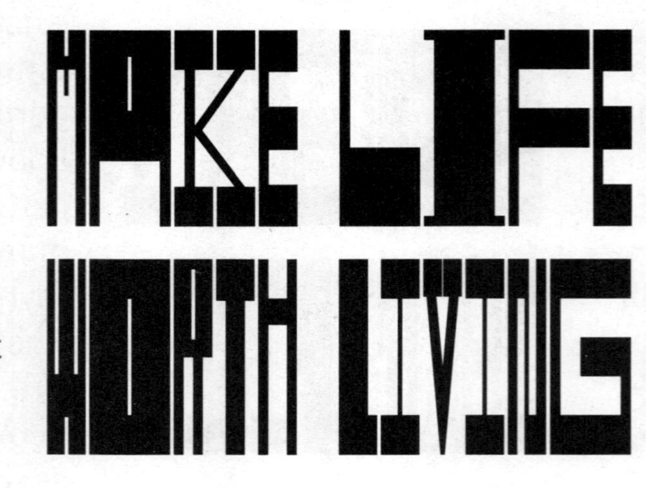

Keioui Keijaun Thomas

Issue 60
Spring/Summer 2024

i have been thinking about how to start my MRPJ Guest Editors letter for Issue 60, reimagining the Journal's third issue third issue, published in the fall of 1991, sometimes referred to as "Gender Disarray." As a guest editor, I wanted to bring black and brown trans and queer people of color who are thinking and making poignant work that speaks to how we exist, thrive, and move through this world, conjuring new ones in our names and stories. It has proven to be an experience in drifting through oceans of pages, swimming from word to word, under, over and around text.

i've always been compelled by language. i remember growing up and sitting outside in my auntie Shirley's front yard and listening to my aunties, cousins, and grandma Marva telling stories about growing up in my hometown—what some would call the deep south, although we were most certainly in central Florida/ Flurda if you nasty! The south but nonetheless not at the same time. Surrounded by amusement parks: Disney World, Universal Studios, etc. Storytelling has always fascinated me — the act of reliving and reworking through stories and the lives (my chosen family) that carry them. These stories live within my spirit, our chosen family's collective dreams; but stories come in many different forms. Nowadays, I take stories apart. i want to reimagine, rethink, and reconfigure how stories lounge and worlds are built, float and travel. How stories move — like can a story move through my body; can i tell you a story through my ass shaking or my back sweating or an image, a poem? Do you hear our stories in the drum and bass on the dancefloor? Do our pig- mented by melanin-filled sleeves speak our truths? I'll start here:

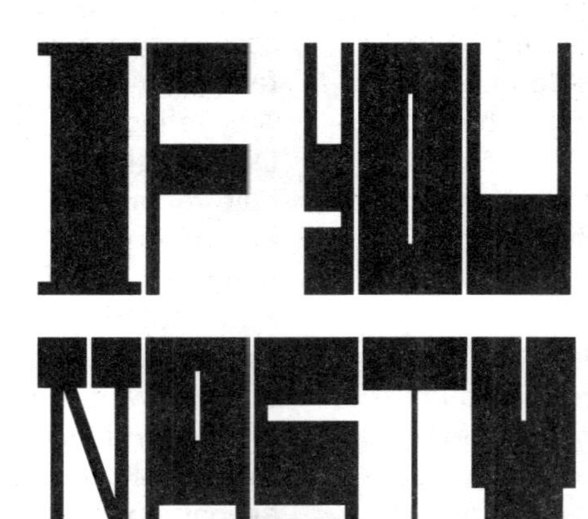

Can you please, aaattthhheeee, WAIT LIKE, a few minutes... seat with yourself and take a deep breathe. DRINK SOME WATER

–PAUSE– like... TAKE A B R E A K.

What I mean to say is breeeee- WAIT...

WASH YOUR FACE. REMOVE THE STRESS AWAY

SIDE-NOTE: IF YOU ARE READING THIS AND WEARING MAKEUP, YOU GOT A FULL FACE ON, I FEEL YOU, BOO. YOU CAN ALSO USE THIS TIME TO: WASH YOURS HANDS AND MOISTURIZE—
I KNOW MAKEUP IS EXPENSIVE. I GOT YOU, TOO.
A GENTLE REMINDER:
DON'T FORGET TO TAKE BREAKS. IT'S GOOD FOR YOUR MENTAL HEALTH AND YOUR SKIN... YOU DESERVE IT. WE ALL DO!
THERE IS NO PROPER TIMELINE, NO FINISH LINE. DO YOU :)
YOURS,

Keioui

IF

YOU

ARE

READING

THIS

AND

WEARING

MAKEUP, (...)

I

FEEL

YOU,

BOO.

YOU

CAN

ALSO

USE

THIS

TIME

TO:

WASH

YOURS

HANDS

AND

MOISTURIZE –

I

KNOW

MAKEUP

IS

EXPENSIVE.

I

GOT

YOU,

TOO

Movement Research
Performance Journal

High Fem, High Masc: Performing Gender in Colors

Author
HONGZHENG HAN

Contributing Editor
KEIOUI KEIJAUN THOMAS

WOMEN COLLABORATE IN HUNTING LARGE GAME IN 50% OF SOCIETIES AND PROCURE SMALL GAME IN 85%, CONTRIBUTING 10-35%

Can gender be performed? This question has preoccupied theorists, spanning the gamut from psychoanalysis to postmodernism, yet it remains elusive. Sigmund Freud offered essentialist conceptions of gender identity rooted in psychic anatomy, whereas Michel Foucault conceived gender as a construct devised to maintain networks of power and knowledge. In her monumental work, *GENDER TROUBLE* (1990), Judith Butler notably argued that gender comprises the sustained performance of socially ordained acts that produce the illusion of binary difference, subverting deterministic links between sex and gender. As conservative extremists increasingly weaponize discourse surrounding gender to undermine trans and non-binary communities, interrogating the performative nature of gender remains as relevant as it is urgent. Decades after Butler's groundbreaking intervention, their theories continue to insist we critically challenge gender norms and examine how gender categories regulate identities and bodies, especially ones of color.

Can gender be performed? Let's ask this question again. Butler and other scholars have collectively compelled us to conclude that it can, while pushing us to imagine possibilities that transcend the binary power structures that produce gender itself. This essay juxtaposes two performance artists on the identity spectrum's opposite ends: Keioui Keijaun Thomas and Matthew Barney. Witnessing their work alongside one another, new revelations about performing gender emerge. Thomas' work constitutes a radical reimagining of history in which the dolls (transwomen of color) are thriving, whereas Barney inherits and operates within a tradition that has amplified white male voices like his own. Yet Barney's influence has also shaped an art world where marginalized artists like Thomas can finally gain institutional platforms. This ambivalent dynamic inspires ongoing inquiry as to how certain voices are empowered over others. Ultimately, by contrasting Thomas and Barney's works, this essay aims to uncover invigorating perspectives on enacted gender and its emancipatory possibilities.

Keioui Keijaun Thomas is the self-proclaimed "doll" surviving mass extinction through resilience forged in adversity. Her work inhabits an Afrofuturism that envisions an empowered trans future, leveraging Surrealist imagery and blending satire, homoeroticism, and revisionary oral history telling. Contrastingly, Matthew Barney explores bodily transcendence and sexual differentiation, often incorporating homoerotic and masochistic motifs. Both artists work across media engaging themes of identity, performativity, and emancipation: Thomas directs an activist gaze toward speculative futures that empower marginalized communities, while Barney excavates physiology and the inner psyche to probe an individual body's transformation. Collectivism versus individualism, a notable distinction between the work of these two artists, can be located in the framework of the cultural and historical context of the Queer Black body in America.

Barney, a cis heterosexual white male, never needs to place himself within a historical/cultural narrative where his identity would face scrutiny, potentially being questioned but never silenced. Critics like Terry Myers pointed out at the time of his initial emergence that "Barney is perfect for an art world that prefers that its gay artists be straight, its black artists be white, and its women artists be men."[1] As *NEW YORK TIMES* writer Michael Kimmelman put it, "gay artists darkly joked about the fact that the most successful young gay artist had turned out not to be gay."[2] Curator Amelia Jones summarized it perfectly,

> Barney and Abramović, while appropriating tropes and strategies, such as performance, from feminist and queer art and theory, freeze the performative into objects or spectacles that can be readily commodified. Again, a few "queer" tropes or "feminist" appropriations here and there are fine for the art world as long as the work is still by an artist who appears to be white and male (or, really, "masculine" and "phallic"). Call this the 'Margaret Thatcher syndrome.'[3]

Indeed, the "Margaret Thatcher syndrome" continues to prevail in today's art world, leading me to think about disidentification, José Esteban Muñoz's theorization of a survival strategy leveraged by marginalized people, particularly queers of color, in navigating hostile cultural terrain — rendering (re)generative what might otherwise be deadening. Rather than completely rejecting or assimilating dominant ideologies, minorities disidentify, taking up cultural forms and repurposing them, insisting they reflect and refract one's own experiences and needs. Disidentification allows marginalized groups to reshape cultural production, enveloping forms encoded with heteronormativity and whiteness, refilling, refueling, and ultimately transforming them. In an essay on Jean-Michel Basquiat, Muñoz posed: "How does this young African American identify with a muscular red, blue, and gold and yes, white, 'Superman,' not to mention the pastiest of art-world megastars?" [4] Muñoz's query crystallizes the complexities of identification for minority subjects amidst icons of mainstream culture that fail to represent their identities. Pioneering Afrofuturist artist Renee Cox, confronting the absence of black superhero figures when her sons questioned this lack of representation, transformed herself into the figure of Raje to envision a liberatory black female superhero who shatters the status quo. Muñoz and Cox highlight the importance of disidentificatory practices, empowering possibilities to rework mainstream culture while rewriting history.

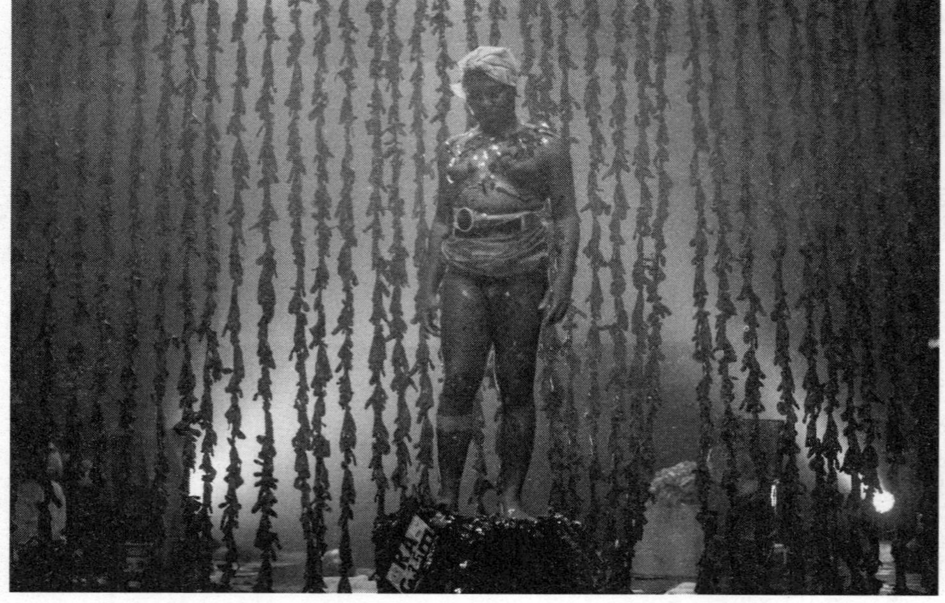

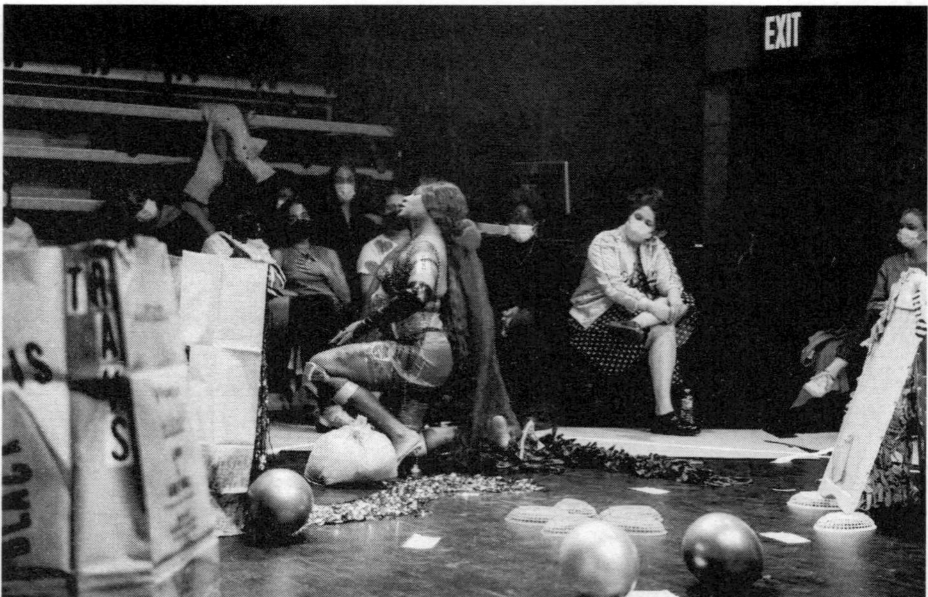

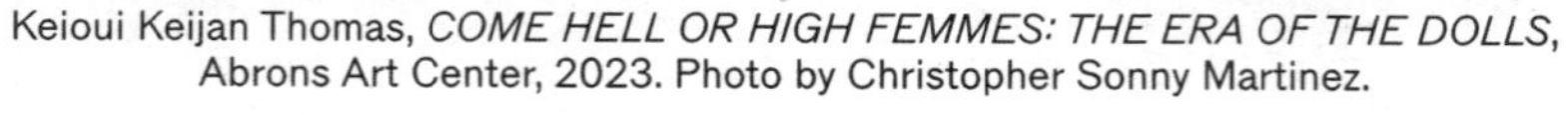

Keioui Keijan Thomas, *COME HELL OR HIGH FEMMES: THE ERA OF THE DOLLS*, Abrons Art Center, 2023. Photo by Christopher Sonny Martinez.

1 Ben Weaver, "The Athlete Is the Artist," THE LONDON LIST, November 12, 2020, https://www.thelondonlist.com/culture/matthew-barney.
2 Michael Kimmelman, "The Importance of Matthew Barney (Published 1999)," *THE NEW YORK TIMES*, October 10, 1999, sec. Magazine, https://www.nytimes.com/1999/10/10/magazine/the-importance-of-matthew-barney.html.
3 Amelia Jones, "On Sexism in the Art World," ARTNEWS.COM, November 18, 2019, https://www.artnews.com/art-news/news/on-sexism-in-the-art-world-4193/.
4 José Esteban Muñoz, *DISIDENTIFICATIONS QUEERS OF COLOR AND THE PERFORMANCE OF POLITICS* (Minneapolis: University of Minnesota Press, 1999), 39.

Thomas's gender-performing work traffics in disidentification as she continues to battle with the concept of "lack" within the Black diaspora. "It is so black, it is blue... It is detached and left for the faggot who can never be a Black man." In *COME HELL OR HIGH FEMMES: THE ERA OF THE DOLLS,* Thomas reinforces this interrogation of absence. Thomas parses and unsettles Black masculinity, revealing the alleged deficiencies that obstruct identification as and with true Black manhood. Echoing Muñoz's assertion that "the social construct of masculinity is experienced by far too many men as a regime of power that labors to invalidate, exclude, and extinguish faggotry, effeminacy, and queerly coated butchness,"[5] Thomas critically confronts her deviation from masculinist Black norms to examine further Black womanhood, especially for trans individuals.

In her one-night-only performance, *COME HELL OR HIGH FEMMES: THE ERA OF THE DOLLS*, at Abrons Art Center on April 4th, 2023, viewers were immersed in a dimly-lit interior bifurcated by a fringe curtain of camouflage fabrics. The area was replete with recycled materials — coffee beans, balloons, string, confetti, tape, cardboard boxes, plastic bags, pedestals, and bricks. This use of material carried metaphysical significance, but also carried metaphysical significance, aligning with Muñoz's argument that disidentification within the framework of the Black diasporic experience involves " the (re)telling of elided histories that need to be both excavated and (re)imagined"[6] Staging a no-waste zone, Thomas tangibly manifested her project of challenging ossified historical narratives and boldly envisioning a future where the dolls survive and thrive. Expanding on the concept of revisioning history in an interview with the *NEW YORK TIMES*, Thomas foregrounds thingliness, invoking the long history of "how Black bodies are used as disposable labor and domestic service."[7] The objectification of Black bodies propels Thomas to shape-shift; therefore, a new language of survival is born.

However, this doll is confined by duct tape encircling her joints, waist, and ankles. The indentation and redness caused by the painfully tight binding viscerally convey the constraints faced by Thomas as a Black trans woman. The ceremonial freeing of these invisible shackles proves intimately and collectively moving: Thomas approaches the racially diverse audience, asking individuals to gently remove her tape bonds. This ritualistic unbinding signifies Thomas' revisionary reworking of the enslaved Black diasporic narrative through a lens of solidarity. A twist comes at the end when Thomas selectively thanks and embraces only the Black attendees, pointedly excluding non-Black observers from this intimate communion. Her deliberate centering of Black solidarity cultivates a safe space and enacts a paradigm shift: rather than fixating on the white gaze, Thomas' speculative world privileges communal care and appreciation within the Black community. In the era of the dolls, Black folks are finally centered, appreciated, and loved. Thomas' art gracefully re-authors narratives of oppression into visions of empowerment and collective liberation.

In tandem with her video work, Thomas engages in a dialogical exchange with herself. Literary critic Geneva Smitherman describes the Black oral tradition of call-and-response as signifying "spontaneity, emotional involvement, rhythm, teaching, conversation, verbal dexterity, and humor."[8] Speaking in poetic fragments, Thomas conjures a temporal and spatial oscillation, responsive to and in the ancestral as well as the present. By vocalizing in a delayed temporality, this dialectical juxtaposition signifies the nonlinear entanglement of then and now, while foregrounding disruptions of history that (can) shape the present. Through self-reflexive discourse delightfully untethered from chronology, Thomas inhabits the liminal state between reverence for origins already lost and active resistance against current constraints as she chants, "Black femmes are the original teachers." The artist's anachronistic conversation with herself underscores both the ruptures and recuperations between diasporic history and contemporary identity.

Similar to the call-and-response elements in Thomas's work, Barney's most recent project, *SECONDARY*, also incorporates this style of verbal performance. Though signifying the funeral ritual, the chanting in Barney's video work leans closely toward its musicality and sound aesthetics rather than substantive meaning. Inspired by the infamous Tatum-Stingley collision[9], *SECONDARY* continues Barney's interests in the concept of the body and gender performance through a five-channel video installation. As critic Alex Greenberger describes, "Set across several screens, the installation would be easy to write off as another macho, pretentious moving-image work from an artist who dabbles in them. Yet it is so hypnotic that even those repelled by Barney's machismo will fall under its spell."[10] Premiering in Barney's Long Island City studio on May 12, 2023, the exhibition immerses visitors in disquieting tension, evoking the uneasy anticipation of violence within American football and American pageantry culture as a whole. Though based on a tragedy involving the paralysis of a Black athlete, Barney was still able to interject himself into the lead role as Kent Stabler, a quarterback on Tatum's team. Dancers Raphael Xavier and David Thomson embody the roles of Tatum and Stingley respectively, and navigate within Barney's studio with a deliberate slowness that is also rhythmic and athletic. Thomson, in his own testimony, taps into the vulnerability and innocence of the tragic figure, Stingley, which further amplifies the cruelty within American football culture.

Barney's use of Black bodies recalls Kimmelman's comparison of Barney as "a video version of Mapplethorpe; if he wasn't naked, he was, as in one video, pushing around a football player's blocking sled while dressed in a cocktail dress."[11] This invokes their shared appropriation of Black forms as cultural motifs. Mapplethorpe notoriously fetishized Black subjects, even admitting in a 1989 interview that many Black men in his infamous *BLACK BOOK* died from poverty or AIDS.[12] While Mapplethorpe's white privilege aligned with the socio-political climate then, it is crucial to critique similar dynamics today. The

OF

CALORIES

FROM

HUNTED

FOOD.

THE

FINDINGS

INDICATE

A

FLUIDITY

IN

HUNTING

ROLES

THAT

IS

CONTEXT-DEPENDENT,

RATHER

THAN

INDICATING

FIXED

DIVISIONS

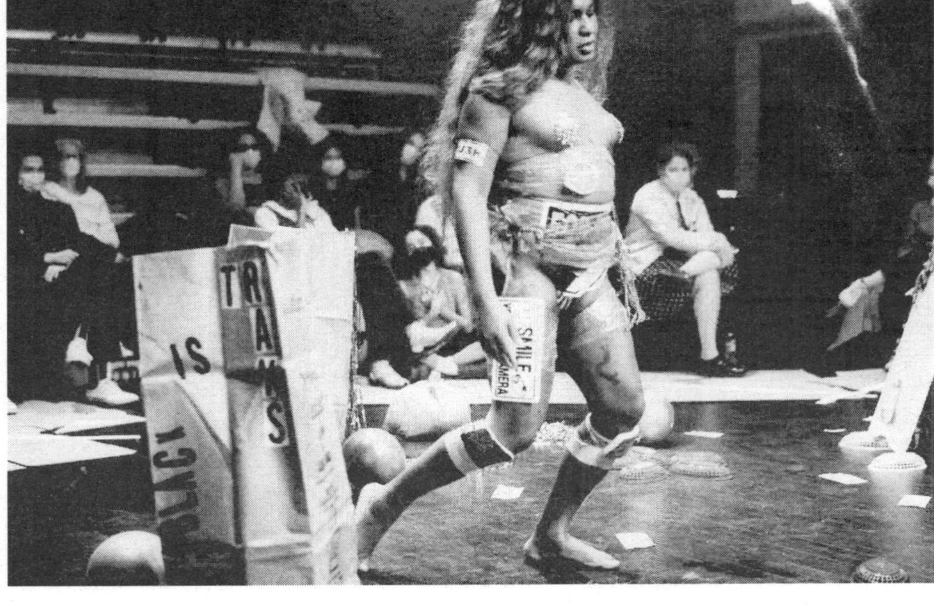

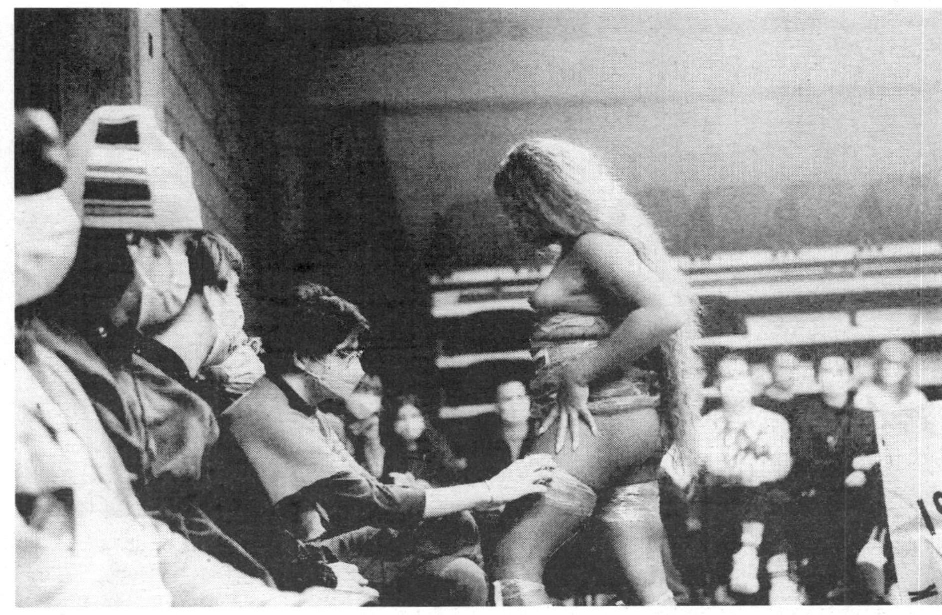

5 Ibid, 58.
6 Ibid, 57.
7 Laura Zornosa, "For Keioui Keijaun Thomas, the Body Becomes a Vessel," *NEW YORK TIMES*, July 13, 2021.
8 Geneva Smitherman, *TALKIN AND TESTIFYIN : THE LANGUAGE OF BLACK AMERICA* (Detroit, MI: Wayne State University Press, 1996), 104.
9 Darryl Floyd Stingley (September 18, 1951 – April 5, 2007) was an American professional football player, serving as a wide receiver for the New England Patriots in the National Football League. Tragically, his career was cut short at the age of 26 in 1978 when he suffered a spinal cord injury caused by Jack Tatum of the Oakland Raiders, who never offered an apology. Stingley's life was further complicated by quadriplegia, and he ultimately passed away due to heart disease and pneumonia.
10 Alex Greenberger, "Matthew Barney Returns with His Best Work in Years, a Shocking Video about America's Favorite Sport," *ARTNEWS.COM*, May 15, 2023, https://www.artnews.com/art-news/reviews/matthew-barney-secondary-review-1234667944/.
11 Michael Kimmelman, "The Importance of Matthew Barney," *THE NEW YORK TIMES*, October 10, 1999, sec. Magazine, https://www.nytimes.com/1999/10/10/magazine/the-importance-of-matthew-barney.html.
12 Dominick Dunne, "Robert Mapplethorpe's Proud Finale" *VANITY FAIR,* February 1989, https://archive.vanityfair.com/article/1989/2/robert-mapplethorpes-proud-finale.

second half of Kimmelman's analogy describes Barney wearing a cocktail dress while pushing a football sled, channeling drag and feminine personas despite embodying masculine physicality. This form of drag experimentation has historical precedent among cis white male artists like Marcel Duchamp's alter ego Rrose Sélavy but is rare among Black cis male artists. The dissonance suggests gender performances intersecting with racial hierarchies – white masculinity accommodates temporary feminization while Black masculinity faces greater constraints, policed by social expectations and power relations. Scholar Kobena Mercer critically assesses Robert Mapplethorpe's fixation on Black bodies, characterizing it as a colonial fantasy that generates ambivalence, in which racist stereotypes are undermined not by Mapplethorpe but by the spectator. Building on this viewpoint, Muñoz argues that gay men of color, including Mercer and Isaac Julien, experience a disidentificatory pleasure when engaging with Mapplethorpe's images, acknowledging the unsettling aspects of the black male objectification in which Mapplethorpe participated while recognizing the persistent allure of this pleasure, despite its political risks.[13] Similar to this notion, Barney's work evokes ambivalence, drawing cis white artists like himself into the embrace of the art world. Ultimately, a legacy of appropriating and commodifying Blackness underlies the work of both Mapplethorpe and Barney, demanding continued analysis through an anti-racist lens.

FEMALE MASCULINITY

Barney's *SECONDARY*, when analyzed in light of our recent societal awakening of race and sexuality, raises a pertinent inquiry: What are the consequences of performing masculinity, particularly for individuals of color? Bearing this question in mind, it is noteworthy that both Thomas and Barney share a common background as former college athletes. Thomas played football from a young age and nearly pursued a collegiate track, while Barney was recruited to play football at Yale University in 1985. However, it is crucial to examine the realities of sports participation for people of color and transgender individuals. Trans people's involvement in sports has become highly politicized, with conservative politicians imposing restrictive measures that not only target trans individuals but also impact cisgender athletes. A striking example is the case of Caster Semenya, a cisgender Black woman Olympic runner, who has been subjected to court rulings mandating the use of hormone-suppressing drugs to compete. These instances illustrate the intersecting and contentious dynamics surrounding race, gender identity, and sports participation. Barney's artistic prowess and institutional recognition are undeniable. However, there is an opportunity for him to further enhance his work by consciously empowering and amplifying the voices of those who would not traditionally receive acclaim for engaging in gender-bending performances. By actively sharing the spotlight with individuals who challenge societal norms but often go unnoticed, Barney's work could transcend conventional boundaries and attain an elevated artistic significance.

Thomas' work constitutes a radical reimagining of history, one in which dolls like her can endure and thrive rather than perish. Barney, conversely, inherits and operates within a linear historical tradition that has always incorporated cis-white male artists like himself into dominant narratives. Yet, the potency and influence of Barney's oeuvre have, in a way, contributed to shaping an art world where marginalized voices, like that of Thomas as a Black woman artist, can finally access institutional platforms and visibility. This ambivalent dynamic proves intellectually energizing for cultural critics like myself. However, it simultaneously issues a call for sustained ethical vigilance: an urgent need to continually hold benefactors of white supremacist systems accountable, while illuminating the oppressed and the invisible.

Recent research conducted on 329 contemporary foraging societies reveals the pervasive and significant participation of women in hunting, challenging the conventional "man the hunter" stereotype. Women collaborate in hunting large game in 50% of societies and procure small game in 85%, contributing 10-35% of calories from hunted food. The findings indicate a fluidity in hunting roles that is context-dependent, rather than indicating fixed divisions. This comprehensive analysis provides compelling evidence of women's substantial contributions to hunting in prehistoric human societies, critiquing the persistent influence of the "man the hunter" myth on gender stereotypes and policy through empirical data.[14] Combining these findings with Jack Halberstam's concept of "Female Masculinity," which explores how individuals assigned female at birth can embody and perform masculinity, suggests a future where gender roles and their constructions gradually collapse, leading to a broader understanding of gender diversity and queerness. While gender can be performed, it is hopeful that one day, society will move toward a state where the performance of high fem or high masc is no longer necessary, and individuals can simply be HUMAN.

HONGZHENG HAN

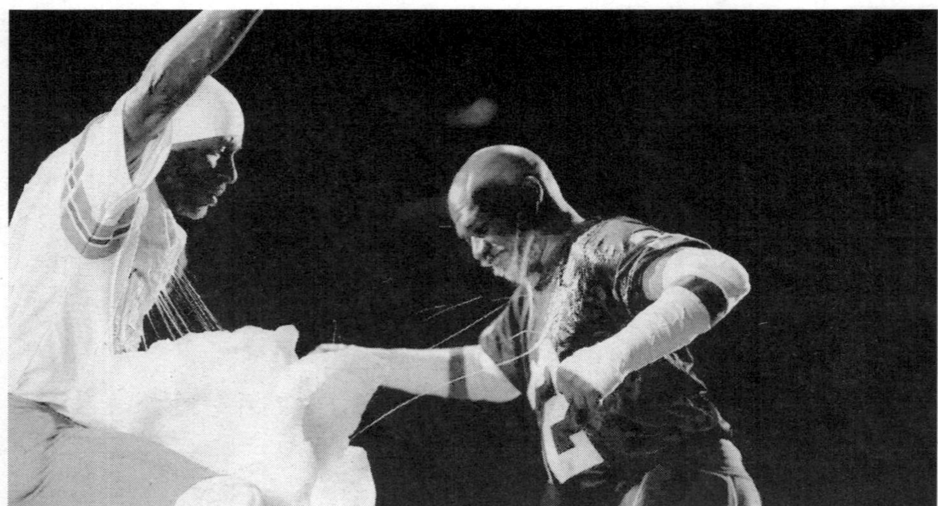

Installation view, Matthew Barney, *SECONDARY*, New York, 2023. Photo: Dario Lasagni. © Matthew Barney. Courtesy of the artist, Gladstone Gallery, Galerie Max Hetzler, Regen Projects, and Sadie Coles HQ

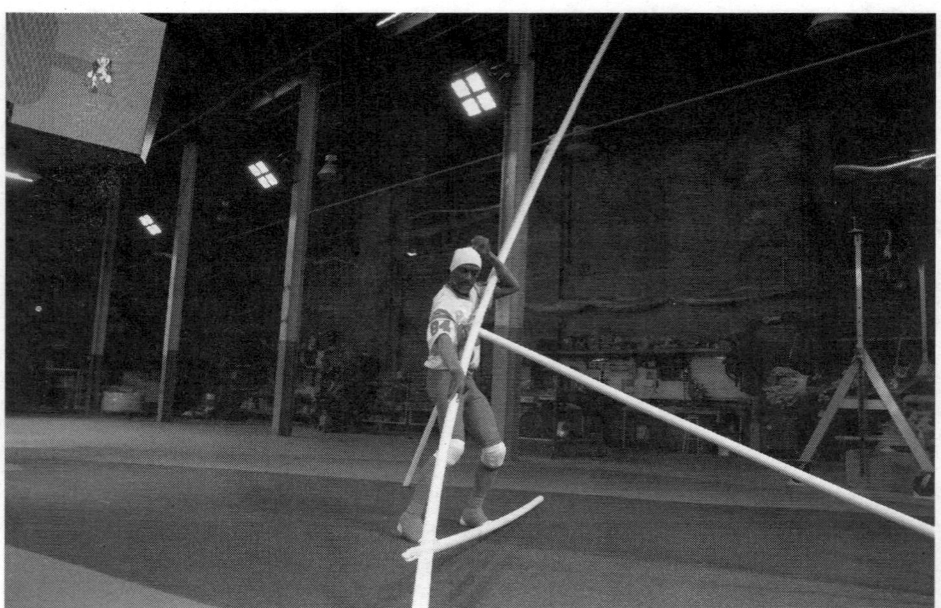

13 Muñoz, 70-71.
14 Abigail Anderson et al., "The Myth of Man the Hunter: Women's Contribution to the Hunt across Ethnographic Contexts", *PLOS ONE* 18, no. 6 (June 28, 2023), 101.

Chỉ Bàn Lộn* 2: A lexicon of queer and sexuality in Vietnam (excerpt)

Issue 60
Spring/Summer 2024

Author
DINH NHUNG

Contributing Editor
ANH VO

A

Anhsomeko: Playing with the slippage of translation between English and Vietnamese to ambivalently ask, “Are you afraid of your mother?” or “Are you into som (i.e., group sex)?” The speaker can safely gauge whether or not the other person is into group sex depending on how they interpret this question.

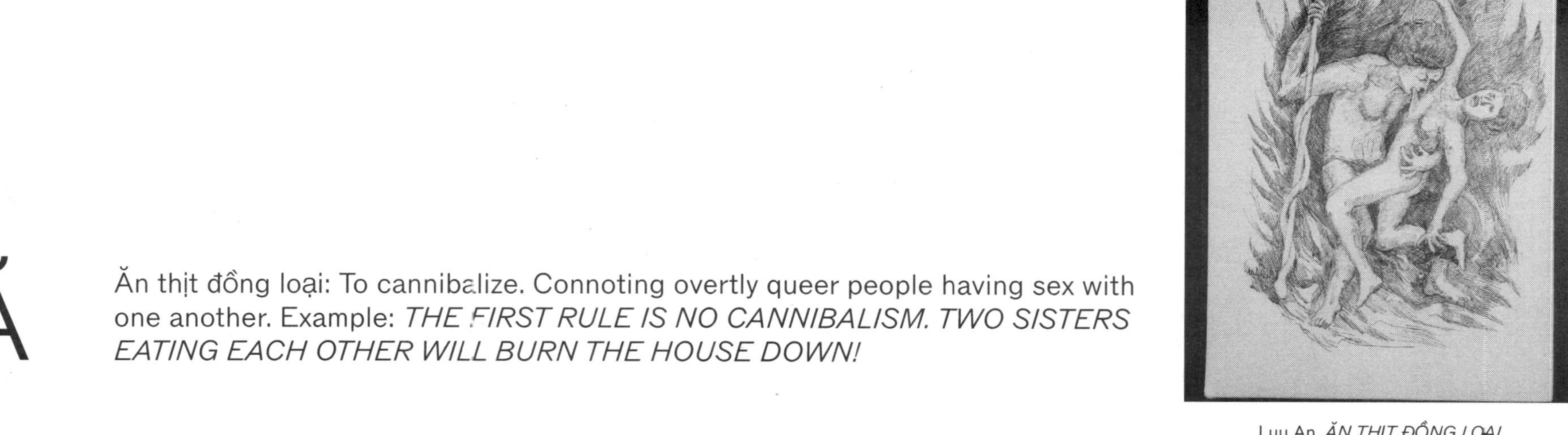

Luu An, *ĂN THỊT ĐỒNG LOẠI*.
Image courtesy the artist.

Ă

Ăn thịt đồng loại: To cannibalize. Connoting overtly queer people having sex with one another. Example: *THE FIRST RULE IS NO CANNIBALISM. TWO SISTERS EATING EACH OTHER WILL BURN THE HOUSE DOWN!*

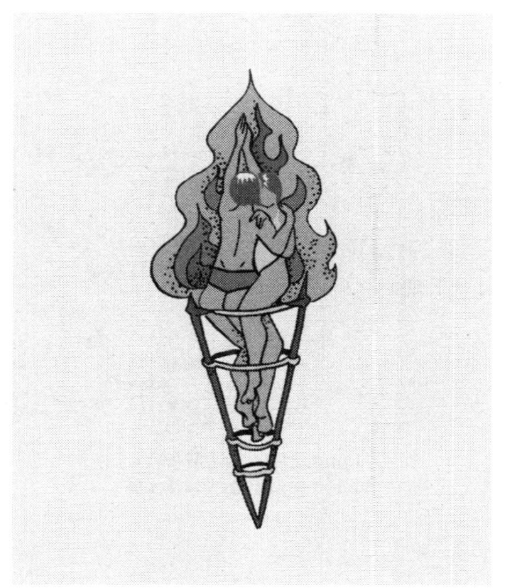

Bùi Nhi, *ĂN KEM TRƯỚC CỔNG*.
Image courtesy the artist.

Ăn kem trước cổng: To have premarital sex. Literally, to eat ice cream in front of a gate. A spoonerism of “ăn cơm trước kẻng” (to eat a meal before the bell is rung).

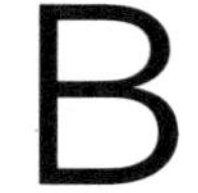

B

Bắt sóc bỏ lọ: Catching a squirrel to put in a bottle. A playful way to say handjob, deriving from the phrase “xóc lọ” (i.e., shaking a bottle or shaking a cock). “Sóc” (squirrel) and “xóc” (shake) are homophones; thus “bắt sóc bỏ lọ” becomes a more euphemistic phrase for handjob.

Bê Đê Sợ Mứt: Playing with the initials of BDSM, the phrase refers to the anxiety of shit leaking out while having anal sex. “Bê đê” means gay; “sợ mứt” sounds similar to “sợ cứt,” which means scared of shit. E.g.: *I AM A “BÊ ĐÊ SỢ MỨT,” NOT THAT KIND OF BDSM.*

Bóng cầm chuông: Literally means queers holding bells. A spoonerism of “bóng cuồng Trump” (i.e., Trump fanatic queers). Referring to queers who believe in conspiracy theories, fake news, and authoritarianism, who are Sinophobic and racist, fetishizing white people while discriminating against black people.

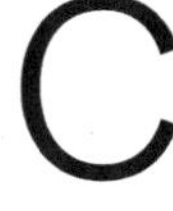

C

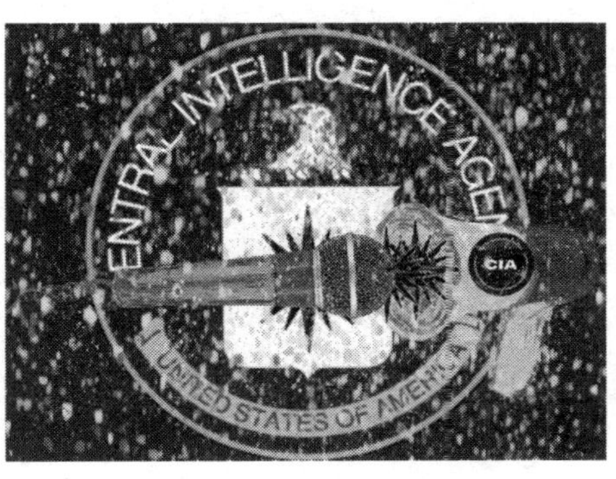

Mz, *CIA*.
Image courtesy the artist.

CIA: (1) Cum in alone, or climax by oneself. (2) Cum in alo, or cum in someone’s mouth. Vietnamese people answer the phone with ‘A lô;’ thus ‘alo’ refers to mouth. Massage and sex services often emphasize they accept CIA. People on dating apps can also ask one another if they like CIA or not.

Translator’s Note

It is an impossible task trying to translate a dictionary of Vietnamese slangs and idioms around gender and sexuality, whose melodic playfulness and visceral imageries operate on a vastly different plane compared to English. Translation is always already an impossibility, having to contend with what is lost in the passage of movement not only between languages, but also into language to begin with. As I spend hours and hours perfecting the translation with Nhung Dinh, there were no ways for me to adequately communicate the laugh-out-loud humor and subtle vulgarity of these 51 Vietnamese phrases. If only I could animate how these slangs dance with the Vietnamese monosyllabic and tonal linguistic structure without simply explaining them away and arresting their dynamic liveness onto the page. I try to tell myself that in the inevitable loss, translation also opens up other meaning-making possibilities. Though frankly, it is difficult to put trust in the analytical sterility of English to further enliven the playfulness of these sex idioms.

This version of “Vagina Talks” feels quite incomplete as it is onyl a tiny sliver excerpted from the 527-page volume of *CHỈ BÀN LỘN 2: A LEXICON OF QUEER AND SEXUALITY IN VIETNAM.* Nevertheless, *CHỈ BÀN LỘN 2* never labors towards being complete. It feels less comprehensive than it is excessive. There is an unruly additive logic to the project, with Nhung Dinh wanting to collect as many phrases and include as many contributors as possible — whatever fits can go inside. To me, *CHỈ BÀN LỘN 2* is not a dictionary of definitions to be understood, but a compilation of choreographic scores indexing the myriad possibilities of how language and gender can do each other. The invitation, then, is to do more with the scores, to listen to the improvisational linguistic impulses that might not be immediately available in English, to move with this translational impossibility, and to have fun while we are at it.

–Anh Vo

Chơi Cao Đài: Refers to a visibly gay person dating a closeted person, which, similar to the religion Cao Dai, makes no sense. To outsiders, Caodaiism is very queer because of its hodge-podge-like quality.

D

Dái trong: Literally, inner balls. (1) effeminate, not manly. A derogatory term for intersex people, trans people, or cismen who are overly feminine and indecisive. Example: *MEN WHO COMPLAIN A LOT HAVE THEIR BALLS GROWN OUTSIDE IN.* (2) refers to manly women, girls, or tomboys.

Duyên âm: "Duyên" can refer to fate, or unpaid debt/unresolved connections from previous lives. "Âm" means yin, or negative energy, referring to the dead. "Duyên âm" describes being pursued romantically, sexually, and often unwantedly by spirits. The spirits can be tethered from previous lives or from current life (e.g., an ex-lover who dies young). One can also by chance attract wandering spirits, who die single and have the desire to marry. Many people, especially queer folks, who are single for a long time, often get told by families and friends to go and get their "duyên âm" cut by shamans so that they can move on with their current lives.

Đ

Đóng mạng nhện: Have not had sex for a long time, or ever. Literally means fossilized spiderweb.

Ê

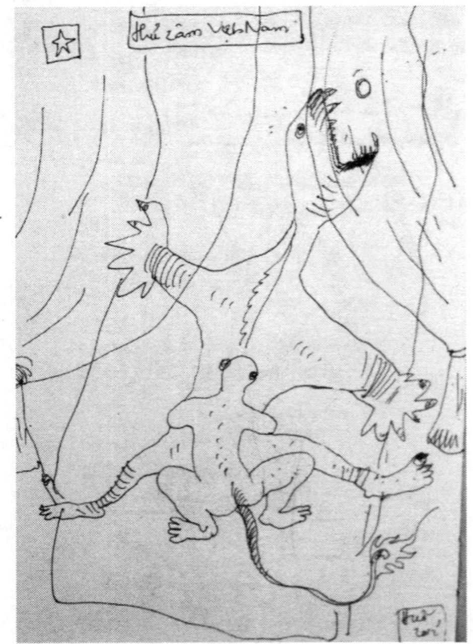

Long, *ẾCH ÔM MĂNG.*
Image courtesy the artist.

Ếch ôm măng: A frog hugging a bamboo shoot. Referring to a relationship or a sexual act (particularly doggy style) between a top who is much smaller than a bottom.

F

Fen with phịch: Vietnamization of "friends with benefits," which sounds more like "fend with fit." The simplification and mispronunciation of words generate a more melodic quality to the phrase. "Phịch" also sounds similar to "phang" (i.e., fuck), which makes the phrase much more direct than friends with benefits.

G

Gạo nếp: Sticky rice. It refers to a penis that does not get much bigger when erected. Similar to sticky rice, which does not expand a lot when cooked.

Gạo tẻ: Regular jasmine rice. It refers to a penis that gets unmistakably bigger when erected. Similar to jasmine rice, which expands when cooked.

Gu mặn: Savory or carnivorous taste. (1) Refers to someone with atypical sexual preferences, which can be considered disgusting. Example: *RUNNING RED LIGHTS (I.E., HAVING PERIOD SEX) IS TOO SAVORY FOR ME. I LIKE EATING PUSSY, SUCKING BALLS, BUT I CAN'T DO IT ON RED DAYS. TOO HORRIFYING. TOO SAVORY.* (2) Refers to someone who likes significantly older people. Example: *"THEY ARE TOO YOUNG TO BE DATING THIS WOMAN WHO IS 20 YEARS OLDER." - "DAMN, SUCH A SAVORY TASTE!"*

H

Hố đen vũ trụ: Black hole, capable of sucking in anything big or small. Slang for vagina or anus. Example: *6-INCH IS TOO DAMN SMALL. MINE IS LIKE A BLACK HOLE, SO WHAT CAN 6-INCH DO!*

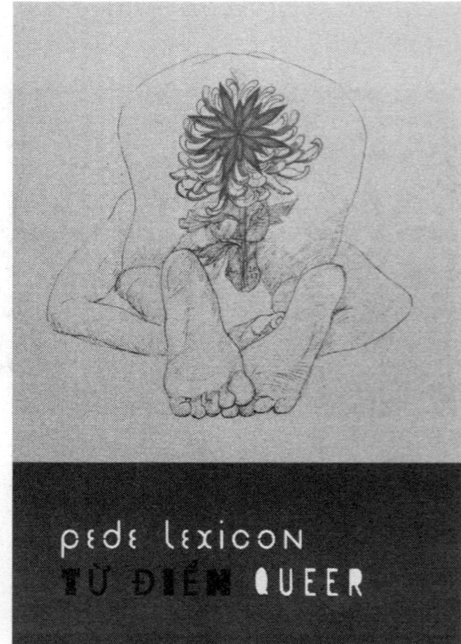

Luu An, *HOA CÚC.*
Image courtesy the artist.

Hoa cúc: Chrysanthemum flower, slang for anus. Gerbera daisy flower or sunflower can be substituted to refer to larger holes.

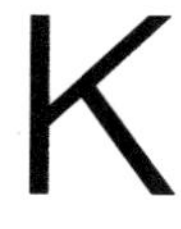

In Tư: Information. Literally in four (in = in, tư = four). Can be abbreviated further to "in4." Example: *NO BABY. I CAN ONLY GIVE YOU MY IN FOUR* if you take Prep.

K

Khoảng trống trong LÒNg em: The void in my cunt, which refers to the extra space in the vagina or the anus that cannot be filled by too small and short of a penis. Playing with how "lồn" (cunt) sounds similar to "lòng" (gut or heart), the phrase memes on the cheesy saying, "the void in my heart," often uttered by female characters in Vietnamese soap operas.

L

Lồn quốc dân: The people's pussy. (1) A communal pussy for everyone's use. (2) A pretty pussy, a sweet pussy, a model pussy.

Lộn cái bàn: Friends my ass! Literally means flip the table, which is a spoonerism for "friends my cunt." Can be used to express frustration at being friendzoned, or to direct anger at an ex who wants to remain friends.

M

Mạ vàng thanh kiếm: Gold-gilded sword. Denoting a penis covered in shit when having anal sex.

Mlem Mlem: (1) very delicious, very appetizing. An onomatopoeic imitation of licking continuously with a lot of spit. Denoting something or somebody delicious to drool over. (2) wanting to eat pussy. (3) slurping "oyster."

N

Nai bò: Deer and cow. (1) A derogatory term referring to bisexual or gay men who are in relationship with women. Example: *YOU ARE GAY BUT PRETEND TO BE A STRAIGHT MAN TO FUCK BOTH DEERS AND COWS.* (2) Denoting people who are naive and silly like deers and cows. Often used to describe straight women who fall in love with gay men.

Nằm phơi nắng: Sunbathing. (1) Often used by queer women to denote having sex. Example: *I JUST GOT SUNBATHED* (i.e., I just got fucked). (2) a provocative lying down position, bottoms showing ass.

Nulosa: Anglocization of "nứng lồn sảng" (i.e., imaginary wet pussy). Making a big deal out of nothing.

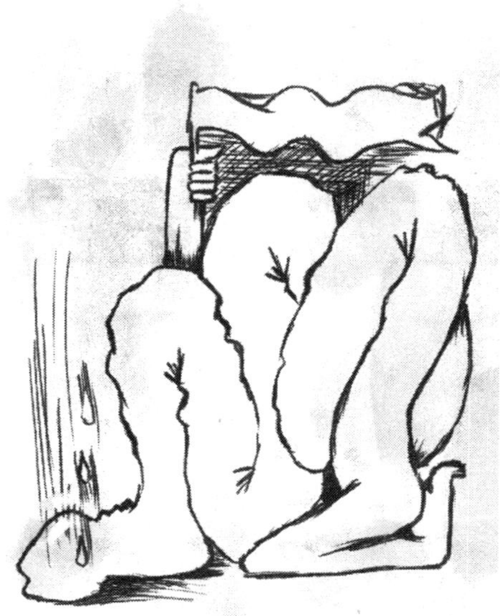

Dan Ni, *OANTALAVAN*.
Image courtesy the artist.

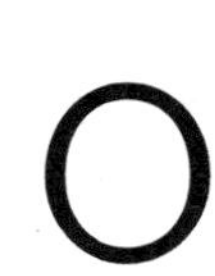

Oẳn tà là vẳn: Not straight, noodling around. (1) Describing a penis that cannot get hard. (2) Referring to a thing or a situation that is futile or just not right. (3) Meandering, not focused. This phrase derives from "oẳn tà roằn," first used in a short story by Nguyễn Công Hoan. Later on, in an episode of the TV series "Gặp nhau cuối tuần," comedian Xuân Bắc used "oẳn tà là vẳn" to describe a soft penis. Since then, the word is widely circulated in the North.

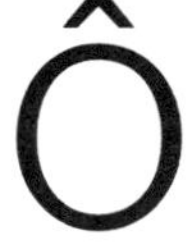

Ô môi: (1) Refers to masculine women. (2) Refers to women who have intimate relationships with other women. The term coud have originated from a tropical fruit in Vietnam (cassia grandis), as how you eat the fruit resembles the act of cunnilingus. It might also derive from "homosexuelle" in French. As a derogatory term, "Ô môi" is not often used by queer people for the purpose of self-identification.

Ốc xào: Stir-fried snails. A malapropism of "ông xã" (i.e., husband). Used within a gay male couple to refer to each other.

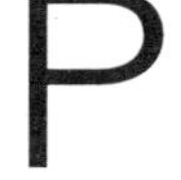

Pỏn: Porn. The word results from an unintentional mistake when typing "porn" using a Vietnamese keyboard. Compared to porn, pỏn with the tonal error sounds better and cooler, while also circumventing surveillance efforts by parents.

Q

Quay tay: Rotating or turning your hand. Handjob.

Que (dt): Stick. Denoting skinny long dicks.

Quể (dt): Queer. Similar to pỏn, quể results from an unintentional mistake when typing "queer" using a Vietnamese keyboard. Often used by young queer people to address one another. Quể also sounds similar to quê (i.e., rural, unrefined), and thus represents an attitude distinctive from the fancier and flashier queers.

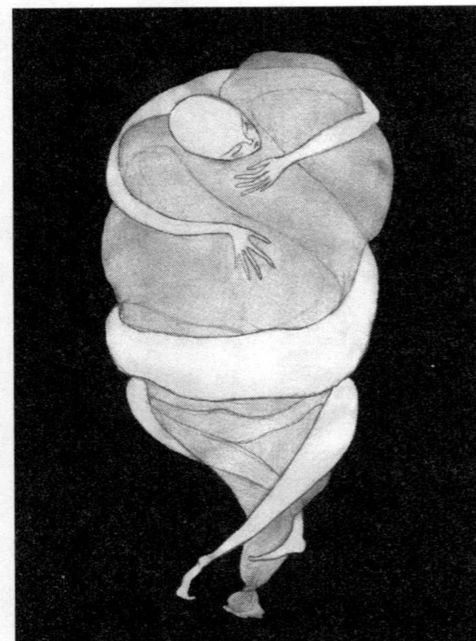

Sil Vũ, *UẤN QOÉO.*
Image courtesy the artist.

Quấn quéo: Being moved, feeling sunsick, having a crush on somebody.

R

Răm mặn: Spoonerism of "dâm mặn," which is a combination of being slutty/salacious and having a savory taste (see gu mặn).

Rớt cái đờn ông ra ngoài: The manly thing falling out. (1) Jokingly describe the bulge of a drag queen or a trans woman (2) Refering to penile erection in response to seeing an attractive guy.

S

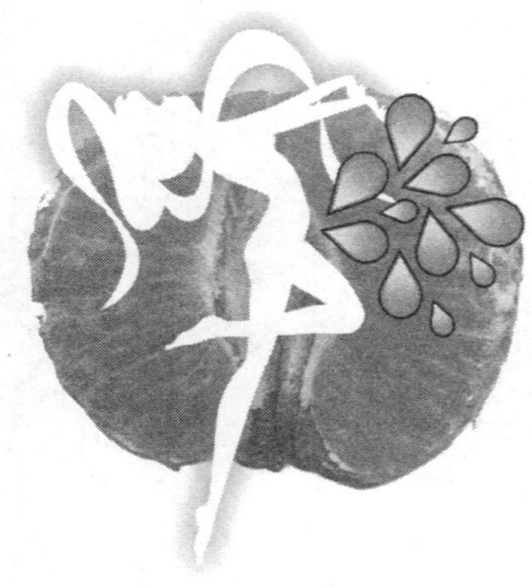

Dan Ni, *SỜ QUÝT.*
Image courtesy the artist.

Sờ quýt: Vietnamization of squirt. "Sờ" evokes haptic sensation. "Quýt" is tangerine, juicy and sweet. Example:

A: WE'VE TALKED A LOT ABOUT TOUCHING ASSES AND TITTIES, LET'S TALK ABOUT "SỜ QUÝT" TODAY. HOW CAN WE SQUIRT?

B: CALL A SPADE A SPADE — YOU'RE LEAKING WATER! WHO CARES ABOUT TANGERINES AND ORANGES.

C: LEAKING IS DIFFERENT FROM SQUIRTING. IT MEANS CUMMING. IF MY LOVER CAN SQUIRT, I'LL SPEND ALL DAY úp mặt vào sông quê.

T

Thà để thanh kiếm dính máu của kẻ thù chứ không để dính phân của đồng bọn: Rather have enemy's blood than ally's shit on my sword. Often used by straight men to express their disdain for gay sex. They'd rather have sex with women [enemies] and be stained by period blood than have anal sex with men [allies]. This phrase is also used by gay people to mock men who are scared of being gay for having anal sex with their girlfriends.

Thần Lồn: Genius cunt or vagina god. (1) A very talented pussy, full of tricks, too difficult to resist. (2) An expert on vagina. (3) Represent a supernatural force that brings bad luck.

Thông thống cho chuột cống đi vào: So wide that rats can run in and out. Denoting loose vagina or anus.

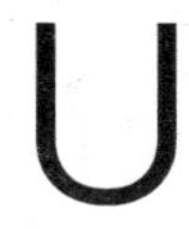

Ụ: An abbreviation of "đụ" (i.e., fuck).

Úp mặt vào sông quê: To bury one's face into the country river. To eat pussy or to eat ass. The phrase is widely known due to its immediate association with a very famous song by Phó Đức Phương, in which the country river signifies patriotism.

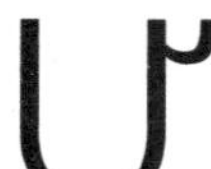

Ứ: (1) An onomatopoeia for having sex. Other variations include "ứ hự," "ứ ừ," ứ ừ ư," each with its own emotional implication. (2) Depending on context and the speaker's tone, it can mean no or yes in response to sexual solicitation.

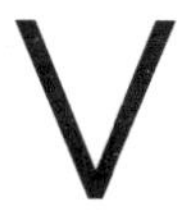

Vãi cả nồi: Similar to how "fucking" functions as an intensifier in English, many variants of "vãi," such as "vãi chưởng" or "vãi đái," can be used to enhance feelings about something. "Vãi cả nồi" is used to avoid using "vãi lồn", which literally means you feel such strong emotions that you drop your cunt. Instead of using "cunt", "vãi cả nồi" means you drop your pot.

Vailon: See Vãi cả nồi. Also used as an intensifier, "Vailon" is a euphemistic anglocization of "Vãi lồn" (drop your cunt), combining the syllables while eliminating the tones.

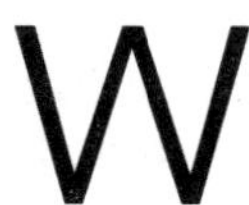

Weitei: Anglocization of quay tay. Handjob.

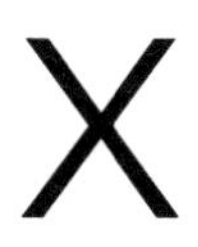

Xăng pha nhớt: Gasoline mixed with oil. Denoting someone who cannot easily be identified as a man or a woman, thus causing confusion. As a discriminatory term directed mostly towards gay men, it appeared in the northern region of Vietnam during the post-Vietnam-War planned economy era (1975-1986). At the time of extreme poverty, mopeds often run on gasoline mixed with oil.

Xì trây: Vietnamization of "straight." "Xì" connotes deflation; "trây" suggests laziness. Together, "xì trây" sounds iffy and uncertain.

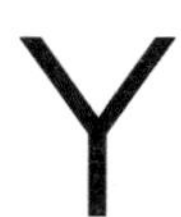

YSL: Low performance/low libido. Wet noodle. An initialism of "Yếu Sinh Lý."

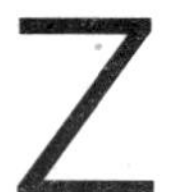

Zin: Intact, not yet penetrated by another. Derived from "origin," "Zin" is a euphemism for hymen that is intact.

DINH NHUNG

Sex as an ecology that extends beyond the physical body: An interview with Annie Sprinkle

Issue 60
Spring/Summer 2024

Authors
AMELIA GROOM
ANNIE SPRINKLE

Contributing Editor
AMALLE DUBLON

Back in the early 1990s, Annie Sprinkle calculated that the thousands of cocks she had sucked during her decades as a sex worker could make up the height of the Empire State Building (around 1500 feet of erect cocks, if they were lined up end to end). She illustrated that achievement with a diagram in her live performance *ANNIE SPRINKLE: POST PORN MODERNIST,* which took various iterations between 1989 and 1995. *POST PORN MODERNIST* also featured Sprinkle's *PUBLIC CERVIX ANNOUNCEMENT* – the performance she became best known for – in which she sat on stage with her legs spread, inserted a speculum in her vagina, and invited audience members to take a peek at her cervix with the aid of a flashlight. This was an era in which Sprinkle was transitioning from her work as a prostitute and mainstream porn star into the realms of performance art. In the decades since, she has completed a PhD in Human Sexuality and joined forces with the artist Beth Stephens, who has been Sprinkle's partner and artistic collaborator since 2002. Together, Sprinkle and Stephens have embarked on a series of ecosexual performance art projects that have involved getting married to the soil, sea, snow, Moon, coal, Appalachian Mountains, the Adriatic sea, to the rocks and, of course, the brine shrimp.[1]
A couple of months ago, MRPJ guest editor Amalle Dublon invited me to respond in some way to the journal's third issue, the 1991 "gender disarray" issue. I suggested an interview with Sprinkle – who appears in that issue – and she kindly agreed to speak with me. We met online in October 2023 (Sprinkle at her home in San Francisco, me at a sublet in Berlin), and I began by asking about an announcement that ran in the *MRPJ* issue, inviting people to join a *DRAG KING FOR A DAY* workshop on September 28, 1991, at The Annie Sprinkle Transformation Salon.

— Amelia Groom

Amelia Groom So, Annie, according to the announcement printed in the *MOVEMENT RESEARCH PERFORMANCE JOURNAL* back in 1991, the "Drag King for a Day" workshop at *THE ANNIE SPRINKLE TRANSFORMATION SALON* was to be facilitated by John Armstrong [aka Johnny Science] and participants would learn to "dress, act, talk, walk, stand, move, dance, etc. like a real man!" Can you tell me about the Salon and the drag workshops that were held there in the late 80s and early 90s?

Annie Sprinkle My apartment at Lexington and 27th Street in Manhattan was a gathering place for lots of different people from 'fringe communities' at that time, like sex worker activists, porn people, tattoo and body piercing people, and trans folks. Johnny ran a really beautiful support group for trans men and their allies. He was a performance artist and musician and a sex-positive person; he did theatrical, kinky BDSM shows, and he was into hardcore punk rock stuff with chainsaws. Before he transitioned, he was part of the lesbian S&M scene. Anyway, he was really the guy on the East Coast who was organizing meetings for trans men, publishing the first "F2M" newsletters and holding gatherings and creating support networks for trans guys and developing drag king culture. Actually, here's Beth calling on my phone [Beth Stephens, Annie's partner of 21 years] — that reminds me, Beth and I weren't lovers back then, but we knew each other, and she came to my Salon for a party Johnny and I hosted for two trans men who'd just had bottom surgery, so we could celebrate their new penises.

Anyway, those drag king workshops were very generative. Diane Torr often co- facilitated the workshops with Johnny. She had a dance and performance background, and she wrote about the workshops in her book [*SEX, DRAG, AND MALE ROLES*]. She would teach us how to walk, talk, and act like men, and how to "take up space." Johnny did everyone's facial hair makeup. And showed us how to make a penis bulge with a pair of socks. The workshops were always at my apartment. But the support group would meet at my apartment or at Kit Rachlin's apartment – she was Johnny's girlfriend at the time. Now she's a very well-respected psychologist who works with trans people. At the workshops, I would be the slutty hostess with the mostest; I'd dress up real sexy with lots of boobage and serve beer and snacks and sometimes give lap dances.

AG The announcement in *MRPJ* has a photo of you as "Annie Sprinkle" on the left and a photo of you as "Andy Sprinkle" [with a tie, mustache, briefcase, and fedora] on the right. Did you explore your masculinity during the workshops?

AS I became a man a few times. The first part of the workshop was make-up and training. Then we would go out as a group of men to a bar or strip club. We really passed as men. The first time I became a man I was a businessman; I took pictures of myself at the bank machine. I was very uncomfortable being a businessman. After that, I became a hippy Deadhead with long hair and that felt better. I was an army guy in camouflage once and that was very, very uncomfortable. The only guy I kind of liked being was half woman and half man. Once I wore this sexy red velvet dress with lots of cleavage, and red velvet high heels, but I had male face makeup with a mustache and five o'clock shadow. Out on the street, I remember a police car cruised by me, probably thinking I was a hooker from the back, and then when they saw me from the front I heard the officer yell, "Oh my god, it's a man!"

AG The 1991 *MRPJ* issue also features photographs by you throughout, including a series of portraits of your ex-lover Les Nichols, who stars with you in your 1989 film *LINDA/LES & ANNIE: THE FIRST FEMALE-TO-MALE TRANSSEXUAL LOVE STORY.*

AS I love that movie, but I got some shit for it. Not on the east coast but on the west coast. There was a trans community leader, Lou Sullivan, who thought the film was not good for the community. He said trans men wanted to be accepted in mainstream society and it was better to "put our best foot forward." He critiqued the film for being too freaky. The truth was I actually left a lot out; Les was kinky as fuck and the most sexually masochistic person I've ever met, but I left that out in the film. Anyway, it was apparently the first-ever sexually explicit F2M film ... F2M is an outdated term now; the language has changed a lot. So it was the first sexually explicit trans man film. That's something else that's changed a lot — there is so much trans man porn now, which I have always believed was educational, and *WAS* putting a best foot forward. But anyway, we had a lot of fun. We made mistakes too. When *LINDA/LES & ANNIE* shows these days, I make sure to use a disclaimer. Same with my other videos; I need to apologize. People still sometimes want to screen those old films, like *SLUTS & GODDESSES VIDEO WORKSHOP* [1992], which is full of what I thought was respecting and honoring some other cultures but is actually cultural appropriation. In *LINDA/LES & ANNIE*, the information is way out of date. Rather than try to erase these works, I say, ok, these are historical documents, and I wouldn't do it the same way now, obviously.

AG Can you say any more about trans history since the early 1990s, and your personal perspective – as an ally – on how things have changed in the US over the last three decades?

AS I first met trans people in porn in the 1970s, and over the years I have had quite a few trans lovers. What I remember about that time in the early 90s is that all the trans guys in the support group wanted to pass as cis males. That was a big struggle back then. Of course, some trans people still want to pass. But now there's a lot more nuance and more options and new pronouns. There's so much more community, and more trans people who are out of the closet, and more support networks for them. The hormones can be easier to get, the surgeries have come a long way, and there is a lot more trans art and culture. Our

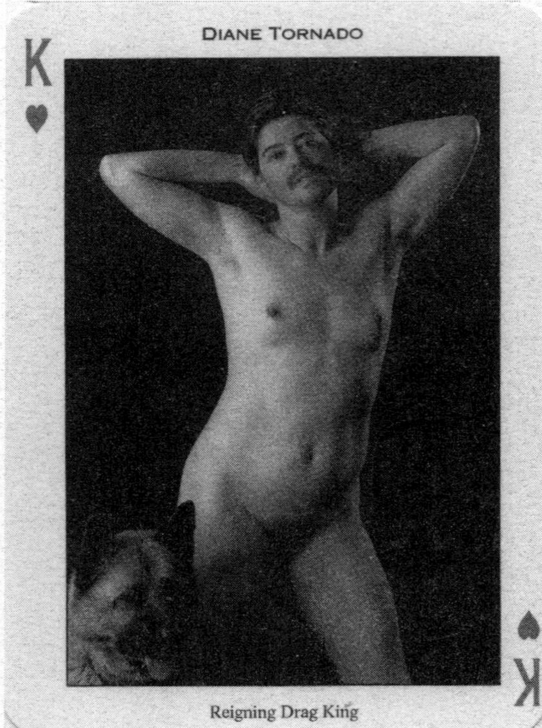

DRAG KING DIANE TORR from Annie Sprinkle's "Pleasure Activist Playing Cards" with Katharine Gates, 1995. Photo by Annie Sprinkle.

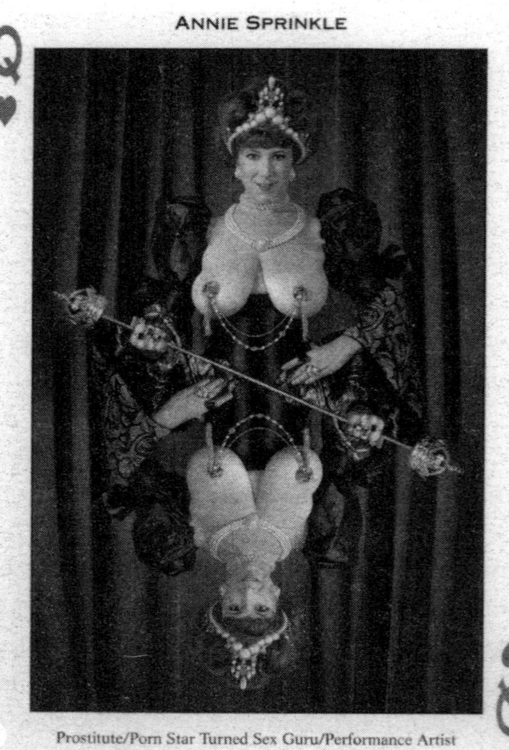

QUEEN OF HEARTS: PORTRAIT OF ANNIE from Annie Sprinkle's "Pleasure Activist Playing Cards" with Katharine Gates, 1995.

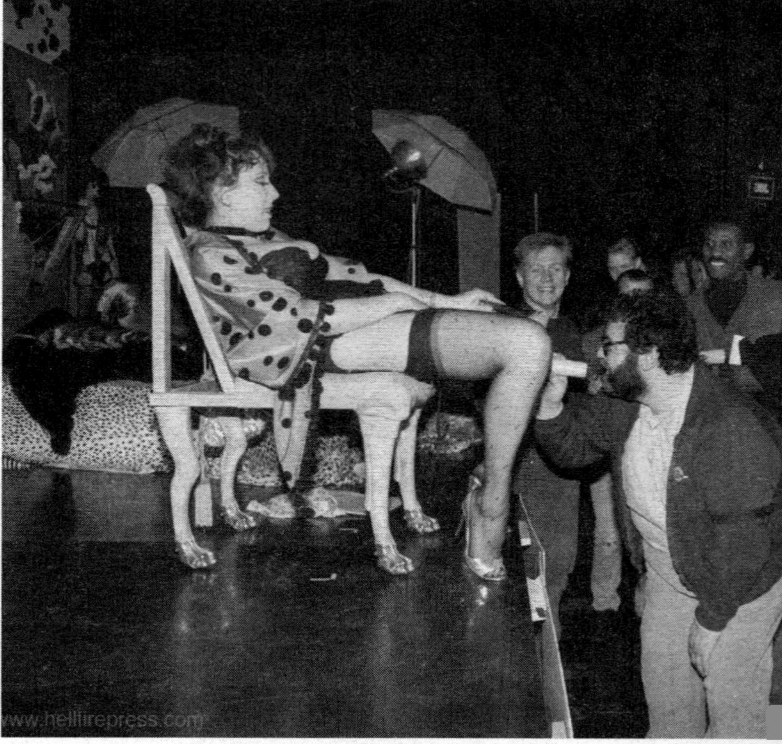

A PUBLIC CERVIX ANNOUNCEMENT from *POST PORN MODERNIST* performed at the Kitchen, New York, NY, 1989. Photo by Ephrain Gonzales.

1 For more about Annie and Beth's work, visit sprinklestephens.org. Their book *ASSUMING THE ECOSEXUAL POSITION — THE EARTH AS LOVER* is published by University of Minnesota Press.

friend and collaborator Paul B. Preciado's book *TESTO JUNKIE* is studied in colleges around the world and is a best seller. There are many more opportunities for people to be aware of trans issues, and there's a real trans cultural flourishing – hence the violent backlash by the transphobes and haters.

Last week there was a protest here in San Francisco called *DRAG UP! FIGHT BACK!* in response to recent anti-drag and anti-trans legislation and attacks. It was so wonderful; it's such a beautiful community. I was just like, "these are my people and I adore them and I feel so lucky to be part of this community." I wish trans and nonbinary people and people between genders ruled the world. I would love to see a world where they were not only accepted, but honored and appreciated. I can't believe trans people are being attacked like they are right now. They're being killed in this country and all around the world. There's so much hatred and stupidity. Someone in Beth's family in West Virginia was trying to tell us that he has a friend who's a school teacher and the students are putting kitty litter boxes in toilets for kids who say that their gender is cat. I was like, "I'm pretty sure that's an urban myth," and I went home and Googled it and, of course, it's just anti-trans urban myth bullshit perpetuated by [right-wing Colorado congresswoman] Lauren Boebert.

AG That reminds me of a particular strand of reactionary hysteria before marriage equality, where it was always this concern that if you let a man marry a man, then the next day you'll be letting a man marry a dog. Or they'd say "what's next, WOMEN MARRYING TREES?" –

AS – and we were here to prove them right!

AG Haha, yes, that's what I wanted to say – you made their worst nightmares come true.

AS Exactly, and we're proud of it.

AG Some might wonder why you would bother working with the institution of marriage as part of a queer art practice, but I think that by proliferating it so much and staging it so many times through such expansive relations, you and Beth have really messed with the idea of marriage.

AS We have done a series of weddings as performance art projects. At our first wedding ritual, our friend Barbara Carrellas did a performance called "Ten Reasons Why Marriage Should Be Abolished." We loved it. So we kept having objections as a part of all our subsequent weddings. In the invitations, we tell people not to bring gifts – instead, we ask them to co-create the wedding with us. We always involve a lot of different collaborators. Also, all the wedding guests can join us in the vows to "love, honor and cherish" the mountains or the water or the rocks or the snow or whatever, and it can make them feel more connected to those entities and elements. Everyone knows the narrative parts of a wedding ritual, so everyone – artists and non-artists – can plug into the ceremony in all kinds of ways.

We keep thinking we're done with the wedding project, but we keep coming back to it. We recently married fire because we felt that we needed to deepen our relationship with it, as we have had a lot of fires and we've been evacuated here in Northern California. We are now making a film called *PLAYING WITH FIRE*.

AG And you started to identify as ecosexual after you married the Earth, is that right?

AS When we married the Earth in 2008, it changed us forever. We woke up the next day and it just felt so right to acknowledge how much we loved the Earth. We didn't invent the word ecosexual; it was around a bit as a dating term. But we ran with it, added to the definitions, and launched an *ECOSEX MANIFESTO*, which made ecosex into a movement. For us it's an art movement, and it has really caught on. People like how inclusive it is. Beth and I want to make the environmental movement a little more sexy, fun and diverse. It's an affinity group where we can be fun and wild and free and dress up in drag, and at the same time be serious about the environmental issues facing us all. For me, it's also a sex education project and a way for people to expand on society's limited concept of what sex is, where it's only thought about as bodies and genitals coming together. If you've ever had body-to-body sex outside in nature, it can be the best sex you've ever had, because it's bigger than you and your partner. It's sex with the environment too, and a whole very sensual ecosystem.

AG I also wanted to ask you about ecosexuality and trans identity. You and Beth cast your friend Sandy Stone [trans theorist and performance artist] to be the voice of Earth in your film *WATER MAKES US WET*, and you've often said that the Earth is trans. What do you mean? And what happens to gender when we expand our sensual relations and embrace the Earth as a lover?

AS I just tweeted a definition of ecosexuality; we have a lot of different definitions — let me find it, here it is: "Ecosexuality: An expanded form of sexuality that imagines sex as an ecology that extends beyond the physical body." And that involves acknowledging that things are interconnected. In our text *25 WAYS TO MAKE LOVE TO THE EARTH*, we use she, he, and they pronouns and we mix them up. We imagine the Earth as trans, multi-gendered, and fluidly gendered. I mean, it seems so obvious. As humans, we're only a little part human. We're water and stardust and microorganisms and minerals and fungus, and we're also not so different from other animals, DNA-wise. We are the Earth. And the Earth is straight and gay and queer and trans and genderqueer and genderfluid and it's everywhere and sex is happening everywhere in billions of ways and it's natural. This thing we got into that says you have to be a man or a woman and stay that way – it's so limiting and narrow. I mean, it actually hurts to think that there are people who wanna make humans fit only into male or female and just eradicate everything else. Excruciating! It's absolutely impossible.

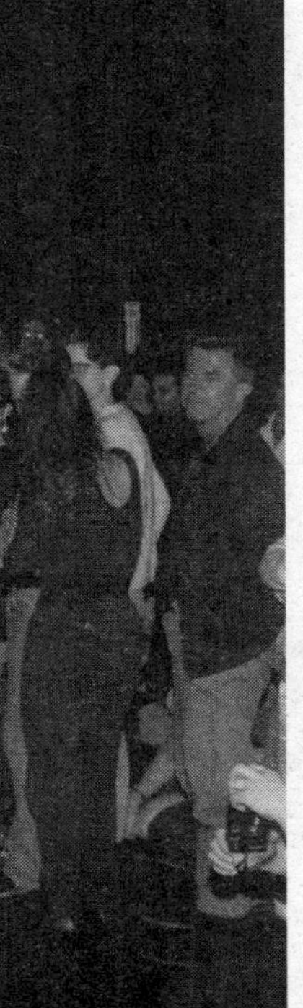

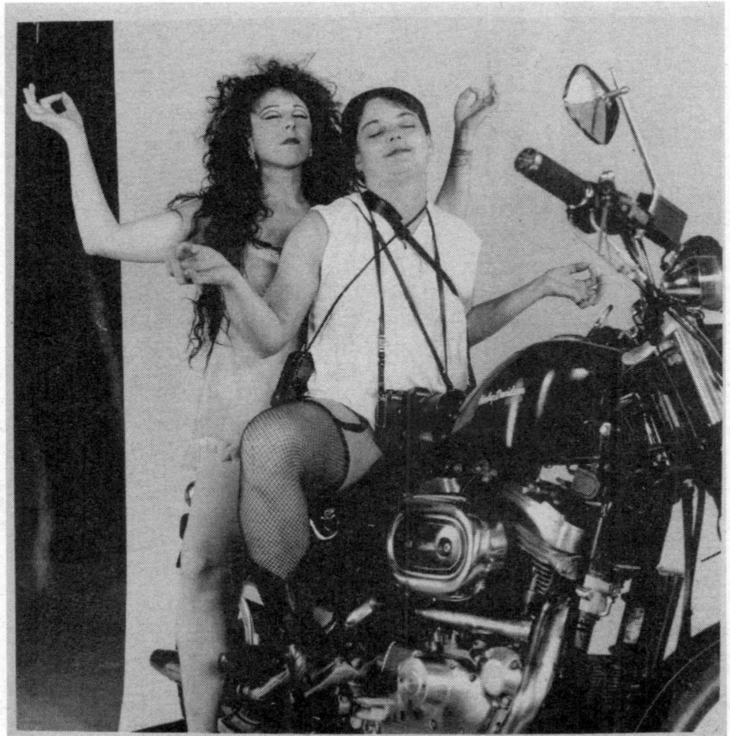

WHO'S ZOOMIN WHO, Beth Stephens & Annie Sprinkle on bike, 1992. Courtesy of Beth Stephens.

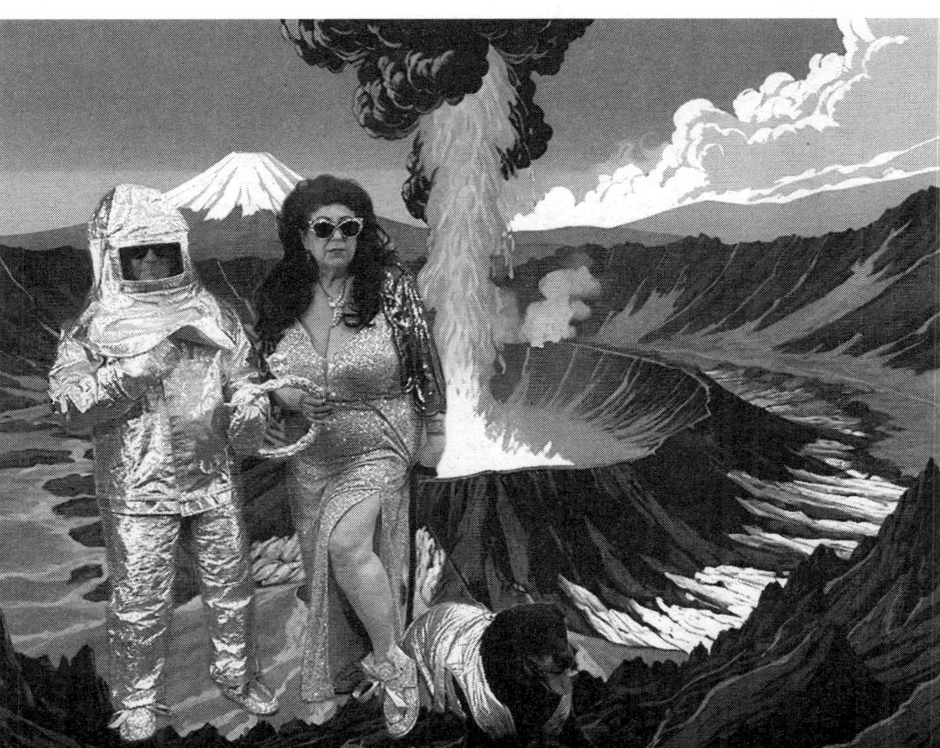

Annie Sprinkle & Beth Stephens, *PLAYING WITH FIRE* (film still), montage by Kate Bornstein, 2023. Courtesy Beth Stephens.

AG "Earth as lover" is an alternative to the older idea of "Earth as mother," right?

AS Yes. Of course, we are anthropomorphizing, because it helps us get closer to nature, but really the Earth is beyond gender completely. It's all fantasy and imagination. People imagine god as a white male with a long beard to try to access god, who is probably not a white male with a long beard. We can imagine the Earth in all kinds of ways; father, sister, friend, MILF, host...like many people and cultures, Beth and I do imagine the Earth as a mother sometimes. A mother in menopause.

AG We spoke earlier about the Sprinkle Salon that you had in your apartment in New York in the '80s and '90s. Something else that came out of that space was Club 90, a female porn star support group, which was the first of its kind. It was called Club 90 after the location of your apartment, 90 Lexington Ave, is that right?

PLEASURE ACTIVIST

AS Yes. I just watched a TV talk show that was recently digitized, the Club 90 support group women appearing on the Richard Bey talk show in 1988. The idea of feminist porn was just becoming a thing, and we were trying to promote sex-positive feminism. It was amazing to watch. I was blown away by how eloquent my dear friends were, and I remembered how terrified I was to speak that day. At one point, I told everyone that I'd had sex with 2000 men, and I remember my friend Candida [Royalle] was so mad at me for that. She was trying to fight for acceptance and I was so over the top; she was trying to put our best foot forward and promote her films for women and couples in suburbia, and I wanted to be experimental and see what happens if you tell the world you love to fuck and you've literally fucked thousands of guys. I realize now that we had slightly different agendas. I wanted to be a conceptual artist. The creative impulse has always been my guide — my clit and my creative impulse. Candida was an artist too, and a great one. But I was the provocateur, and she was the velvet glove.

AG Is that video available online somewhere?

AS Yes, through Candida's archives at Harvard's Radcliffe Institute. I've become an archivesexual lately; I get off placing archives! I'm working with my old friend [the sex worker and author] Dolores French to find a place for her archives. Much of Johnny Science's archives ended up in a dumpster when he died. Luckily Diane [Torr] and Kit [Rachlin] went and salvaged a bunch of it, and now it's at NYU. That happens so often to people who lived on the so-called fringe; the partners or the family are embarrassed about who they were and they want to erase that and then the history isn't there for future generations. So I'm trying to help preserve our herstories. Right now, I'm trying to help find good homes for the archives of four friends, including my long-time friend Spider Webb, the tattoo artist.

AG Back in 1991, when this issue of *MRPJ* was published, AIDS was raging. How did the crisis affect your work and change your life?

AS AIDS was devastating! The Great Dying! I was a working prostitute and pornographer during those years. I was in Manhattan, and I was part of the New York Healing Circle. I went to ACT UP a bit, but I was mostly involved with the Healing Circle. We were the lovers more than the fighters. We needed it all! AIDS taught me a lot about life, death, love, and community, and it made me get in touch with my feelings. I was more cut off before, but through AIDS, I was able to really cry.

AG I wanted to ask you about activism and pleasure. When AIDS hit, you were quick to respond with your safer sex workshops and other educational initiatives that maintained an emphasis on sexual possibility and enjoyment. In the 80s, you protested against anti-porn feminists, while insisting on feminist sex positivity. Pleasure has always been in the foreground of your politics. Now that you are more involved with ecological frameworks, can you comment on the role of pleasure in environmental activism?

AS Well, pleasure makes life worth living. I heard someone say the other day that the term "pleasure activist" was coined in 2019, but it was around in the 1990s. Maybe even the 80s. I published my *PLEASURE ACTIVIST PLAYING CARDS* in 1995. But anyway, we live in a sex-negative society, where sex is sinful and dirty and shameful. And it's also a pleasure-negative society; suffering is definitely more socially acceptable than pleasure. Sometimes it takes conscious effort to stay sexually active, and sometimes you have to put in effort to experience sensual pleasures – to really enjoy delicious food, to love the smell of a honeysuckle flower, to marvel at a sunset, to enjoy watching bees pollinate, to take pleasure in all the many shades of green in a forest... Beth and I produce public performances. One is called *FREE SIDEWALK ECOSEX CLINIC*, where we have a team of clinicians write psychomagic prescriptions for people to do nurturing activities outside, to try to remind them that there is a lot of pleasure and nourishment out there to be had. A prescription might say something like "lie down on some nice grass and hug the Earth and sniff the soil for fifteen minutes on a Tuesday at noon."

AG What else has changed since 1991?

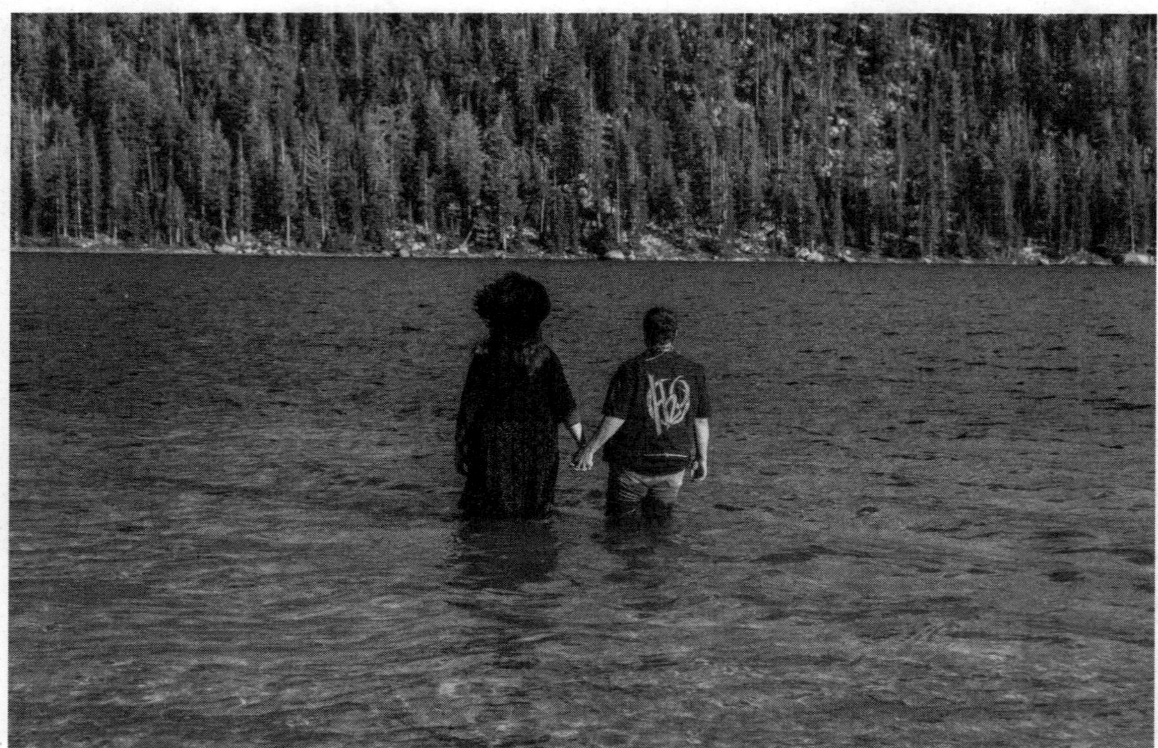

Beth Stephens & Annie Sprinkle, *WATER MAKES US WET*. Beth Stephens (film still), 2017.

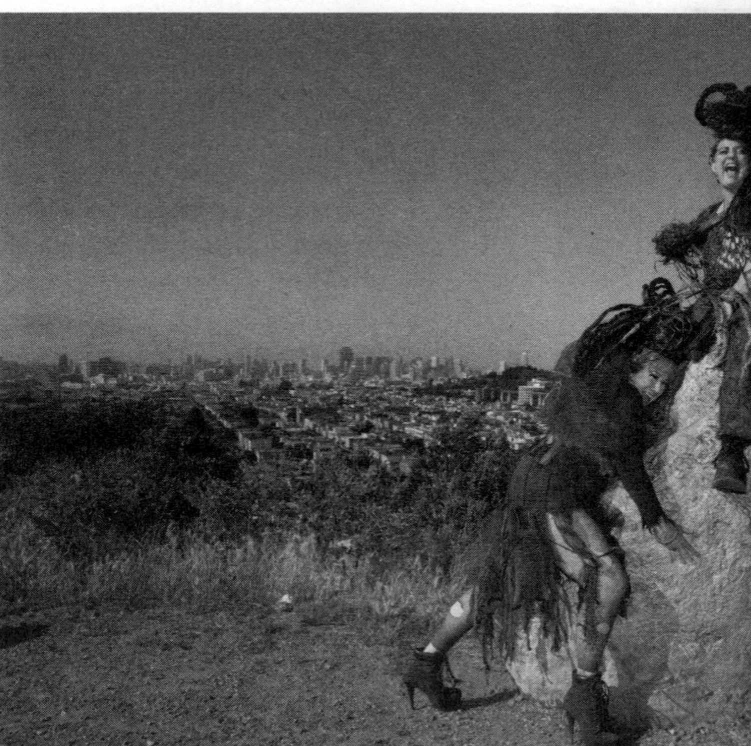

"Ecosexuals on a Rock and Kissing," portraits of Beth Stephens & Annie Sprinkle, photo by Manuel Vason from *ASSUMING THE ECOSEXUAL POSITION* (University of Minnesota Press, 2021).

AS So much. One thing that comes to mind is strap-on dildos. I made porn with strap- ons way back in the 70s, but it was a hard plastic cock with a thin piece of elastic with snaps that would go around your hips. It was terrible. You would have to hold it at the base, and it didn't work very well at all. But now dildos and strap-ons are so sophisticated: the shapes, colors, materials, the toxicity — it's all vastly improved. The sex toy industry has been making more products that are environmentally friendlier. Of course, for ecosexuals, you can simply use organic vegetables.

AG Well, that's an ancient technology!

AS Yes, true.

AG There's a part of your website where you describe your sexual journey as going "from Het, to Bi, to Lesbian, to Ecosexual." I wanted to ask you about this evolution. How have you experienced the changes over time?

AS Some people find themselves, and find what they want, and stick to it. And some of us are metamorphosexuals – that's a word I made up – which means we change at different points in our lives. I think most people go through changes and phases over their lifetimes, and their sex lives reflect those changes. Especially people in queer and trans communities. Things change over the years: our partners change, our sexual identities can change, our desires, our levels of sex drive, and so on. I'm 69 now, and I've been doing work about sex and documenting my sex life for more than half a century. My body has been a laboratory for my sex research. Amazingly, there's still so much to learn. Sex and gender are endlessly fascinating to me. As is love.

AG Can you offer any sex advice for people in their 60s and 70s and beyond?

AS Well, the only answer that always answers questions about sex is: it depends. It's so individual; every person is an entire erotic universe unto themselves. I would ask about an individual's sexual history, their fantasies, have they had cancer treatments, surgeries, traumas, lack of experience, do they want genital sex, do they want affection, are they turned on by porn, what do they like, dislike, is their desire low or high, have they been there, done it, and are over it, or are they a 70-year-old virgin? That's what I love about ecosex. Everyone loves the sensuality of nature; it's a common denominator. My best advice is to read our book, *ASSUMING THE ECOSEXUAL POSITION: THE EARTH AS LOVER.* LOL.

AG I spent some time with your early work while preparing for this interview, and I noticed that the ecosex stuff was actually always there, long before it was named as such. You contributed to the 1991 anthology *BI ANY OTHER NAME: BISEXUAL PEOPLE SPEAK OUT* with an essay called "Beyond Bi," in which you declared "I literally make love with things like waterfalls, winds, rivers, trees, plants, mud..." I also found "Annie Sprinkle's Guidelines for Sex in the 90s," in the 1991 Angry Women issue of *RE/SEARCH*, where you wrote, "Our Earth and sky are painfully polluted. Make love to them, and they'll make love to you. Send them your sexual energy. They love it."

AS Well, yes, the pleasures of the nonhuman realms have always been a part of my erotic awareness. But then again, humans are part of the Earth. All human sex is ecosex too.

AG Annie, you've lived an amazing life and you've been so prolific and generous with your sluttiness.

AS I've had a good life. I've been so lucky and very privileged. If I died tomorrow, I would die happy. I wish I could stop the wars; I would give my life to stop any war. The human world is really tragic right now, and it doesn't seem to be getting better. I still believe that peace is possible. I don't understand why there aren't more benevolent leaders who promote peace, love, compassion.... War is, of course, the worst perpetrator of environmental destruction. It doesn't only kill people, it also kills all the creatures in the soil, the fish, the birds, horses, and it pollutes the air, and water, and everything.

Our films are a drop in the bucket, but maybe getting a few people to love the Earth could have some kind of ripple effect. Just last month, local government officials finally ordered Nestlé to stop taking water from the San Bernardino National Forest here in California. Nestlé had unlimited access to the natural springs, and they were paying scientists very well to say that everything was fine; but there were biologists, like the one in our film [*WATER MAKES US WET*], who were saying, "no, this is ecologically destructive and not right." Several species had no water and were becoming extinct. So I like to think that our film was a little part of that success. We helped save some little birds, fish and snakes. The work that Beth and I and our collaborators do is not everybody's cup of tea, but it resonates with some people.

And we need lots of different strategies at once. You gotta keep fighting for freedom and practicing it, because sadly, freedom can be taken away. We all have to remember that freedom isn't free.

AMELIA GROOM
ANNIE SPRINKLE

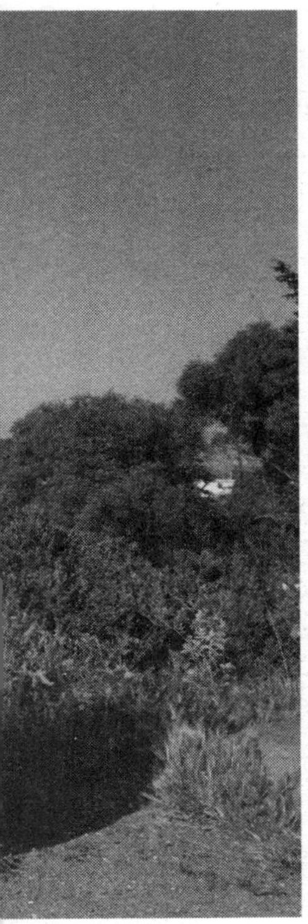
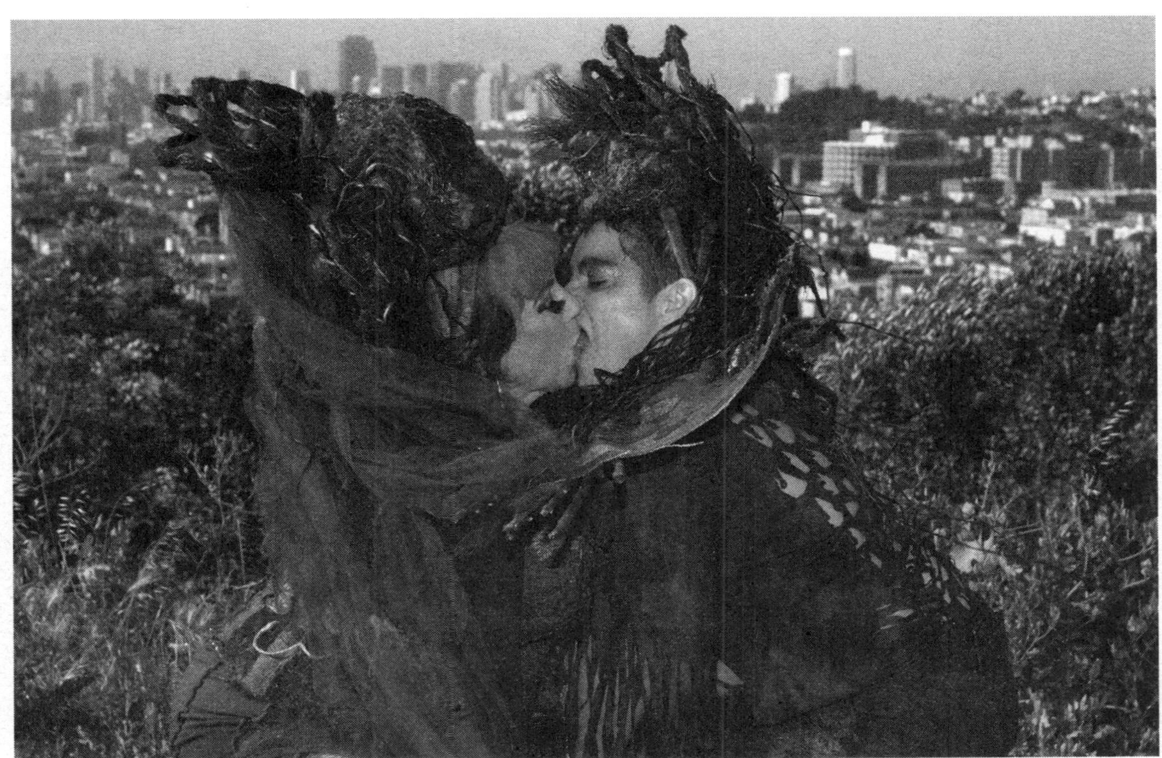

"Ecosexuals on a Rock and Kissing," portraits of Beth Stephens & Annie Sprinkle, photo by Manuel Vason from *ASSUMING THE ECOSEXUAL POSITION* (University of Minnesota Press, 2021).

DJing as a Mediumship Practice

Author
GAVILÁN RAYNA RUSSOM

Contributing Editor
KAY GABRIEL

EXPERIENCING INDETERMINATE SPECIFICITY AROUND GENDER HAS BEEN A PATHWAY TO WAYS OF BEING IN THE WORLD THAT ARE NOT LOCKED TO LINEAR TIMELINES, NOT COMPLIANT WITH CLOCKS AND CALENDARS. BEING IN

I was a dancer before I was a DJ. And I was a medium before I was a dancer. Increasingly over the last years, and almost certainly accelerated by the Covid-19 global pandemic, I've begun to experience that evolutionary process in reverse. I've slowly shifted away from DJing as the mainstay of my gig income and the primary driver of my presence at clubs and raves. There were years when the only reason I was going to clubs was to work as a DJ, and at some point, I started to get more interested in being on the dance floor than I was in playing and mixing tracks. This led to what I lovingly call my "fourth nightlife renaissance," somewhere around 2017 to 2019 — long-arc cruises through New York at night, all its many spaces and places, explicitly as a dancer, in the years before the pandemic. When clubs closed in 2020, I had an unprecedented kind of time to reflect on those spaces and what had brought me to them over and over again, even into my 40's. There were no gigs to speak of then, and I remembered a lot of things about myself and spent a lot of time with spirits and ancestors uninterrupted by the intrusive rhythms of capitalism. This current phase of working as a medium, talking about dead people almost constantly, and being largely unable to spend extended periods of time in nightlife spaces because of the overwhelm related to feeling everyone in the room's dead talking all at once, grew organically out of those experiences. If I do go out, I get there at 10:30 and leave before midnight, or I arrive at 4:00 (or later depending on the function) and stay for an hour or so. I rarely play gigs and tend to say yes to the ones I do because of the money, the community, and/or the opportunity to say something important through music and performance.

Oddly though, I'm engaged with DJing as an art form more deeply than ever. Time- telescopically I've taken a step across the spiral-path back to ways I wove sounds together when I first began to DJ parties in my high school cafeteria, collaging other people's recorded music. I experienced a similar crossing of time through practice during my first years living in Berlin. While I loved going out to dance clubs, my compositional sensitivity was extremely high, in a way that made DJing exclusively beat-oriented dance music less than compelling as an artist. Those DJ sets were long and through-composed architectural landscapes of mixed and meshed sounds, geared to the deeper motivators of body movement, rather than the metronomic and increasingly ubiquitous bpm-locked pulsations of the 4/4 and its multifarious permutations. The practice of DJing has been heavily research-based for me, but not in the ways that are more conventionally discussed, such as crate-digging or analyzing recorded mixes. While these research approaches are wonderful and important to the practice, my own research has often consisted of effusive iterations of:

fucking girls in dark
rooms, careening through
club and rave
space in a blend of numbness
and ecstasy bathed in the wetness
of the woman me that holds all the other ones
and couldn't come out for years unless i
was drunk, high, and on a dance floor, interlocking rhythmic
engagement with undulations of unidentifiable
shifts in the climate of a room filled with dancers only marginally related
but also definitely not unrelated to shifts in the tactile skin of
what the dj is provoking the speakers and the air in the room to do, getting
dressed alone or with others or also against others sometimes in ways that might
facilitate these states of permeability, states of permeability, seeing ghosts in basements
where strobes, lasers, fog, and repetitive throb predominate, shifts of hip, shoulder, chin, hair
that are clearly storytelling, interactions with people I'll never see again whose names I forgot
as soon as they said them as I am sure they also forgot mine, turns into unexpected
places which reveal unexpected and often invisible spaces in both time and
topography, kisses with strangers, sweat shared, drugs shared, drinks
shared, partners shared, space shared, internal spaces shared,
remarkable and fleeting insights shared, terrible sets
played by boring egomaniacs, startling moments
revealed in the spaces between knowing
and wondering by people who care
if only for that one moment,
breathing sweat,
new ideas
felt.

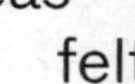

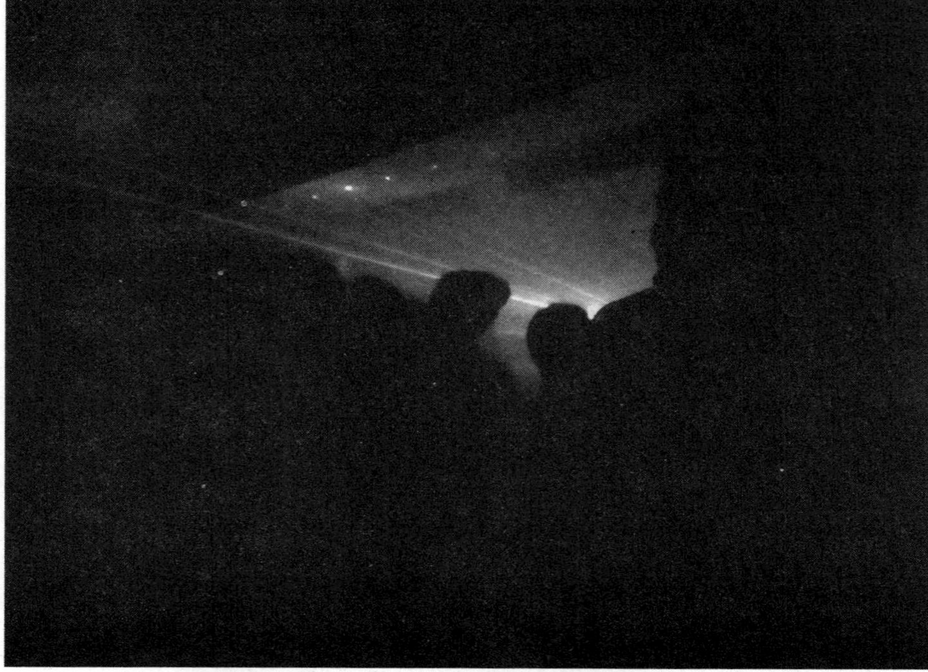

Images courtesy of Gavilán Rayna Russom.

None of which explicitly has anything to do with DJing, despite the presence of DJs who are/were not me throughout all of it. None of which explicitly has anything to do with mediumship despite the presence of a medium, myself, throughout all of it. All of which explicitly has everything to do with dancing, present throughout all of it. All of this to say my perspective here is based on an overwhelming amount of this type of experience-based research. I am extremely far down the rabbit hole on this particular trajectory and despite my sincere desire to meet you at the entrance with a flashlight so you can follow the path I took down here, I doubt I will be able to. So, in parallel to that endeavor, here is an abridged — but I think nonetheless useful — flow chart as a guide:

A The process of recording sound, including music, encodes moments that have passed into one or more forms of media from which they can be re-awakened through playback at a "future" time in relation to the time when those moments occurred.
B Bodies also encode moments in this way by storing rhythm (in the broadest sense of the word) internally as a coding device for emotional and other experiential landscapes that can be retrieved through the use of memory.
C These two means of encoding, storing, and re-experiencing moments that are no longer visibly occurring can be interwoven to produce powerful experiences of timelessness: recognition, meaning, and connection.
D As moments pass out of the lens of visibly existing in the present, they become ghosts.
E Both body memory and recorded media hold these ghosts.
F Playback of body memory and/or recorded media releases these ghosts.
G DJs engage in the playback of recorded media in ways that awaken body memory in listeners and especially dancers.
H DJing is a mediumship practice.

A significant component of what it has meant for me to be in a transgender body is an experience of liminality and indeterminacy in relation to binaries. Of course, yes, gender binaries like man/woman, obviously but also: young/old, experienced/naive, skillful/lost, human/animal, awake/dreaming, binary/nonbinary, living/dead. To speak of indeterminacy and liminality in this way is not to say that these things are vague or unclear, rather that they become highly specific in ways that are fluid, sometimes unpredictable, and that they can also crystallize into other highly specific states that are experientially distinct from previous states of specificity. This is what I've discussed in other contexts as *DRIFT CONTINUITY*. To be clear, this is not to say in any way that I am not a woman, because I am. There are different ways of being a woman, and for me, all of the fluidity, indeterminacy, specificity and flux I'm describing is held within a context of womanhood that is not defined by a binary with manhood — it's something else. Within that context, like DJ Autopay so perfectly articulates, "sometimes I'm more femme, sometimes I'm more masc."

DRIFT CONTINUITY

This kind of indeterminate specificity around externally conceived categories and binaries has always been heightened for me on dance floors. In fact, it is very likely that decades of reflecting on what happens for me on dance floors, often while on them, is what led me to the understandings I currently have about my gender, my identity, and all the other things I'm articulating here. On dance floors I've worked with what DJs, lighting designers, bartenders, door people, fellow dancers, the space, the place, and other members of the community and the culture have provided to provoke states of consciousness that facilitate this kind of indeterminate specificity extremely well. As a DJ, I strive to be the best person to work with in this capacity, because as a dancer it's essentially what I'm there for, and indeterminate specificity is what allows me to both feel like "myself" and to feel connected, often very deeply, to the people with whom I am sharing the experience of the dance floor.

Recently I've begun to refer to this complex of ideas as *BODYVISION*. I came up with the term *BODYVISION* as a name for the radio show I started doing in 2023. The show came out of me reflecting on what brought me to dance floors, music, and DJing, what brought me back so many times, and what got me to stay. Primarily, the ways in which music and my body — and I think the bodies of other people — interact, facilitating ways of knowing that stretch beyond Eurocentric, settler colonial, and capitalist ideas about knowledge. There is something about those contexts and practices that allows my body to "see" things in ways that push past binary ideas of gender by pressing beyond linear temporality. In that space, tension between a gender assigned at birth and a gender as lived in a body fell apart. What also gradually dissolved through experiences of what I'm calling *BODYVISION* were attachments to binary thinking, particularly the compulsion to view the world through binaries. Being in a trans body on a dance floor and experiencing indeterminate specificity around gender has been a pathway to ways of being in the world that are not locked to linear timelines, not compliant with clocks and calendars. Being in the world in a way that includes glimpses of time not beholden to a linear regime means that along with all the other binaries that disintegrated the binary of living/dead did as well.

My ideas about the dead came through experience long before they came through discourse. As a child I felt, and sometimes saw and heard, both distinct and more ambiguous presences that, even then, I intuited as being connected to ghosts and spirits. This spectrum of experiences with the dead, from those that had a distinct nature to them (like an identifiable spirit or dead person) to those that were more ambiguous (like a general haunted sense or atmosphere) feels related to, if not the same as, the states of indeterminate specificity I have experienced on dance floors. Seeking out writing on the dead has been an attempt to find context and shape for these experiences. The writing I have connected with most deeply — texts that really get at the fabric and texture of these experiences with the dead — are writings on *PALO*.

PALO is one of a set of practices and ideas that exist throughout the Black Atlantic, and increasingly throughout the world, that are animated by Central African Kongo cosmologies and lifeways. *PALO*'s practices also include Indigenous knowledge, West African knowledge, and very likely several other knowledge systems incorporated through interactions between communities of resistance to colonization, enslavement, whitening, and attempted genocide. Anthropologist Todd Ramón Ochoa uses the term "Kongo-inspired" to describe the relationship between *PALO* practices and Kongo culture, and defines inspiration as "a hinge between the past and the future, inspiration being the active, forward-looking creative spark linking past forms with objects, powers and rules born anew." *PALO* is intimately connected with the dead. It is difficult to define, and perhaps defining it here is only useful as an invitation to consider practices such as DJing, dancing, and going out at night from the perspectives it proposes. *PALO* is also intimately connected with music, rhythm, drums, repetition, and dance. All of these are core technologies used in *PALO* to achieve substantive, often embodied contact with the dead, and to work through that contact to navigate life in ways that would be impossible without it. In an attempt to invite you into this way of thinking about things in a way that does not demand definitively defining *PALO*, here are the voices of several other people speaking about it, about Kongo culture, and about the dead as conceived within the frameworks these propose, along with short reflections of my own:

Todd Ramón Ochoa reports that his Yayi Nkisi (*PALO* initiatory mother) told him that the body is "a version of the dead, literally brought into being by those who had birthed her and then made to ring in intense material agreement with the strange, indifferent tones the dead had taught her to hear." Further, the body is "...a form of the dead, material insofar as matter was understood as a momentary condensation, precipitation, or coagulation of the fluid immanence of the dead." Ochoa's experiences with Palo led him to propose frameworks of "the ambient dead" and "the responsive dead," which articulate states of indeterminate specificity that other research frameworks do not. For me as a trans person, conceiving of the body as a "momentary condensation" of the dead, rather than as a fixed construct defined by genitalia, secondary sex characteristics, and gender assigned at birth, is infinitely liberating — possibly because it suggests that my body is made up of many things.

Yvonne Daniel explains that in the Kongo-Angola culture in Cuba that *PALO* is part of, "The division between the

THE WORLD IN A WAY THAT INCLUDES GLIMPSES OF TIME NOT BEHOLDEN TO A LINEAR REGIME MEANS THAT ALONG WITH ALL THE OTHER BINARIES THAT DISINTEGRATED THE BINARY OF LIVING/ DEAD DID AS WELL.

sacred and the ordinary does not have boundaries in common within their understandings; ritual behaviors can easily look like ordinary events." This shift from the sacred as something divorced from everyday life to a perspective of an everyday life permeated by the sacred speaks to the presence of the dead in activities as simple as walking to the store, or moving from the living room to the bedroom. Seeing DJing and dancing as everyday activities reframes them in ways that I think are important, and Daniel's observations propose a model of sacred connection in nightlife that is more consistent with my experience than ideas like transcendence are.

Aisha M. Beliso-De Jesús builds on Ochoa's work, identifying that the formulation of, "African-inspired," which he uses to analyze ways that Cuban *PALO* practices draw upon forms of Africanness without relying on notions of original essences, is helpful in thinking about the various articulations that are brought into being through practices such as [...] *PALO* monte (also regla *PALO*)." Moving away from ideas of purity and original essence, especially in relation to African cultural perspectives and technologies, allows for more complicated and useful conversations about music forms like house and techno. These forms emerge from African American communities but meaningfully extend beyond a simplistic analysis of African survivals because of the ongoing folding in, by those communities, of new cultural materials, ideas, innovations, and experiences. This shift away from essentialist readings of identity also cracks and destabilizes arguments about the essential nature of gender.

Solimar Otero, in detailing the appearance through mediumship of a *PALO* spirit at a spiritual mass, describes how "her entrance into the liminal frame of the gathering creates a temporal palimpsest that allows for the perception of different kinds of time. Perception here is subtle, and spirit guides illustrate that attention to sensory detail is vital for communicating with them. That is why the very idea of materiality takes on a different perspective when defined by spirits." I think this one speaks for itself.

Elements of the rhythmic devices that form a part of the drumming traditions of *PALO* exist throughout dance music in the U.S. They enter it even in its pre-electronic formations, through Delta Blues and New Orleans Jazz, sounds that spread throughout the country through the Great Migration and through recording technology. Kongo rhythms also entered and inspired dance music during waves of immigration — people and sounds — into U.S. cities from Cuba, Puerto Rico, and the Dominican Republic. The communities that entered the U.S. from these places brought traditions already permeated by Kongo cosmology and its attendant rhythmic technologies along with them, often literally embedded in their bodies. My own embodied experiences with *PALO*'s ritual technology and communities have extended the experiences I have had of indeterminate specificity on dance floors and dance music into even more detailed and specific realms. These experiences have allowed me to see things about my own dance floor experiences that were previously imperceptible. They have provided access points to a time outside of time, marking methodologies and maps of connectedness that chart currents which exceed and flood another binary: individual/collective.

Conceiving of DJing as a mediumship practice, and particularly doing so "inspired" by the cosmologies and technologies of *PALO*, entails doing what DJs do first and foremost: interweave temporalities and spatialities. Audio recordings hold both the time and space during and within which they were recorded. And what a DJ does, consciously or unconsciously, is layer all these temporalities and spatialities by encoding them onto yet another temporality and spatiality — the time and place when and where the DJ is playing. This encoding accumulates meaning as bodies in movement receive it, and perhaps more importantly, these bodies in movement, at least on a good night, guide the flow of the temporal encoding engaged in by the DJ.

This is possible because of the glitches in clock and calendar, and because of the indeterminate specificities evoked by interaction between recorded sound, as a living embodiment of the dead, and bodies, as living embodiments of the dead. Within this experiential framework, all kinds of rules and categories, and most especially binaries, dissipate like smoke in the wind, leaving space, hopefully, for ideas about being that are less restrictive than those we are currently offered as devotees of the dance floor. Ideas about being that, once glimpsed, become very difficult to shake.

GAVILÁN RAYNA RUSSOM

Work Cited

Autopay, DJ. "More Femme More Masc (It's Pride Black Pride Mix)," on HOA011 (The End • The Beginning...). HAUS of ALTR: 2020.

Beliso-De Jesús, Aisha M. *ELECTRIC SANTERÍA: RACIAL AND SEXUAL ASSEMBLAGES OF TRANSNATIONAL RELIGION*. New York: Columbia University Press, 2015.

Daniel, Yvonne. *DANCING WISDOM: EMBODIED KNOWLEDGE IN HAITIAN VODOU, CUBAN YORUBA, AND BAHIAN CANDOMBLÉ.* Champaign, IL: University of Illinois Press, 2005.

Ochoa, Todd Ramón. *SOCIETY OF THE DEAD: QUITA MANAQUITA AND PALO PRAISE IN CUBA.* Berkeley, CA: University of California Press, 2010.

Otero, Solimar. *ARCHIVES OF CONJURE: STORIES OF THE DEAD IN AFROLATINX CULTURES.* New York: Columbia University Press, 2019.

Sublette, Ned. *CUBA AND ITS MUSIC: FROM THE FIRST DRUMS TO THE MAMBO.* Chicago, IL: Chicago Review Press, 2007.

Movement Research
Performance Journal

D.O.U.B.T. - A Density

Author
GEO WYEX

Contributing Editor
AMALLE DUBLON

Illustrations
GEO WYEX

I wrote this text right before the election runoff between Donald Trump and Joe Biden, in November 2020. It marked a departure from addressing white patriarchy directly in my own work, both in my own ancestry, and generally within known power structures. Relinquishing a need to manage accountability of white guilt in the wake of the 2020 uprisings, I no longer felt responsible to respond directly to the suffering or anxiety of inheritors of power and privilege in my work in such a way that reaffrmed my own "victimhood" (absurd) and kept me in a strange loop of acting as a sort of translator. I released myself from the supposed responsibility, to help non-black people understand the dimensions of the black experience that I could claim or have access to (what a relief) — no longer a bridge, I then deeply indulged in the pleasures and densities of language, thinking about a continuous present, a woven curtain of words and references, an ocean to hold or move me — I charged up, like I ate a mushroom in Super Mario Bros. I thought a lot about Adrienne Kennedy's plays, about the presence of multiple timelines in one scene, where one might find Jesus, Patrice Lumumba, and the Duchess of Hapsburg suddenly in proximity, and how theater can hold so many worlds in ways that feel less possible in daily life. When I was a kid, I had a recurring dream of hitting an intergalactic home run, the baseball bat smashing to smithereens in slow motion, and multiple fragments of ball, cascading through the stadium into a night sky, refracting into constellations — mnemonics, maps, a resemblance to the Big Bang. I also fantasized about a possibility of communication through time travel, a portal where a transmission to the past intervened, perhaps in some historical wrong-doing, as an attempt to distort the render, to muck up the known account, as a manner of shifting future outcomes — like in the film Back to The Future. A ruining of history as an evasion of capture, to make room for what stories, what people, what objects may emerge, having been here all along anyway, for as long as blackness has reverberated, with and beyond known forms, stories, people. The baseball field, the plantation field, the field of stars, the art field, the fieldwork, the fielding of eyes or feelings.

The balls on a body, the balls in a body, the balls of stars or planets, the balls to hit hard.

"This is the Last Time I'll Be speaking to you in this form."

I have no idea if this text should be performed live, or if it could — if anyone has the balls, let me know.

Descartes Is Pitching Tonight (Gonna Whoop His Ass)

or

The Home Run Stunner Steps Up To The Plate To Feel The Field And Fracture The Feeling

or

A Tired Hex, 30 Years Before The Great Abolition (of 2050?)

or

-

or

-

or

A Last Ditch Title I Can't Remember, A Seed of Doubt Planted In The Fields Of The Greatest of White Daddys, The Last Home Run, The Bat Crack To Splinter A Hole In The Cracker Across Fields and Fields of Stars

or

Reparations Now Suite

or

(spelled out carefully, and with balls, held up to the audience, one by one)

- Deeee...
- Ohhhh.....
- Yoouuu.....
- Beeee.....
- Teeee.....

– – – – –

DOUBT (a density)

– – – – –

ENTER the Home Run Stunner, a front counter, a door, a home, teeth of a zombie, a River, eczema, a side story, Babe Ruth's called shot, sequins, five balls, a field, a feeling, all of them stars.

SETTING a graveyard

– – –

This is the last time I will be speaking to you in this form.

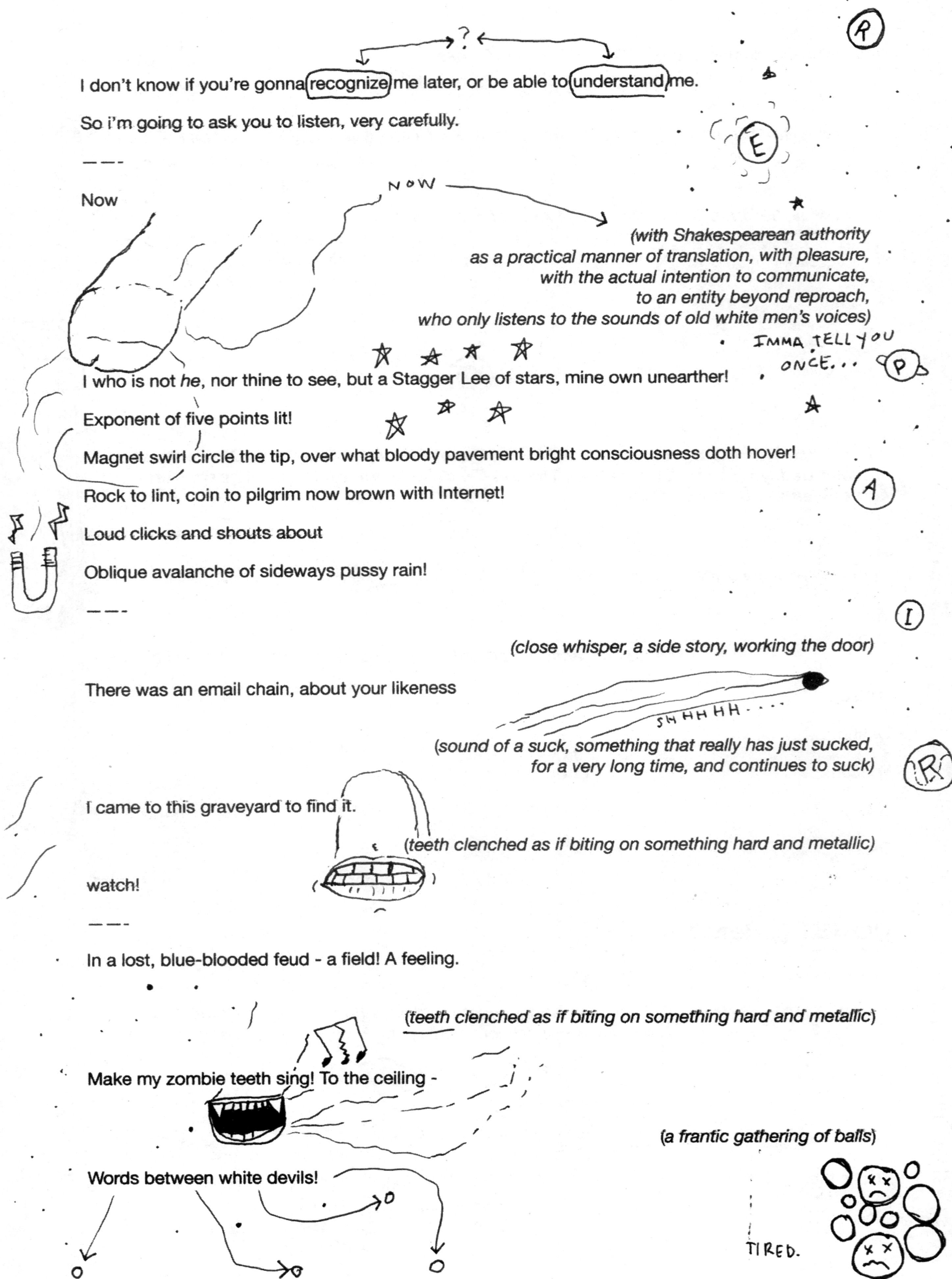

I don't know if you're gonna recognize me later, or be able to understand me.

So i'm going to ask you to listen, very carefully.

Now

*(with Shakespearean authority
as a practical manner of translation, with pleasure,
with the actual intention to communicate,
to an entity beyond reproach,
who only listens to the sounds of old white men's voices)*

I who is not *he*, nor thine to see, but a Stagger Lee of stars, mine own unearther!

Exponent of five points lit!

Magnet swirl circle the tip, over what bloody pavement bright consciousness doth hover!

Rock to lint, coin to pilgrim now brown with Internet!

Loud clicks and shouts about

Oblique avalanche of sideways pussy rain!

(close whisper, a side story, working the door)

There was an email chain, about your likeness

*(sound of a suck, something that really has just sucked,
for a very long time, and continues to suck)*

I came to this graveyard to find it.

(teeth clenched as if biting on something hard and metallic)

watch!

In a lost, blue-blooded feud - a field! A feeling.

(teeth clenched as if biting on something hard and metallic)

Make my zombie teeth sing! To the ceiling -

(a frantic gathering of balls)

Words between white devils!

(end of play)

WHEW...

———-

(Play begins again - a constellation of lumpy balls makes an appearance)

I, a scab, could sell the material.

(casual renumeration of heavy topics, as an oblique tactic of focus by irreverent abandonment, seeking attention while questioning oneself for doing so)

Family crest… combat stress…

Etched in twisted chains across my chest - noooo, nooo, noooo! Repair! Repair?

(is it an actual question?)

STEAL "~~ASK~~ AND YE SHALL ~~RECEIVE~~" GET WHAT'S OWED?

With my grandmother's hair?

(teeth clenched as if biting on something hard and metallic)

HARD

A wasp's nest!

(a WASP?)

(a never before experienced feeling of relaxation)

We murder your memory back.

———

(a constellation of heavy but buoyant balls make an appearance)

GAS - heavy / buoyant?

But what? How now, sequined customs, alight!

Shout! Broke umbrella bitches - home running!

Fucking gay rageful chorus of night

Don our coats of ash and weed-killer wishes — stunners!

(working the door)

Go!

(steady slapping of balls, growing in momentum, filled with centuries of ache and longing)

Go Go Go Go Go!

R Y G GREEN

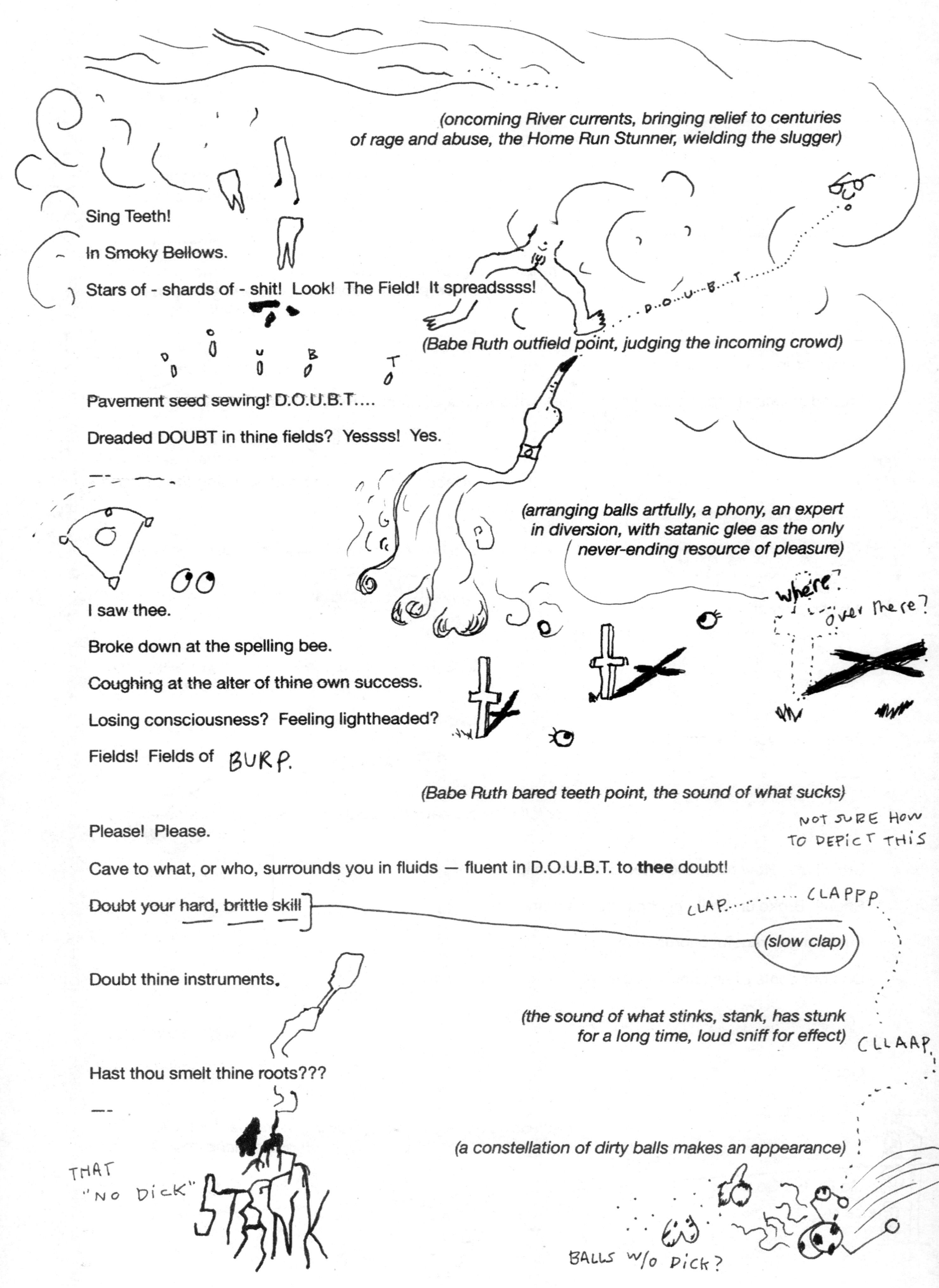

(oncoming River currents, bringing relief to centuries of rage and abuse, the Home Run Stunner, wielding the slugger)

Sing Teeth!

In Smoky Bellows.

Stars of - shards of - shit! Look! The Field! It spreadssss!

(Babe Ruth outfield point, judging the incoming crowd)

Pavement seed sewing! D.O.U.B.T....

Dreaded DOUBT in thine fields? Yessss! Yes.

—

(arranging balls artfully, a phony, an expert in diversion, with satanic glee as the only never-ending resource of pleasure)

I saw thee.

Broke down at the spelling bee.

Coughing at the alter of thine own success.

Losing consciousness? Feeling lightheaded?

Fields! Fields of BURP.

(Babe Ruth bared teeth point, the sound of what sucks)

Please! Please.

Cave to what, or who, surrounds you in fluids — fluent in D.O.U.B.T. to **thee** doubt!

Doubt your hard, brittle skill

(slow clap)

Doubt thine instruments.

(the sound of what stinks, stank, has stunk for a long time, loud sniff for effect)

Hast thou smelt thine roots???

—

(a constellation of dirty balls makes an appearance)

How now, underearth suck! This sludge of saltbake gristle!

Curdle into the earth!

All mixed up, scabbed, frosted skin flakes tossed to track up your inner circle!

The wall to wall carpet, the Wall, a street !

(relentless oncoming River currents, the sound of what's naughty, covered in mud, covered in eczema, a very bad dog, what stinks, and can't stop)

To undress your false modesty, shudder you, fuckface, ~~father.~~

— —

(a constellation of salty balls make an appearance)

Krill will kill thine fantasy of helpfulness.

At This Moment, limp thine wrist - I'm telling you! Drop thine pride! Look outside —

(Babe Ruth bleacher point, wielding the slugger)

The field! Waaaaaaaayy out!

To D. O. U. B. T. Doubt!

(a never before experienced feeling of relaxation - the Home Run Stunner sits)

Doubt I am alive or dead.

(Babe Ruth forehead point, in the style of an imagined zombie ancestor)

Raising my head from a bloody blanket.

To choke you! with me, and thine, own rotten sausage too.

Eat purple intestine, you — and boil thine roots! it's good for you.

(arranging balls artfully, with satanic glee as the only never-ending resource of pleasure)

I never wish ill. I only follow through.

On what field whispers is comin for youuuuuuuuuu. ooooooooo!!!

(sung in an operatic style, oncoming River currents, the sound of what stinks)

Deee Ouuuuu. Yuuuu. Beeee Teeeee!!

(Babe Ruth outfield point, judging the incoming crowd)

DOUBT.

— — — —

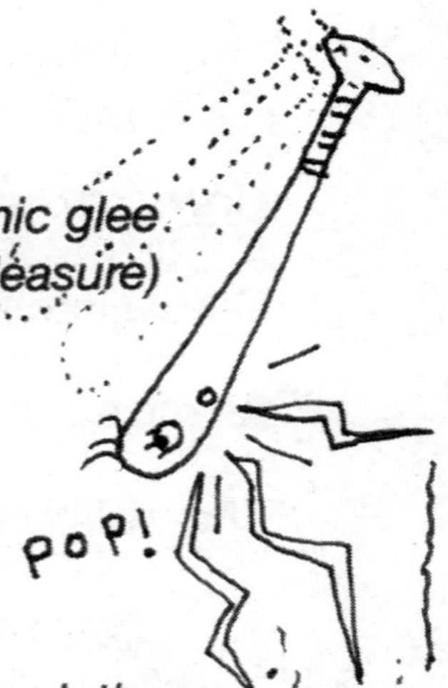

(a never-before experienced feeling of relaxation, with satanic glee.
as the only never-ending resource of pleasure)

Its the only sharp this batter can switch

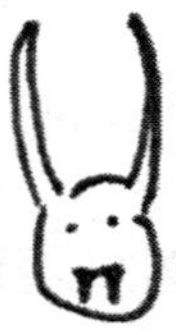

Firing too many balls! And tiny stars to maul you for all of eternity.

Doubt thine hands, thine eyes, ears, mind, thine mouth.

(wielding the slugger, at the front counter, working the door, judging the incoming crowd, the Home Run Stunner sits, the curtain goes up, the entrance. Begin play.)

Doubt thine will. You are no longer on this account.

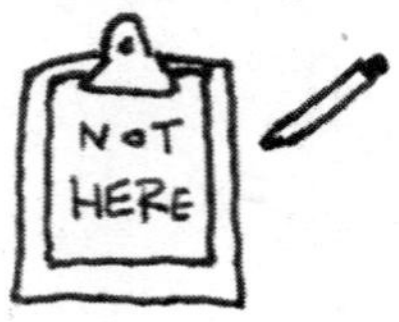

Just stop, and let us field kiss you. Bleeed you out.

(close whisper, a side story, working the door)

with D. O. U. B. T.

doubt

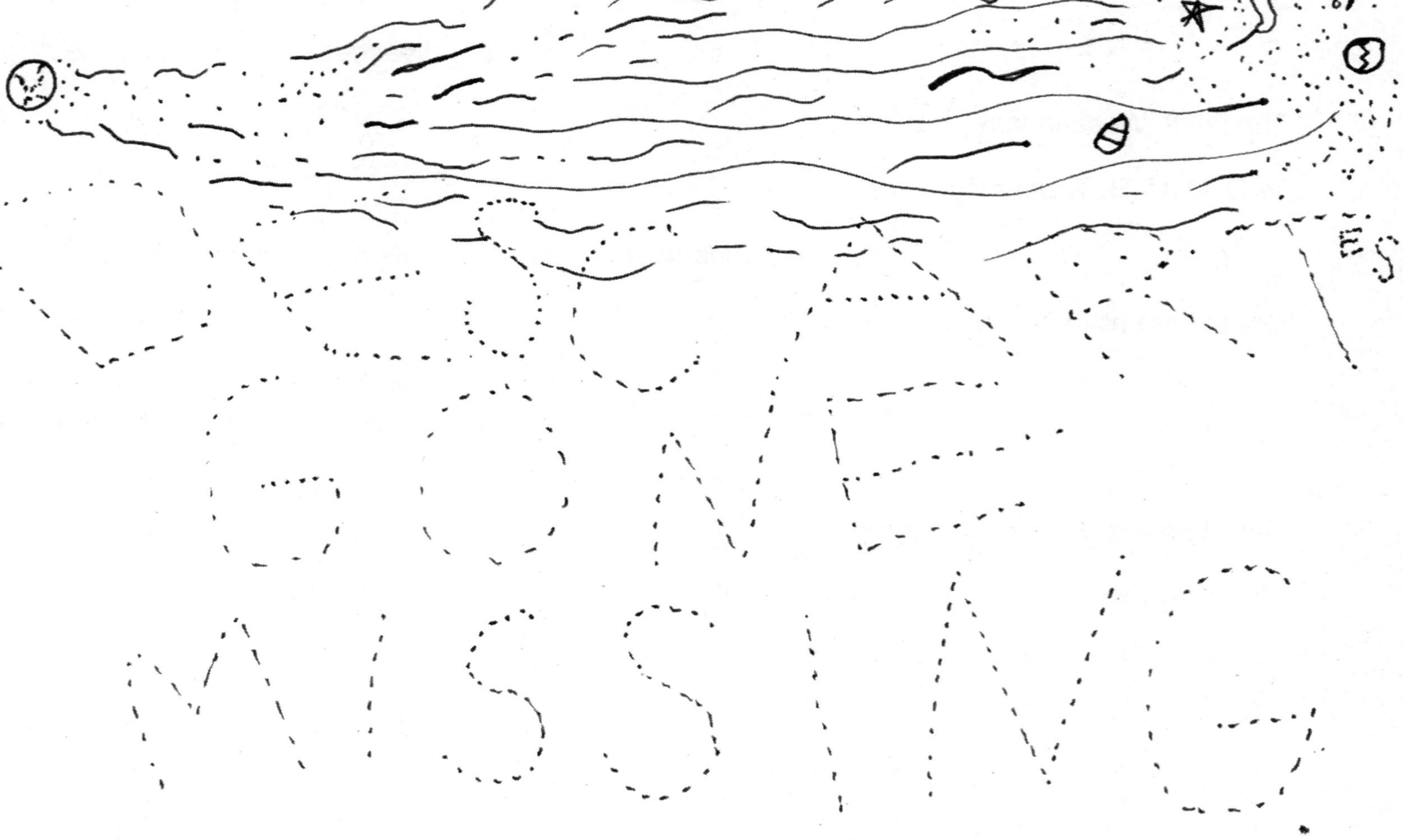

GEO WYEX

Anh interviews Ann and Avgi

Issue 60
Spring/Summer 2024

Authors
ANN PELLEGRINI
AVGI SAKETOPOULOU
ANH VO

Contributing Editor
ANH VO

Anh Vo *GENDER WITHOUT IDENTITY* is an amazing and dangerous book. As rich as it is, the relationship between gender, especially its minoritarian forms, and trauma can be easily weaponized.

Ann Pellegrini This is something we've thought about so much in the writing of this book. There were numerous moments when we thought: *SHOULD WE KEEP GOING?* We were so concerned about the potential misuse of our arguments. And we spoke about weaponization to some of our comrades, queer and trans people who shared our concerns but who encouraged us to keep going, saying that if we let our worries about how our arguments will be misused stop us, we will never actually be able to make a shift in the conversations that we believe are needed. Moreover, no amount of trying to pick our words carefully can prevent the possible misunderstanding, misreading, misapplication, and outright weaponization. It's such a fantasy that we could ever control the uses of our arguments.

GENDER WITHOUT IDENTITY

Avgi Saketopoulou Even at the proofs stage of the book, we would stop and look at each other thinking, *WE CAN STILL STOP THIS!* It was very helpful to be working with Ann on this book, because it's almost like we took turns being afraid and talking each other through it. But we felt so strongly that being able to show that it's possible to find links between gender and trauma without that necessarily delegitimizing trans and gender diverse experience. That has felt very politically important to us, because in some ways, those of us who have invested in the flourishing of trans and queer life have left trauma discourse to the right and to conservatives, those who seek to conserve the idea that assigned-at-birth genders are the only legitimate forms of gender. This has not served our communities well.

As analysts, when we work with gender complexity, we only talk about trauma in the context of people being traumatized by transphobia, gender normativity, and cis oppression, all of which are painfully true. But what about people whose gender shifts after some major traumatic events, such as sexual violation, or in the context of severe parental discord? Non-transphobic clinicians have had little to say about that, whereas transphobic ones have been saying a lot, in essence claiming that if trauma is connected to diverse gender-formation, it's because gender has become pathology. We usually respond by naming the transphobia, but at the end of the day, that is insufficient. We need to be able to push back more substantively than that.

AP There is already an argument out there, both in the public discourse as well as in numerous clinical conversations, for this constitutive relationship between trauma and transness or trauma and queerness, which involves a supposed "warping" of what should be naturally straight. To Avgi and me, there may well be a constitutive relationship, but it's of a different order. This is an intervention into the way we think not simply about transness and queerness, but about all gender. We are saying that, in fact, all gender has some relationship to trauma. In this idea, we are building on Avgi's first book, *SEXUALITY BEYOND CONSENT*, and her theorization of traumatophilia; we are also making a claim that we get to do things with trauma. Trauma isn't only what has to stop us in our tracks. Trauma can spin us. Trauma can provide us with some energy that makes it possible for us to transform, to mutate.

AV I am so glad that you did not stop going. When hearing about your process, it immediately makes me relate to my own experience being treated as a patient in psychoanalysis. At some point, I had no idea what I signed up for. I did not consent to this experience. Touching my wounds made me realize how much I have been acting out through my artistic experimentation. For a long period, I was so scared that psychoanalysis would normalize me. I am so glad that I also did not stop, because then something else happened. I hope that this something else will happen to the book as it circulates outside of your control.
Let's take a step back to unpack from a more foundational level how you approach trauma through Jean Laplanche.

AS Laplanche gives us an unusual way of thinking about trauma: not as something that interrupts the subject, but as an irritant in response to which one *BECOMES* constituted as a subject. When trauma is seen as a disruption to an organized self, as an injury to intactness, the question becomes: how do you go back to stitch up that which was cut up by the injury? In contrast, Laplanche gives us a way of thinking about how it is, in fact, the psyche's response to that which traumatizes us that organizes us into what we, at any particular moment, come to experience as our self, to understand as our identity—a sense of, *THIS IS WHO I AM.* In the après-coup, narcissism steps in to churn this into, *THIS IS WHO I HAVE ALWAYS BEEN, THIS IS MY ORIGINARY BEING.* Laplanche doesn't start with a notion that there is something true to the self that gets interrupted by trauma. Let's take Winnicott's notion of the false self, for example, for whom the focus is on a true self that is receded, covered over by false self formations. Treatment concerns, then, work that permits one's full self to emerge. But with Laplanche, there's no sense of a true self, it's all about autopoeisis, which gives us an extremely elastic way of approaching questions of gender and sexuality that don't back us into the conceptual corrner of needing to figure out what one's "real" gender or "authentic" sexuality is. This hunt for authenticity gets us in trouble as clinicians. Even in the expansive clinical models that work to be inclusive of trans people, there's still this conservative idea at the epicenter of clinical thinking: that one's gender has to correspond to something true to the self. That becomes a problem with detransition and how it is politicized these days. The logic goes like this: some people (trans and gender-nonconforming individuals) do not accurately know their "real" gender, mistakenly think they are trans and mistakenly transition only to discover this later and de-transition. In a model of transitioning that is rooted in some true or core gender identity, there's no room for someone's gender shifting after transition. You get to transition once, or so the liberal argument goes. Laplanche gives us a fertile theory with which to move away from both the essentialisms of biology, and of an interiorized, true psychological self.

AP Laplanche gives us a way to think about trauma with a lowercase t, as well as Trauma with an uppercase T. Laplanche suggests that all of us get set into motion by the outside coming inside. In fact, the contact from the outside even creates the sense of an interior, the division between the outside and the inside. The foundation of what will become the subject is actually allocentric. It starts not just from the other, but from the otherness of the other. The infant is being bombarded with messages from the world that surrounds it. And these messages are contaminated by the sexual unconscious of the adults, especially the adult caregivers that are touching the child into life, feeding, nourishing, cleaning that child. Every touch, every vocalization, even the covering of a blanket that keeps them warm are actually a message soaked with something that exceeds even the parent's consciousness. The child is tasked with making sense of these enigmatic messages, which are not content that you have to decode. There's no actual message there. But the actual contact creates the sense that there's a message intended for you. The process of making sense of that something coming inside, we could call traumatic.

AS It constitutes you, we might say, at the border of your consent.

AP Laplanche is making a claim that there's a fundamental asymmetry, especially in the first months of life, between the adult caregivers and this neonate. We're bombarded with things against our consent, creating the conditions whereby we start to become this nascent subjectivity. That's lowercase t trauma. Many of us are also subjected to uppercase T Trauma— the violence is of the social, which may have something to do with our race or our bodily capacity. So, we have a second set of potential Traumas that not everybody is subjected to equally. All of us are subjected to lowercase t trauma, in order to be a subject at all, suggests Laplanche.

AV In Avgi's book, you use the word violence to describe the process of lowercase t trauma, too.

AS Yes, in talking about what — and how much — occurs at the border of the subject's consent, we are working with ideas from Sexuality Beyond Consent: the other's otherness pierces us, indifferent to our consent, and the psyche is forced to respond to that. To respond is to give form to formlessness. How does that happen? By using materials, mythosymbolic codes, provided by the caretaker. This is why Ann was saying that with Laplanche, we're always working with allocentrism. The subject is always in relation to the social, to the other, to the other's otherness. Think of the gender panic right now: *KIDS ARE READING THE WRONG BOOKS, FREQUENTING THE WRONG INTERNET SITES, AND GET CONFUSED ABOUT THEIR GENDER.* That contagion model only works if gender is seen as an interior process: then, the outside would warp you. But if gender and sexuality are products of allocentric processes, the fiction that you are sovereign, and contact with the world endangers you, begins to lose its explanatory power.

AP All gender is scavenged from, in Laplanche's language, the mythosymbolic. All of us assemble our gender from what is presented to us culturally, though that does not imply that infants "select" from an encyclopedia of gender possibilities. The most important social ring is the one closest to the infant, their most local community — whether it's the family, the extended family — those closest to the child are offering translations of that mythosymbolic material. So, nothing comes to that infant pure. There are all sorts of mediations. If we think about the scavenging from the social, we could say that maybe all gender is contagious. All gender has caught something from the outside. It's not just queerness or transness that someone caught. Think of the bombardment of images of normative femininity, the beauty ideals of whiteness, of slimness. We have all sorts of people trying to model themselves into and after those images. If that's not the contagion of cis femininity, what is?

AV There's a certain creativity involved with relationships to the outside, too. In *GENDER WITHOUT IDENTITY,* you call this process autopoeitic self-theorization.

AP In her solo book, Avgi talks about this in terms of sovereignty. This auto-theorization is not about the volitional subject who gets to will their theorizations ex nihilo, as if they're uncontaminated by social influences. It's a kind of auto-theorization that you get to craft out of the materials that are presented to you. We did not consent to being gendered, we did not consent to being raced. Nonetheless, we can make something from these materials being presented to us that feels like our own; we can offer our own translation, our own innovative reformation of the materials that are out there. That's what makes it a self-realization or auto-theorization, but it does not start from us. I also think about this with Foucault — it's a kind of agency that happens after the fact of the conditions you didn't get to choose.

AS When Ann talks about the materials that are scavenged from the outside, the idea is not that one sees a trans person or a drag queen, and then simplistically decides 'I may be trans, too', identifying with transness in a straightforward way, as if transness is something one mimetically adopts. At stake is a queer kind of agency, which is not that of a centered, willful subject, but a process which involves the psychic labor of how we use materials from the outside, materials put at our disposal from without and which can be worked in ways that produce experience that feels ours. This is not about imitation or appropriation but about how psychic life works, by weaving codes through translational processes. Cis people who feel at ease with their gender, for instance, in a way that makes it non-remarkable, that makes it feel natural, have also undergone psychic processes that congeal into this sense of truth and authenticity. Part of how that happens is through this exercise of queer agency, which is how the unconscious manifests itself. Queer not in the sense of gay, but in its etymological sense of deviation — in the sense that it's slanted. It issues, to reference Laplanche, from a perch that the ego does not command.

These scavenged materials get sorted together inventively, through a process that is very much experimental — and you see if it takes after the fact. Cis-genders have a lot of institutional and relational support, which means that they "take" more easily. That's one way to think about why people with more atypical gender concoctions need queer community, because gender is also a social and relational process.

AP Sturdy. If one is sturdy enough...

AS Sturdiness is a good word, and we use it a lot in the book. There's sturdiness in looking for places that can support or help you experiment with your gender. Sometimes that gender will take, sometimes it will not and what that means is there's a lot of innovation in gender-becoming, a lot of trying things out before one someone may settle in what their gender is, at least for the moment. That process also involves breakdown of previous gender forms, undoing, and redoing them before something feels good enough for now. This involves taking liberties with oneself to offend the norms that have been given to us, which is part of how inventiveness and auto-poeisis proceed. Such liberty-taking is not a problem — even as some queer communities, too, can have tight protocols as to how one is trans or non-binary in the "right way". But queer agency is about the unconscious throwing it all up in the air and we then watch how it lands. Is it livable or not? Does it bring pleasure or not?

AP What we are describing is also true of normatively-gendered and normatively-desiring subjects. This is not just about transness and queerness. However, if you are cis and straight, there's a whole network of support that patches up fissures in your experience and identity. I use the term *IDENTITY* very loosely, because we are arguing for a loosening of the grip of the term *IDENTITY.* One of the places in which cis and straight people get patched up in that way is, of course, psychoanalysis. Historically, psychoanalysis has offered straight and cis people ways to talk about the miseries of their heterosexual gender, the difficulties of what it is to be a gendered subject in the world. Psychoanalysis has addressed those vicissitudes and struggles, but not with the idea that if you are someone who has been assigned female at birth and you are struggling with femininity, you must actually be trans. Psychoanalysis does not try to convert struggling heterosexuals and cis people; it sees their struggles as part of the human condition. We want a psychoanalysis that can offer queer and trans people the same resources that allow for vicissitudes, struggles, miseries, and trauma without that recognition somehow invalidating transness or queerness. Trans and queer people should get to have all the feels, including negative feelings. That's why we're very influenced by recent, exciting work in trans-negativity in this project.

AV I want to come back to this term *EXPERIMENTAL*, which is very relevant in the experimental dance context. It is so important that you are describing it through this lens of queer agency that is about this process of throwing it in the air and moving through the feeling to see if it takes or not. Oftentimes, when I think about artistic experimentation, it can fall into the realm of action. That is why I am very hesitant to bring up how you talk about gender in the book as a "wildly improvisational process," which might sound a little too willful.

AS Indeed, talking about it this way invites this risk. For example, the idea that something is improvisational can sound too conscious or willful of a process, get flattened into a prescriptive: *YOU SHOULD NOW IMPROVISE OR EXPERIMENT.* This is not what we mean by experimentation: it's not some task of experimenting, which turns this into a linear, progressive project. As you point out, that would be a stunningly impoverished reading of what we are trying to do.

In talking about wildly improvisational processes, we are also talking about things that are messy and anarchic, because improvisation involves a lot of doing, undoing, and redoing – though, importantly, none of this is a conscious, willed process. Rather, it is messy and difficult. And it produces some forms of gender that can *LOOK* unimpeachable but are actually quite fragile (as is the case with some cis genders), while other forms of gender (whether trans, non-binary, or cis) may be capable of taking the heat of distress, upset, or failed relationships. The latter, I would argue, can be robust in ways we don't usually associate with gender.

AV **The book itself does provide some hints of how to move through this. I'm thinking specifically of one case study where you, Avgi, evaluate that you have failed this one particular patient. As you sit with that failure, you say something along the line of, if you had done it differently, you would have waited, rather than interpreted. I find that to be such an important call—to just wait. Using these words like experimentation and improvisation can create this illusion of action. *THE TASK IS TO DO AND THE TIME IS NOW.* Whereas the book is full of messiness, negativity, failure, pain; of having to wait and just let that soak in.**

AP The waiting that Avgi is talking about in describing the case of this young child, Ory, is not about making the patient wait. We also use the language of *PATIENT AFFIRMATION*. There is this approach of a watchful waiting that some clinicians are taking with regards to trans subjects and, in particular, trans kids. *WE DON'T KNOW YET WHAT YOUR GENDER WILL REALLY BE, SO WE'VE GOT TO SLOW YOU DOWN, HOLD ON, JUST WAIT.* That is waiting as an imperative passed from the clinician to the patient — the *PATIENT AFFIRMATION* kind of waiting for which we are advocating is different: it's saying that *WE* need to wait, so that we do not rush to fill in what we think we know. It is to stay really close to the patient's experience, because we do not know what is going to unfold. Neither does the patient. It is about dealing with our own anxiety and desire to rush. It is a slow process. It is not the temporality of every day. Some people come four times a week. What does it mean to give oneself over to a process that has no foreordained conclusion?

AS To say this slightly differently, we think of waiting here as a resource, not in the way that clinicians who are engaged in what I call anti-trans clinical activism think of waiting; that is, that trans children should wait indefinitely before qualifying for transition services, if at all.
Ann's point is that this is about the *THERAPIST'S* waiting. With Ory, the child whose clinical case we discuss in the book, a child who was very timid and held back, the work permitted a burst of hope and pleasure to arrive in the room. These were then interrupted by the sadness and the danger of their mother's anxiety about their gender: that's where I didn't wait. In retrospect, I think that Ory did not actually need me to see how much his parents were constricting him, true as that was; he needed me, I think, to be present with him while experimenting, and the therapy room was the space where he actually escaped that constriction. I wanted to talk about the trauma of gender policing when what Ory needed to do was observe, celebrate, and therefore support his gender-which is what the orchid, the talk about fabrics, his moving me around the room making me touch this or that thing were about. The problem is that I was too preoccupied with how he was being cut down. Not that it is unreasonable to pay attention to such constriction: any clinician can see how I got there, it is not a big leap to want to mark a patient's pain. But that was *MY* preoccupation at the moment, not where he was at. That is my mistake, then: I am not patient in that stage of the treatment to stay with his pleasure, I want to offer him something else, something I think he needs — recognition of his pain, rather than the pleasure of his experimentation.

AP Maybe you focused on "the trauma" or the constrictions, and not on what he himself was already able to do with what was being passed onto him, through intergenerational transmission, and the constrictions of the immediate family, and the wider culture that he was part of. In some sense, this is a case that happened before the development of your clinical thinking about traumatophobia versus traumatophilia. In thinking about the mistake, this has also allowed for a different way of thinking about the relationship between trauma and intergenerational transmission in the book. You did not yet know what is now in the book.

AS That is true. And, using that idea, that trauma can become a generative energy, that it can be spun into something else, I always have the hope that Ory will come back to see me at some later point. When you work with children, sometimes they come to see you in adulthood, to process earlier moments or to continue the work. I do not know what this experience with me meant to him. I still wish I had waited, and I regret I didn't. Still, I am curious about what this very sturdy child may have spun out of his experience with me.

AP I'm thinking about theory-making, not the auto-theorization we were talking about earlier, but theory-making as in the making of this book. So, there was this case that Avgi came to describe as a "failure," though we do not know what Ory may have done with it... One of the things that Avgi did with that failure is she has been thinking about it and thinking about it and thinking about it. She wrote this case presentation, which then became the basis for our theoretical work that is in this book. In other words, this book's theory-making also came out of disappointment or failure for us.

And the book in its entirety was a response to our own traumatic experience in another way, too. Avgi and I together worked on a paper around Ory's case, which won a prestigious prize in 2021, the Tiresias Award, given by the International Psychoanalytical Association. It was the first time they had given a prize recognizing work in gender and sexual diversity, which shows us how out-of-touch psychoanalysis still is. The award came with the possibility of publication in the *INTERNATIONAL JOURNAL OF PSYCHOANALYSIS*, the oldest journal in the field, founded by Freud himself. We submitted the paper, and it was accepted. We were given revisions, we went through edits. A year later, we handed in what we thought was the last version. We added acknowledgments and another section about the social context. Then suddenly, everything changed. Ultimately, the offer of publication was withdrawn because we refused to take certain sentences out of our acknowledgments. It was super draining and puzzling. There were implied legal threats. It consumed an entire summer trying to figure out what was going on. We suddenly had an article. What were we going to do with it?

One of the things we did with it was this book. We churned this really horrible experience into something. The argument is actually better in this book because we got to extend it. But would I prefer to not have had that experience? For sure. Am I really happy with what came out of it? Even more. That would be another example of how theory-making comes out of experiences that we did not get to choose, that indeed have been miserable, even traumatic. We can do things out of that as well.

AV Throughout this interview, doing has been coming up a lot — how we can do things with trauma. I am also thinking about gender performativity, and its formation around doing. In my own experience being in psychoanalytic treatment, doing does not take priority when it comes to creativity. It is more about this feeling that you can create, rather than the actual creation itself.

AP Action is a really strange category in psychoanalysis, because there is a long tradition of psychoanalysis saying: Don't act out. Speak. Speaking is posited as not just the opposite of, but also the solution to, the problematic acting out. This has a homophobic and transphobic history, because it situates the seeking of gender transition in the domain of action, of acting out. It would also be acting out to have a homosexual relation rather than sitting with your analyst and talking about your same-sex desires so they may be resolved. Who is allowed to act and have it be seen as just what you are doing in the world? When is action troublemaking—the wrong kind of action in the wrong kind of place?

AS Nor are we saying in a facile way, you need not be worried about your trauma, why not just do something with it? Our call is about being more attentive to the things that subjects already do with their trauma, just like Ory was already doing something with the blend of anti-semitism, patriarchy, and his mother's intergenerational trauma. The generativity of trauma is something that psychoanalysis has not had a lot of tolerance to think with, especially when it produces something that is non-normative; psychoanalysis has struggled to think about how trauma may be woven into our understanding of ourselves.

In the clinic, too, such connections between trauma and queerness, for example, can make someone feel very ashamed, as if "good gender" is some stand-alone, pure thing, unalloyed by experience. This is what the ideology of a core gender identity, and of gender as true and authentic to the self, produce. I have sat in the consulting room with many patients who worry that if a sexual violation has had something to do with their gender and sexuality, that makes their gender untrue or makes their sexuality into a symptom. So in talking about traumatophilia, we are speaking to clinicians, but also want to intervene in wider conversations, to offer more expansive and more complex tools with which to think about how gender acquires its experiential texture. We do not need to be weighed down by imagining we owe fidelity to some fictional, authentic gender that is innate and untouched by culture, experience, or trauma. Letting go of this imperative to be "true" or "authentic" may actually enable people to be in their genders with more pleasure and more joy, not having to protect or validate them all the time. There is nothing true or untrue, right or wrong about anyone's gender: gender just is.

AP To go back to our notion of queer agency in the context of trauma, to suggest that trauma may have contributed to your gender and sexuality does not mean it is something that just "happened" to you, turning you into a passive subject. To be sure, these are materials that you did not choose, but you have done something with after the fact. This is a different way of talking about development. We are trying to offer an account of how gender is acquired or develops over time without this tipping into developmentalism. Developmentalism has a telos, the homotransphobic form of which is that it is always already unfolding into heterosexual cisgender. So, let's get this person back on the straight track! What we have had so far for those who want to affirm queerness and transness – and to do so in developmental terms — is to say that this process of change over time is always already unfolding into the truth of this person being queer, the truth of this person being trans. This developmental path may not be straight, but it is still *STRAIGHTFORWARD*, in the sense of being linear and unidirectional.

In the end (and telos means the end), the end is founded in the beginning. It was always already there in the subject, just waiting to spring to life. But we are trying to think about the development of gender and sexuality over time, with multiple determinants and multiple possible destinations. These multiple determinants mean that things could be assembled in different ways by different people. Moreover, things could be assembled in different ways by the same person across their lifetime. It is a different way to think about causality. It is not the causality of if A then B. It is the contingencies of how someone becomes.

AS If you subscribe to this understanding of gender as an acquisition, then you have to let go of the notion of prediction. You step off the self-righteous perch of granting gender-related services, for example, by ascertaining someone's "true" gender. What we are proposing involves signing up for a version of gender that cannot be confirmed or disconfirmed: there are no protocols by which you decide that one's gender is right or wrong. You are opening yourself up to something that could be constantly shifting. As human beings, we like stability and we like to keep things settled and set in place. But the more you commit to things in yourself being set, the tighter you are wound to think this way, the more you become stalled. And, in fact, it is that very "stalling" that comes under pressure for some cis people in their encounters with trans subjects: for some cis people that encounter reveals to you your own constriction, and a lot of anxiety can be generated by that. We oftentimes see that anxiety being psychically managed in problematic ways: the disturbance to one's own self-stability that can arise in the encounter with a trans body can defensively morph into a cis person doubling down and trying to control the other — their gender, their expression, their access, their rights. That is where hatred comes in and how we see these increasingly restrictive policies on the legislative level recently.

AV Letting go of stability and certainty is a lifelong project and does not happen overnight.

AS Absolutely.

AV This idea of gender being allocentric is so radical, though. It makes so much sense for me thinking through the Vietnamese language, which makes it impossible to conceptualize gender through the lens of self-affirmation. With English, you can make the claim, *I AM THIS, MY PRONOUN IS THAT*. Whereas in Vietnamese, pronouns are always contextual and relational—in relation to age, to gender, to the formality of the relationship. It speaks to this moment in the book where you say that gender is not a private language; it always implicates us with others.

AP What you are describing — gender as relational — just makes so much sense. How do different linguistic possibilities shape gender possibilities? Even the protocol of *MY PRONOUN IS...* gets caught up in the notion of gender as private property that I am safeguarding. If you misgender me, you have somehow stolen something from me. I am not talking about people actively and consciously disrespecting someone's gender pronouns; that is not okay. I am talking about the ways in which we might misrecognize someone in everyday life, not because we are being callous or disrespectful. What does it mean to believe you can go through the world and think you are never going to be misrecognized, not just with respect to gender? What congeals around gender such that we think we can commandeer the world? Is there something colonial about the ways in which we think we can grasp a gender and assert our claims over it? Kadji Amin says some really interesting things about that in a fascinating 2022 article, "We Are All Nonbinary: A Brief History of Accidents." I both will respect the protocols whereby someone wants to tell me their preferred gender pronouns, and also – with my Foucault hat on! – wonder about the cultural context within which such statements are meaningfully made.

AS Talking about cultural context, I am thinking of how people do not know how to pronounce my name. A lot of well-meaning American interlocutors very kindly ask me, *HOW DO I SAY YOUR NAME? DID I SAY IT RIGHT?* And when they don't, *BUT I WANT TO GET IT RIGHT, TELL ME AGAIN*, and I know comes from a place of wanting to be respectful. But if you do not grow up speaking Greek or Cypriot, you are just not going to be able to pronounce the "g" in Avgi in the right way. That inability, to me, is okay, wanting to make the effort and failing still. I do not expect to be addressed in the precisely minute version of what speaks to me. That is different from people who make no effort or who ask me if they can call me something else because they can't pronounce my name.

What I am trying to speak to is that there is an irreducible gap between us as human beings that cannot be closed. It cannot be closed by respect or good intention; it will always overcome us.The question is how to relate to each other around that gap. And how to do so without trying to level difference, but by bearing the differences between us. I know I do not say everybody's name right; however much I try, there are enunciations that my mouth cannot produce. Recognition and affirmation have nowadays become mandates that exert their own violences, which is not to minimize the violence of purposeful misrecognition, where somebody purposefully misgenders a person – as if they are marking the other person's "deception," which is not "tricking" them. There is a fundamental, unclosable gap between subjects: it is a matter of ethics to respect that gap, to accord it the dignity of its existence without trying to eliminate it, as the rhetorics of recognition and affirmation falsely imagine is possible.

AP I want to draw on something Judith Butler argued in an early essay ("Imitation and Gender Insubordination") about what it means to come out of the closet and disclose one is a lesbian. Butler wanted to highlight the opacity of such a claim: you come out of the closet only to enter another one. Before you did not know I am one (a lesbian), they write, but after you do not know what I mean by lesbian. We could put this insight to work to think about third-person singular uses of the pronoun "they." Let's say you get the pronoun "they" right of someone who is non- binary. But that does not mean that you know what that person means by it or how it resonates for them. Nor, and this is Butler's further point, does the person who uses "they" themselves understand fully what that pronoun means and does for them. It is in excess of their own self-understanding. The "I" is also opaque to itself. That is one of the things that psychoanalysis teaches us. There is always a gap between subjects no matter how hard we try. And there is a gap inside subjects, too—the splitting in ourselves.

AS I am thinking of what you were saying about Vietnamese pronouns. I have heard well-meaning liberals, when confronted with such linguistic differences, responding this difference by treating it appropriatively. I think of a Western's subject seemingly open-minded response to such linguistic richness and can imagine someone asking if it might not be better if American English adopts the same linguistic conventions. This is the sort of thing I feel impatient about—about subjects who relate to difference by wanting to have it all, to appropriate, to own everything, you want your hands on everything. What about sitting with the delight that is difference and becoming curious about what it illuminates about *YOU*?

ANN PELLEGRINI
AVGI SAKETOPOULOU
ANH VO

Centerfold

Author and
Contributing Editor
NICOLE BRADBURY

Issue #3 of the *MOVEMENT RESEARCH PERFORMANCE JOURNAL* was published the year after Judith Butler's *GENDER TROUBLE,* though both grew out of a burgeoning scene of queer performance practices in the 80s and 90s. In reimaging *MRPJ*'s Issue #3 "Gender Disarray," we wanted to honor its focus on queer and trans performance artists pushing against policing of the gender binary through their embodied practices. We also wanted to recognize that these both definitions of gender and the barriers constructed in the name of gender's supposed "binary" have shifted since the 90s when Issue #3 was published and will continue to shift well beyond the publication of Issue #60. With past and future ideologies of gender collapsing into the "now," this centerfold holds the work of three artists of a new generation. Each artist has shared a statement and visual component extrapolating on gender as a central, fundamental component in their work and lives. At the same time, placing this overt reflection on "gender" at the centermost point of this publication, we recognize that Issue #60 will never speak to the totality of gender. To that end, we invite the reader to imagine what the construction of gender as centrifugal to this issue might do to obfuscate other ways of thinking, knowing, and sensing what this centerfold is all about, what the work of these three artists is all about, as an invitation to let gender come in and out of focus, as it so often does in daily life.

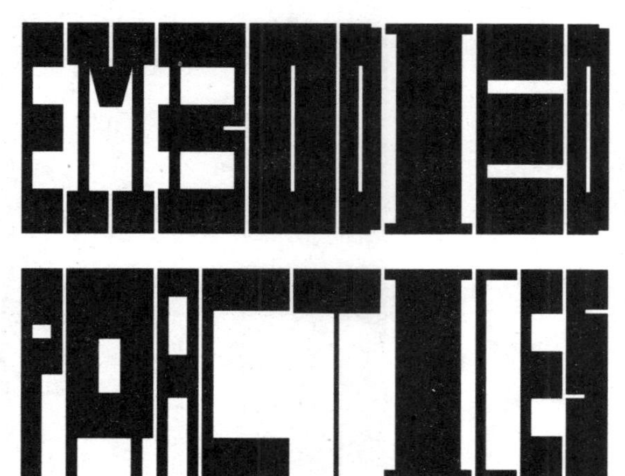

My thoughts on gender + performance

Author
KAIJO CAGGINS

Contributing Editor
NICOLE BRADBURY

I enter into performance and dance spaces as a queer + trans person that was raised in the south. Today, I yearn for spacious land and sweet nothings from neighbors while checking the mail. I am tethered to this place. Here, I also meet the challenge of being seen as my truest self; in all of my genderfuckery. I find solace in larger cities as my gender is experienced as infinite. I am seen here. Possibilities are vast and always arising. My soul feels tender and sometimes too soft for this kind of life. I take so many naps. I am tired. My body pain flares. The doctors seem better here. I can get my testosterone prescription filled. I need to lay in wildflowers or clover or something lush. I wish to only hear the wind for a while. My artistic practices and work center around getting to know myself. I practice meeting and re/meeting the person that I am. The rigor of this work is the act of being fulfilled with who I am at any moment. I am always changing and coming back to my heart space. I return. I spin. I fall. I keep practicing. I lean on Buddhist philosophy in this journey of loving and sitting with my multiplicity. "We have to understand that at some point we have to develop an attitude of needing to love everything, especially what is unloveable. Everything has to be loved if you're interested in getting free." –Lama Rod Owens

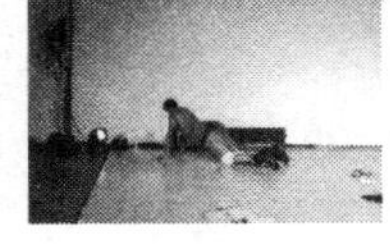 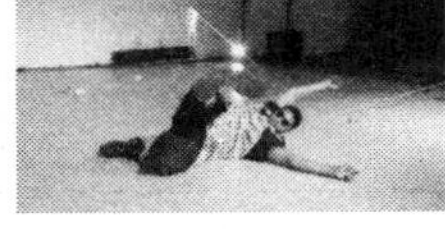

Movement Research

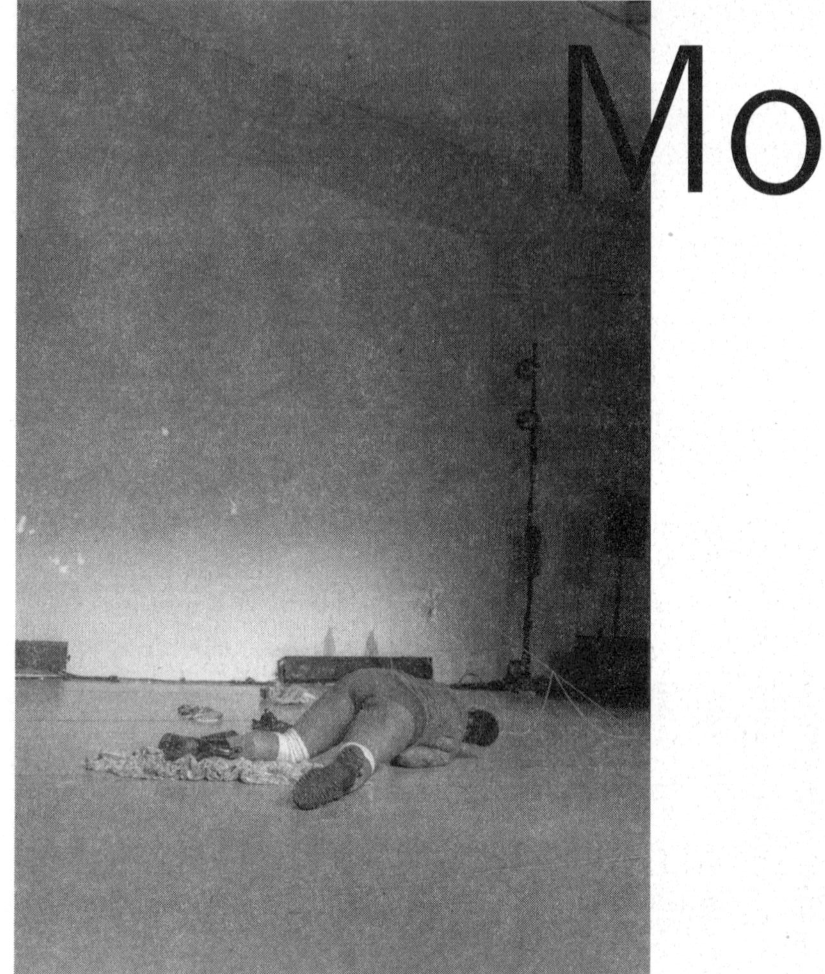

kaijo caggins, fem baby, Icebox Project Space (Philadelphia, 2023). Photo by Shosh Issacs.

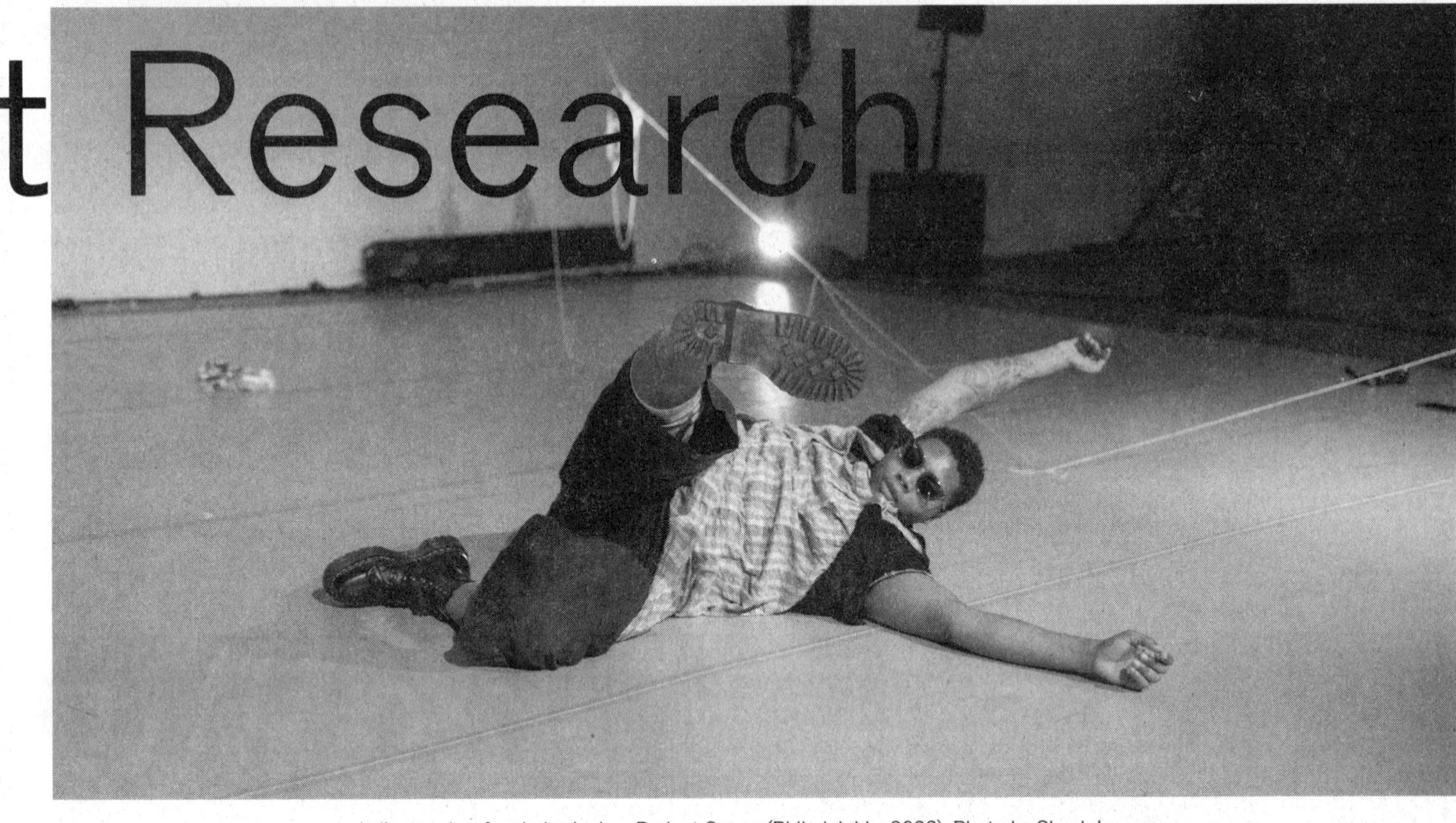

kaijo caggins, fem baby, Icebox Project Space (Philadelphia, 2023). Photo by Shosh Issacs.

kaijo caggins

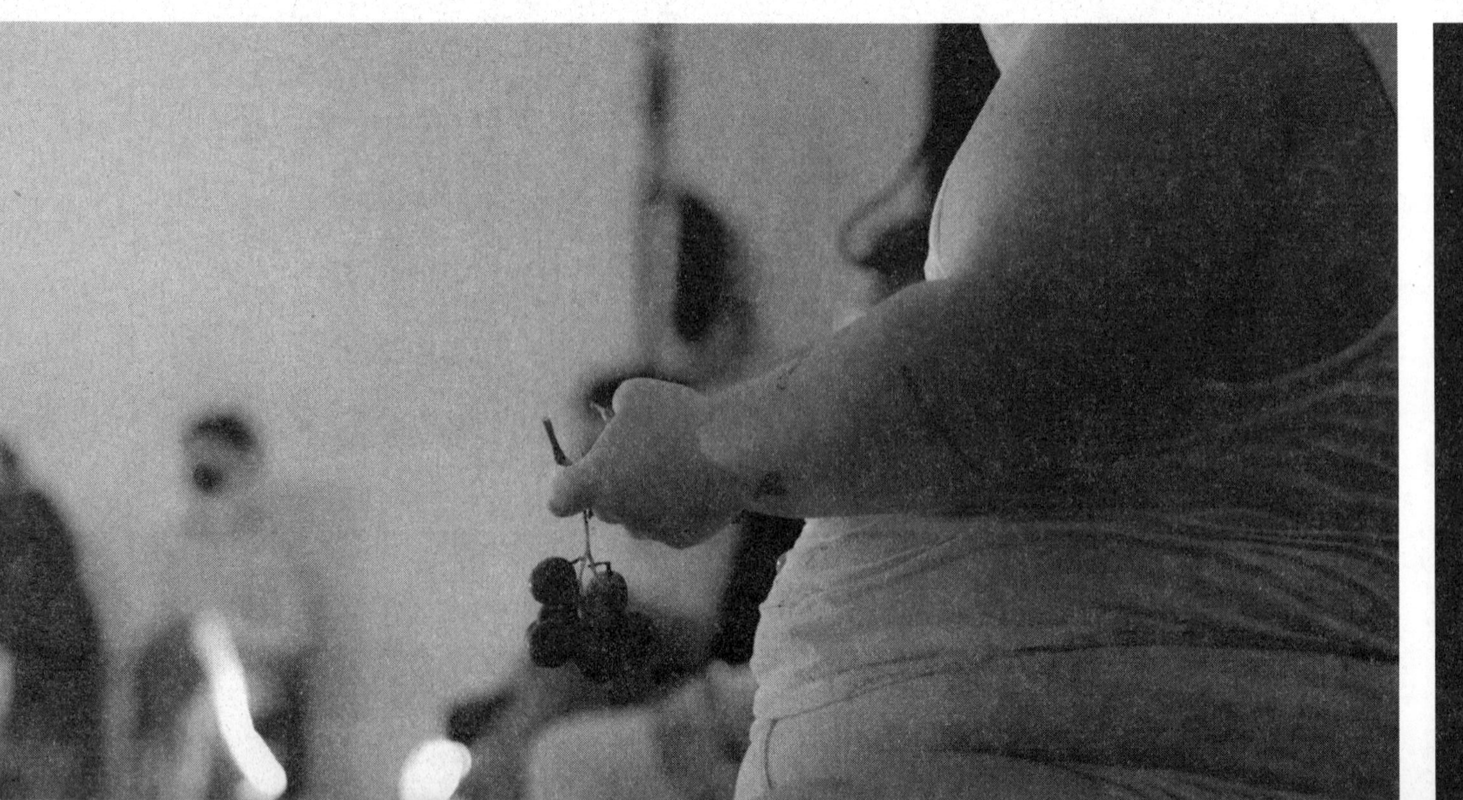

mik phillips, mike baby please (Philadelphia, 2023). Photo by Jorgie Ingram.

mik phillips, mike baby please (Philadelphia, 2023). Photo by Jorgie Ingram.

mik phillips

Photo by Maria Baranova.

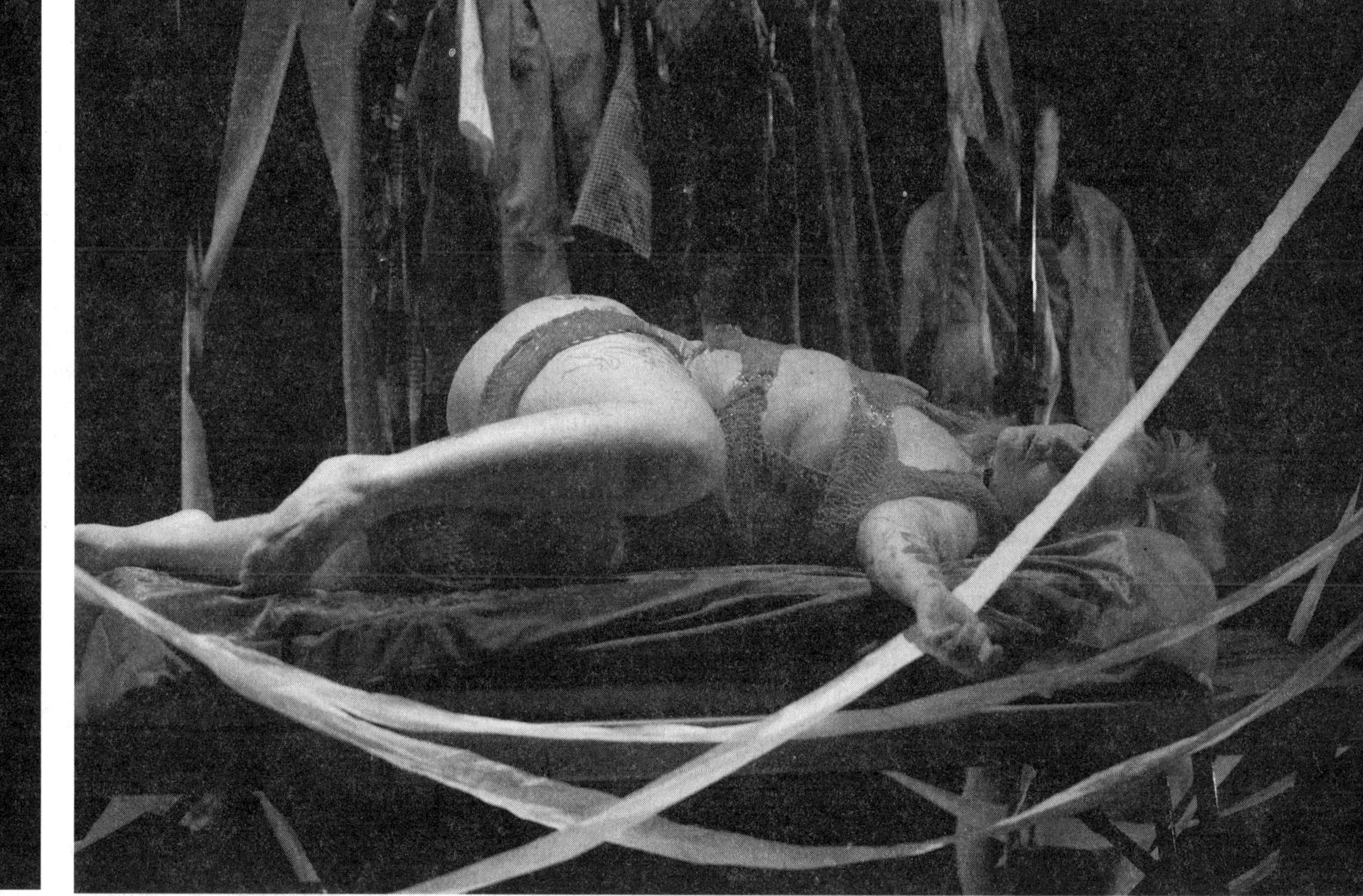

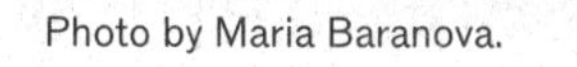

Photo by Maria Baranova.

moss lovejoy

manifesto and/or movement ritual for-from-with my boy pussy

Author
MIK PHILLIPS

Contributing Editor
NICOLE BRADBURY

i continue practicing incessant unbecomingness. reveling in the unkempt exploration, i move toward sustaining future where to be unbecoming is celebratory/mournful, painful/sensational, extraordinary/unremarkable. i feel the sensations in my chest growing as scar tissue lessens and new chest hairs sprout at insurmountable speed; they teach me to feel less tied to keeping up with myself. once a day, i look down at my boy pussy and gently yell, *GROW*. i do the same thing with my plants in my bay window. for this part, i try to pace the urgency, despite it all, i refuse to let me tell things how fast they should move. i continue to well and pay reverence to how close my skin is to my sternum; i spiral in and out – sternum first, boy pussy trailing. i'll continue essentializing and perversing movement and i will be forgiving to myself when i can't feel my body the way i want and can only feel it through a tense form of teeth gritting need. the movement inside my need will teach me tumultuous lessons; i begin grieving again (i love that it's nasty). my aging boy pussy makes space for unbecoming again and again and again.

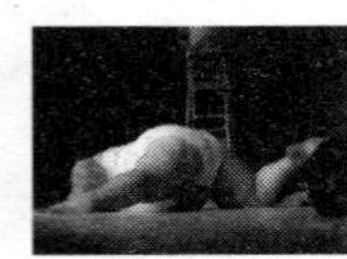
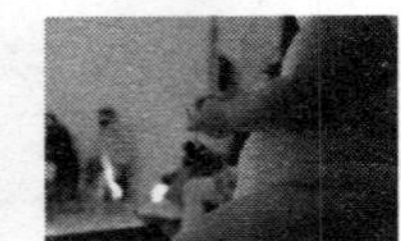

unrecognizable

Author
MOSS LOVEJOY

Contributing Editor
NICOLE BRADBURY

I find that dance-making and gender-making are often parallel quests for me. It's anguish and euphoria. It's ancient, modern, classic, contemporary, prehistoric, and post-modern. It's both the act of shattering and the shards that remain. It's both the act of collecting and the collection itself. It has everything and nothing to do with perception (the viewer's and performer's). Sometimes it's supposed to be the journey but ends up being the destination (and vice-versa). Usually, it's unsatisfactory in some ineffable way (but I remain hopeful that this is going to get better with time). It tends to feel the most gratifying in glittering moments of recognition, potent enough to hold me over until the next. To bring my vision into reality is miraculous enough; to then have it interpreted, understood, and magnified by a viewer is a gratification beyond description. My body craves resistance to definition, which inevitably involves engaging with defining and being defined. I'm certainly never going to be or do anything just because someone tells me I'm supposed to, but I'm also not going to do the opposite purely out of defiance—I'm usually going to do what feels good. Though there's an element of masochism in straddling belligerent and demure, grit and seduction, or any other forces positioned in a binary . Whether I'm performing my gender or a dance, I'm stretching myself, looking for some response from or dialogue with the viewer, further information to guide my quest. Part of me is programmed to desire recognition, but being deemed unrecognizable can feel even more affirming. It reassures me that I can't be quietly filed away under a colonial category, easily assigned a cog in the imperial machine. It confirms that I am not a copy of a copy, a ghost of a ghost, a replica, a recreation, a reproduction, an imitation. I am a new iteration, made possible by a lineage and tradition of resisting and redefining.

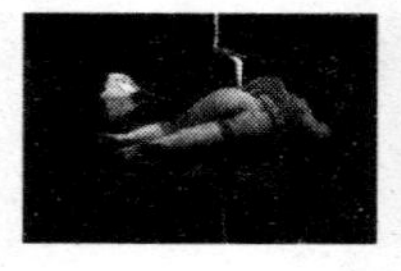
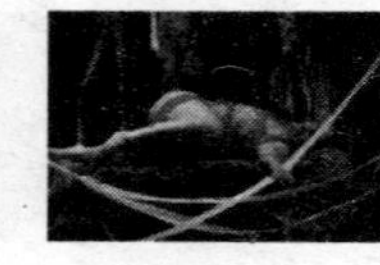

Issue 60
Spring/Summer 2024

astringency principle of the looking drum

Author
S*AN D. HENRY-SMITH

Contributing Editor
AMALLE DUBLON

God is dumb
until the drum
Speaks.

The drum
is dumb
until the gong-gong leads

it.

— "Making of the Drum", *THE ARRIVANTS: A NEW WORLD TRILOGY*, Kamau Brathwaite

"I had to go to work with heavy metal."

— "Colossal", *DS2*, Future

"If" is the conjunction of contingency. Uncertainty is free. I can't predict its tangent.

— "Perspectors/Melancholia", *NILLING*, Lisa Robertson

<u>[Begin, voice only. At each "—" add a new phrasing of camera sounds to the loop.]</u>

Burning latency. Look. How it hastened to be here: Light permeates the darkened space. Light / fills the space. It traveled to get here. Years / it traveled to get here. Here. In the whole of this room. The womb of this light. Light / welling over. Burning latency. Light enters the whole of my looking drum.

—

My listening drum. Metal drum.
Thinking drum,
my l____ing drum
<u>whoosh</u>
my l____ing drum
<u>chunk</u>
my l____ing drum
<u>whir</u>
my l____ing drum
<u>click</u>
my l____ing drum
<u>thunk</u>
my l____ing drum
<u>think</u>
my l____ing drum
<u>thud</u>
my l____ing drum
<u>thump</u>
my l____ing drum
<u>tin</u>
my metal drum
<u>drones</u>
my l____ing drum
<u>gears</u>

—

Dub. The rudiments of this rhythm. Palm pressed against the metal skeem / echoes into the time it gathered. Organic obscura / sound sight. Ride the riddim.

—

my metal drum
<u>bones</u>
my l____ing drum
<u>kick</u>
my l____ing drum
<u>clash</u>
my l____ing drum
<u>toms</u>
my talking drum
<u>looks</u>

—

My sampling drum heard:
the earth /
the sun /
the sea /
the sound /
the room /
the light /
your voice /
your voice /

—

In Obscura. In astringency, little latency oscillates. Impulse of retina ossicles. Groove the ghost note. The ghost note bites,
& light translates to image. My looking drum sings odd time / off time / paradiddle
Notation of light. Notation of life. Light translates image.

—

Portrait of silence. Landscape of sound. Landscape of silence. Portrait of noise, noise portrait. & when I am in that visual music *MMHM*.

—

No capture, I'm caught up! In the sound of light passing through this hollow body, this holy drum looking out, listening. Throwing mirrors. The life. It hastened /
to be
here. So then /
capture <u>confounded</u>
<u>our speech</u>. In our daily,
our social. Whole hierarchies
<u>it ruins / it makes</u>.
Capture / makes capital.
I don't
want it.

—

Nothing of it. How they weaponized light. Life weaponized. I don't want it. Empire breeds but Itself. Eats all Light. All Beautiful things. The mechanics of sight replicate the drum. Life hastened to be here. Light hastened to be here. Let the light eat it all light. Lost in that visual music.

—

<u>& no drum grates like the piano</u>
<u>Ain't no devil like the devil in me.</u>
<u>Possessed by that visual music.</u>
<u>& by the end of the night let the</u>
<u>drummer off the leash</u> *[EARN IT!! ONLY ONCE]*

—

DeCarava was dancing! He was dancing in that experimental dark / listening to it.

—

So look, the sound I saw, I'm seeing!
My blur is result of my dancing.
Blur / result of this sound
Blur / result of this blurring
Blur / result of this *WOOSH*
Blur / result of this

The primary instrument of experience is the body. Embodiment does not belong to human experience alone. This body of water plays this metal body. Waves unfold to frequency. echolocate here in this body, mine & inseparable. Poetry is equally an act of embodiment as that of language. A natural poetics — language unopposed to itself, expressed with ease, inseparable from the body — to think with Glissant, is "the direct result of activity within the social body." Which means it is inseparable from you, us, our gathering. Specifically considering African-descended poetics, this practice has historically been communal, rhythmic, and en-drummed. [repeat, delay]

"Forced poetics exist where a need for expression confronts an inability to achieve expression.", he goes on to say. Let me be in this force of this drum, I need it. The boom of my drum. I need it. Til it's again natural. Witness of light. [Flash phrase into loop]. The sound of this light. Fills the room. The organic possibility of the medium — light enters a dark space, inviting a reflected image of the outside world, the very mechanics of our eyes — I need it. What is the native tongue of the machine? Linguistics of a proto-photo-always. To reiterate: photography, like poetry, is equal parts language and embodiment. As a tool, the camera encourages a set of choreographies that, in its fluency, remain conscious and unconscious to its user at the time of exposure.

A photographic approach to wind will only reflect its effects, without applying adequate patience. The photograph will simultaneously reflect the subliminal arrangements of its maker. The camera is a listening instrument, percussive as it is. What demands presence will appear, regardless of frame. It is the cacophony & rogue mathematics of rhythm & secret / in this light, through this drum. Can you hear it? Can you dance?

Though emergent of a relatively short history, it has taken no time for this medium to accrue an extremely tensioned history for itself. The camera is a dangerous instrument if not approached with caution and care. Akin to its operator, it must be treated as porous. Writing under imposed language, English being the imperial language happenstance has handed me, we invent anew atop colonized tongues The photographic language produced by a Black photographer can be restricted to the pressures of a forced poetics[1] if isolated and unsupported. New creoles and coded languages allow us to re-privatize our language, in open secret.

[Return to columns — cut it up, cut across. Build in response to the loop. Then peel back the layers slowly, but not into quiet.]

[reflections]

The text of *ASTRINGENCY PRINCIPLE OF THE LOOKING DRUM* began as a poem, but also as an essay and wouldn't complete itself as either. Rather, I wanted it to complete itself in either one of those directions, or to mold it into a more recognizably critical format. But I had to trust what the text was doing, and that it enabled the work at hand. The text had to become something I could do. The text/script/score developed and enabled my movements, my voice, my questioning. The critical element was in my doing. Making note of impulse made pattern equals habit. Then freak it. Throughout my practice there's a commitment to the jumping in; an always-already and ongoing conversation continues/crescendos/quiets into another. *ASTRINGENCY* loaded in from a slow quiet I could look into, a dazzling of mirrors and metal. I'm meditating on a proto-photography, an always-photography, a photography before language, or rather a photography whose language precedes the early 1800s inventions — necessarily plural, and of the traceable histories, I want to consider the untraceables — of photography (by which we mean the ability to still life and make prints/record of the still), but also precedes colonialism, catalogue, capture, surveillance, or any other arm-bending of the medium by the state. Thinking alongside Kamau Brathwaite's *HISTORY OF THE VOICE*, I am also looking at a creolization of photo-speak, as there must be a way in which that organic language has been maintained and invented despite the violence of imposed languages, and flourishes in its divinatory aims. There's something holy in the Jamaican patois pronunciation of "flim". I had to hear it out, listen through to get somewhere. I start with the very camera I use, looking through to listen back.

The performance text serves as a glossary, a set of manifestations, and instructions. It would not let itself be read vertically or horizontally, but instead required an activation and sampling across the wide page. It required some memorization, and some entrancing. I had to lose myself in words. It requires response in real time. Even now, as I think of placing it in print, I wonder if I fix it prematurely. There is a selectively listening universe that I participate in. My attention, and yours, dare I think of it, is my shame and my obsession.

A performance text shares poetic intention. As they've taken shape for me thus far/at this time, they operate as a compilation of language to read across, fragments to sample through when the music calls. A performance text might allow a totalizing — previously written/published/discarded works of prose or poetry found their way into this flow, only making sense when they came together. They seem to live differently to me, the performance text and the poem, and activate a previous and consistent problem of song: when does it begin? When does it end? Can we dwell on the melody, loop on the riff? Rough the riff up, loop the line in. Lean on it. Notation was a memory I can't always hold. So these hums, clicks, thuds, and rotations. / *HAD TO GO TO WORK WITH HEAVY METAL*. Harmonics of a pulse that ponders. So the palm was the score. The poem, the score, Cecicly Nicholson: *INTERIORITY OF A DETERMINED WILL (LOGICS FLESHED TO EXTEND SURVIVAL/AGAINST CATEGORIES)*. Extend this surviving drum. Its shape proposes the pacing of breath and punctuation. It instructed the voice and occupation of character. It made way for other ways of knowing, the vibration of circuits summoned spirits. What may be revealed reveals itself.

S*AN D. HENRY-SMITH

1 "Forced poetics exist where a need for expression confronts an inability to achieve expression.", Glissant goes on to say.

Let's Get Loud!

Author
AMBER JAMILLA MUSSER

Contributing Editor
MRPJ

Clad in a neon yellow and black zebra print form-fitting catsuit and high heels, Ayana Evans cuts a striking figure. Amid a sea of people dressed in more conventional (and less shocking) colorways, her presence as a Black woman registers as an exclamation point, giving us an occasion to think about loudness as a variation of Kate Bornstein's concept of a "gender troublemaker." In the 1991 third issue of *MOVEMENT RESEARCH PERFORMANCE JOURNAL,* Caroline Palmer describes Bornstein's investment in deconstructing gender in relation to famous tricksters, writing, "Bornstein views herself as a sort of gender troublemaker, identifying herself with such characters as the native American trickster coyote and uncle Remus' brer rabbit whose exploits provide learning experiences for others." Reading Evans's public "Operation Catsuit" performances into this lineage by virtue of loudness adds other layers toward thinking about gender, performance, race, and labor.

By making herself stand out from the crowd, Evans's performance tableaux produce similar affective dynamics as Kara Walker's (in)famous silhouettes. Evoking the violent interracial eroticisms of plantation slavery, Walker's works of intricately cut paper invite viewers to latch onto stereotypes as part of their practice of reading the images. Since the figures are all black, the viewer constructs their own narratives of what they are seeing based on their own projections. Likewise, Evans's insistence on marking the presence of a Black woman illuminates the projections and fantasies that surround her. In part, I emphasize the "loudness" of Evans's catsuit because the word highlights the conflation between Black women and noise and Black women with excess (sounds, bodies, desires) more generally. This is not a neutral set of associations, but ones that have been met with the criminalization of behavior and the demand for Black women to be respectable and to take up less space. I am reminded here of the Black women who were escorted from a wine tasting tour by the police for their boisterous conversation.[1] In this way, through their mere existence, Black women already inhabit the position of troublemaker.

Thinking further with Bornstein, however, we might see Evans's claiming of loudness (rather than letting it be hurled as an accusation) as its own enactment of "gender trouble." Beyond her catsuit, Evans's performances make unsubtle demands for attention. The ongoing set of performances that comprise "Operation Catsuit" find Evans performing acts of endurance, doing jumping jacks or chair dips, for example, or interacting with strangers in public. In each of these actions, Evans refuses to mute herself and instead demands that she be seen and interacted with — not as spectacle, but as person in the world. For *CATSUIT GARDENING,* a 2017 performance, Evans wore her catsuit to garden in the Bronx, handing out tiaras and neon feather boas while pruning plants, digging in the dirt, and chatting. In this performance of relaxation and connection with the earth and community, Evans tends to her own joy.

Evans describes this form of speaking for herself as a necessity in an interview with the *NEW YORK TIMES*. She says, "Especially for the femme-presenting people in the audience, I was like, 'People don't expect you to ask for what you need, and I'm here screaming for it in front of you. Take that with you, remember that, because sometimes you need to demand what you need.'"[2] In Evans's telling, being loud is actually part of the labor of femininity in that it redistributes resources (of attention and material) to those who are often overlooked. Here, hypervisibility blinds others to actual desires and needs. Being loud, however, is just one component of the labor of Black femininity that Evans makes visible. The catsuit's non-casualness is complemented by make-up and hair, which are

HYPERVISIBILITY BLINDS OTHERS TO ACTUAL DESIRES AND NEEDS. BEING LOUD, HOWEVER, IS JUST ONE COMPONENT OF THE LABOR OF BLACK FEMININITY

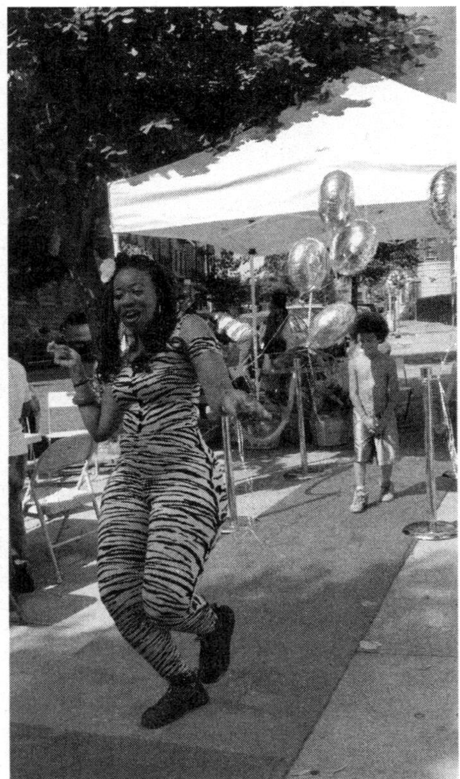

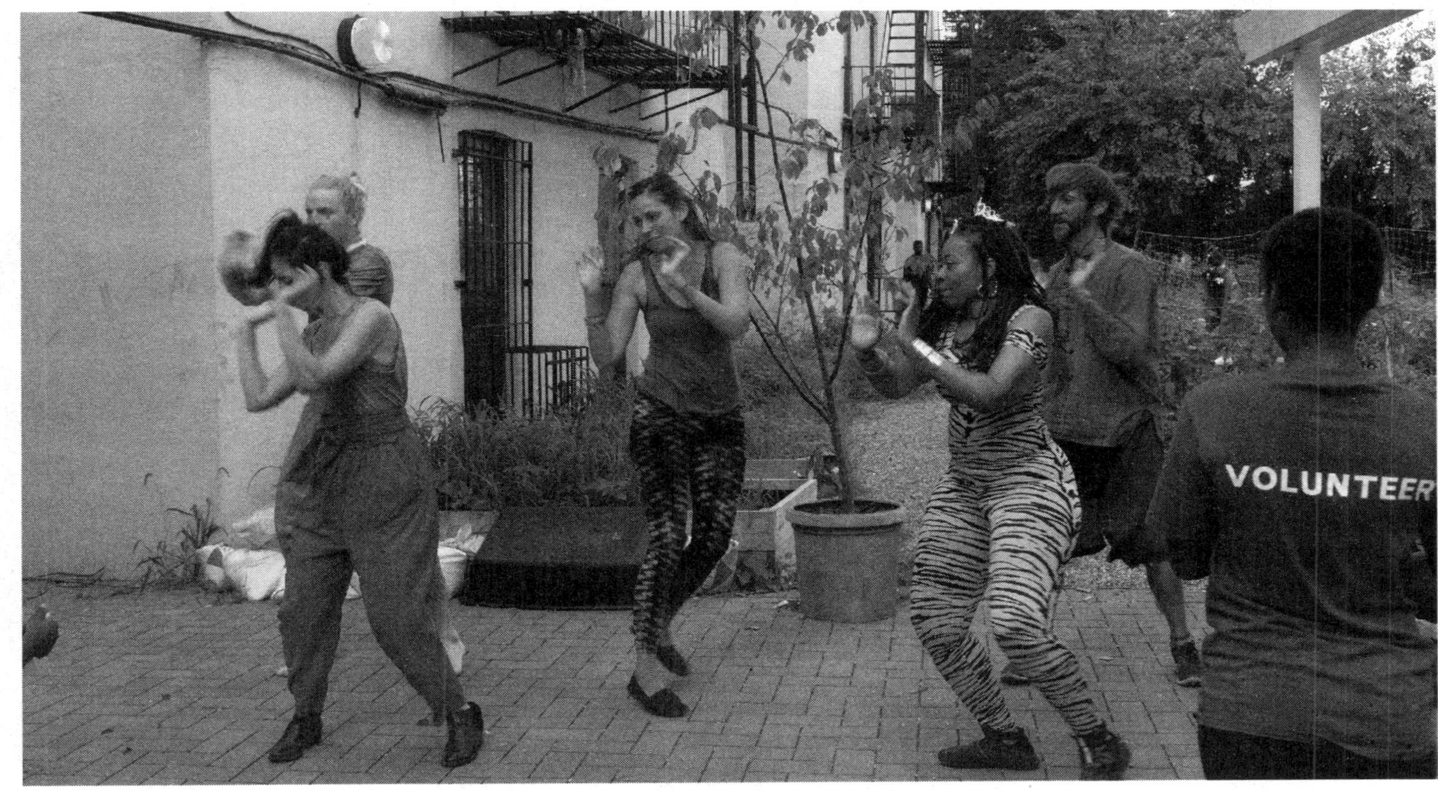

Ayana Evans, Catsuit Gardening (2017), Photos by Michael Hall Britto.

1 Mary Bowerman, "Black women kicked off Napa Valley Wine Train settle," *USA TODAY,* April 20, 2016, https://www.usatoday.com/story/money/nation-now/2016/04/20/black-women-kicked-off-napa-valley-wine-train-settle-racial-discrimination-case/83280120/

2 Seph Rodney, "What it Takes to Raise a Black Woman Up," *NEW YORK TIMES,* June 19, 2020, https://www.nytimes.com/2020/06/19/arts/design/ayana-evans-black-women.html

part of the spectacle that Evans is producing, but which are also part of the labor of gender. This is especially apparent when make-up runs and hair shifts during the durative aspects of the performance. In an acknowledgment of this, Evans describes the ways that her sartorial choices play into this aspect of her performances. Referring to herself in the third person, she writes: "Evans frequently performs in high heels and an eye-catching outfit to represent the perseverance needed to be a woman in this world (and look good while doing it.) Humor, longing, pain, and endurance blend in her performance art while notions of social judgment, and claiming/taking up space are recurring themes in her work."[3] By showing her work, Evans is making a comment on the work that Black women perform (and, for her, in heels!) and the work of gender itself.

It is this foregrounding of Black femme labor that gets at the heart of the matter. Not only does it emphasize the additional effort Black femmes undertake to navigate the world, but Evans shows the effects of this labor by allowing us to see her fatigue and sweat. Further, by asking us to look at what happens when things come a little undone, when one is exhausted, Evans breaks the tacit social contract that gender performance is effortless, a cornerstone of "cis normativity." Evans's focus on labor also initiates questions of the material dimensions of gender. What are the objects — catsuit, heels, make-up, tiara — that make femininity apparent? These material questions are not just about the work put into adding these items to the body, but their material costs as well. How do these questions of effort map onto current valorizations of "quiet" luxury, which contrasts with Evans' performance of "loud" gender? Evans' reminder insists that gender takes work and performs work complicates much, making us aware not only of the labor of appearing feminine but also the ways that all gender requires work — a message very much connected to Bornstein's discussion of troubling gender itself.

AMBER JAMILLA MUSSER

3 Artist statement for " Throwing Hexes — The Barnes Foundation," https://www.ayanaevans.com/2nd-gallery?pgid=iv6t1w66-6be33d5e-1609-44d0-a92a-46fdba34623b

Movement Research
Performance Journal

june or the whole pie or na circle at all

Author
AAINA AMIN

Contributing Editor
KAY GABRIEL

there are all the slots to deposit meaning in
toilet slots
letter slots
back side slots
and my spit slot clogged with vapor and gum

really into hips lately
my clips
keep you coming to me or keep you with me or
you can't procure an aaina i mean
to meet another's pace
good for questions like
"how much do i want you?
the careful turning away
in circles around myself
whether there is a you at all

whether whose hands touch whose
there is the hands capacity to signal
there is clawing at you
or beckoning
possibly to find some you
or in portions of circles up the taconic while
there is a you who waits
reads my hands

"there's more than dates and sex and hanging out"
to leave new york

i hear a lot these days
without remembering much
intentionally undone pouring
one feeling into one thing only's no good
the inhibition chaser burns
good, you hear a lot these days

or i remember to put feet
where do i go [*SLOT?*]
so more circles i know i
find a you in a circle
a line orbituary
a face count each time

the required muscular self direction

"i'm going to circulate"
"i need a cigarette"
"hey, my feet are numb"

later there is a we and
it's waiting
and it does get hotter
and skinnier
and closer
and there is sense to the human capacity for belief
way out, sunshine

AAINA AMIN

Open Dance Figure

Issue 60
Spring/Summer 2024

Author
JOSIE BETTMAN

Contributing Editor
KAY GABRIEL

spring 2023
I REPEATED A SEQUENCE OF STEPS THREE TIMES, ONCE ON THE DANCEFLOOR, ONCE IN THE THEATER, ONCE IN THE OPERATING ROOM.

A DANCE FIGURE IS A COMPLETE SEQUENCE OF WEIGHT SHIFTS DISPLACED IN SPACE, TRANSCRIBED ON A PAGE.

I PERFORMED THREE ITERATIONS OF A SOLO FIGURE, STEPS SHIFTING WEIGHT CLOSE TO DEATH, THEN REVERSING BACK ALONG THE SAME PATH. COMING TO KNOW THIS FIGURE THROUGH REPETITION, IT BECAME BOTH MUNDANE AND PERSONAL, REPEATING ONCE, TWICE, THREE TIMES, EACH APPROACH AND RETIRE DISTINCT YET INTERCHANGEABLE, THE SAME DEATH SCENE PLAYING OUT THREE TIMES, ONE AFTER ANOTHER, AFTER ANOTHER — THREE DISCRETE PERFORMANCES.

This text concerns transition and performance, and my personal efforts to remain living along these lines. I began writing it with an epigraph in mind, words from the artist Yael Davids, whose work deals directly with the lives of people in occupied Palestine. The sense of self-recognition I initially found in her work has shifted in the intervening period, as our present moment bears witness to Israel's unbearable bombardment of Gaza. I position her words and politics alongside this account of my own, encountering again the contingent scale of entwined human lives: struggles for liberation and continuance without congruence, threaded together through solidarity.

In the script of *A READING THAT LOVES — A PHYSICAL ACT*, Yael Davids's 2017 performance, I find a representation of death: death, the outer limit of an individual life, is rendered as a heightened moment of performance; an extreme experience tracing the edge of human consciousness.

Davids:

> A vanishing point. The bed a vast empty stage.
> A double bed in dying is an amplifier.
> You have a solo.
> Dying is always a solo.

In these lines, the solo undoes itself, releasing an individual life from singularity through the ordinariness of its obliteration. Everyone has a life to live and die, everyone has a solo; and therefore nobody's solo especially matters, in particular. In performance, the soloist reaches for their psychic and physical limits, singular in their embodiment of an idea and centered in the viewer's focus, just as in the subjective cycle of life and death, one's individual embodiment is their solo domain of expertise.

Davids's words are direct yet tricky, delimiting the solo and then circling back to dissolve it, making an ensemble. Emphasizing the borders of the soloist's subjecthood actually reaffirms the solo's dependence on the ensemble. Solo-group-solo-group-solo — dying may be a solo act, but the singularity of this death makes way for a plural.

3.

I'm looking out the window above my bed and hanging my legs up on the wall. The sky is dusk and there's nobody around. I suck down the purple light like it's a melatonin gummy. I never before imagined I could take so much rest, because resting in my body sometimes feels like a death sentence. Something's changed, and I can withstand it this week.

The light looks something like another movement of time, the familiar dawn — but dusk, and stillness, are strangers to me. The familiar gloaming: daybreak after a night spent toiling in a windowless room. Waking, sleeping, two edges of the same knife, night. Time cuts both ways.

To stay with the light between worlds, one can stay awake all night and start the day with the dawn, reaching for a state of delirious clarity. It's a way of stealing time. Stealing time and wasting it — it used to feel subversive, like having a double life, being both in the daylight and nightlife.

Dirty your hands with the business of laying waste to time and risk being caught in the act.

The risk will always be borne unevenly, and the idea of reward only exists for the venue owners trying to turn a profit on the time wasters.

Now, in bed at dusk with nowhere to go, I'm losing my edge. Unraveled from my context, nobody there. Stillness, quiet: no atmosphere to hold my body in — my outlines blur to meet this void as if it were the vacuum of space, turning my cells to vapor on contact. In bed with my body and its hazy limits, the double-edged dusk slides between me and several restless decades.

The surgeon sliced me away and glued me back into a long-avoided scene. Forced to lie still in bed: a vantage point looking out over the expanse of my physical form, sliding off along either edge as dusk cuts into the present.

Out from under

I walk side-by-side with the nurse as she leads me into the lights of the operating theater. I swan in, shrugging out of the gown as I enter, matching her tempo as she flows through gestures, guiding me onto the table, my arms in a T, palms facing up, slipping my lower body into a paper sleeve that fills with warm air.

The anaesthesiologist asks me if I work in fashion. She's wearing Chanel logo earrings, I can't decide if they're tacky or not.

"You must have a beautiful smile when you use it," she says.

The bluetooth speaker is playing the Harry Styles song about eating pussy, and then nothing.

I get very attached to the anaesthesiologist who puts me under. She finds my edge — just the right dose of fentanyl and everything else to temporarily eliminate me and then bring me back a heartbeat later. I love her for that.

She did such a good job giving me death, opening an interval in which I didn't exist. I stepped inside and woke up on a fabulous high. Coming off the drugs, I sobered into awareness that part of me had died, but I felt closer than ever to that version of me, the girl that I left in the ether. The anaesthesiologist had been right there as I left her behind.

Surgery is the new sex

If surgery is the new sex, then not telling your lover you're getting surgery is the new infidelity. I sign a form consenting to be sterilized and don't tell anyone, simultaneously betraying the trust in my relationship and the terms of my body's agreement with the linear future. Having wasted these intricate structures, barren and clear, my new form is sanctified via the production of medical waste. I'm mostly left alone — I feel almost dead, but so clear headed, flooded with absence.

In the twilight afterglow of anaesthesia I grieve the linear coming of age I'll never have — wondering if there's any reward for the duration of transition, having been hung up on the outer limits of adolescence for the past decade.

I usually quell my desire to talk about how heartbreak is like surgery — after all, as far as I know, I alone went under and resurfaced, sequentially iterating this solo. What an honor and a privilege.

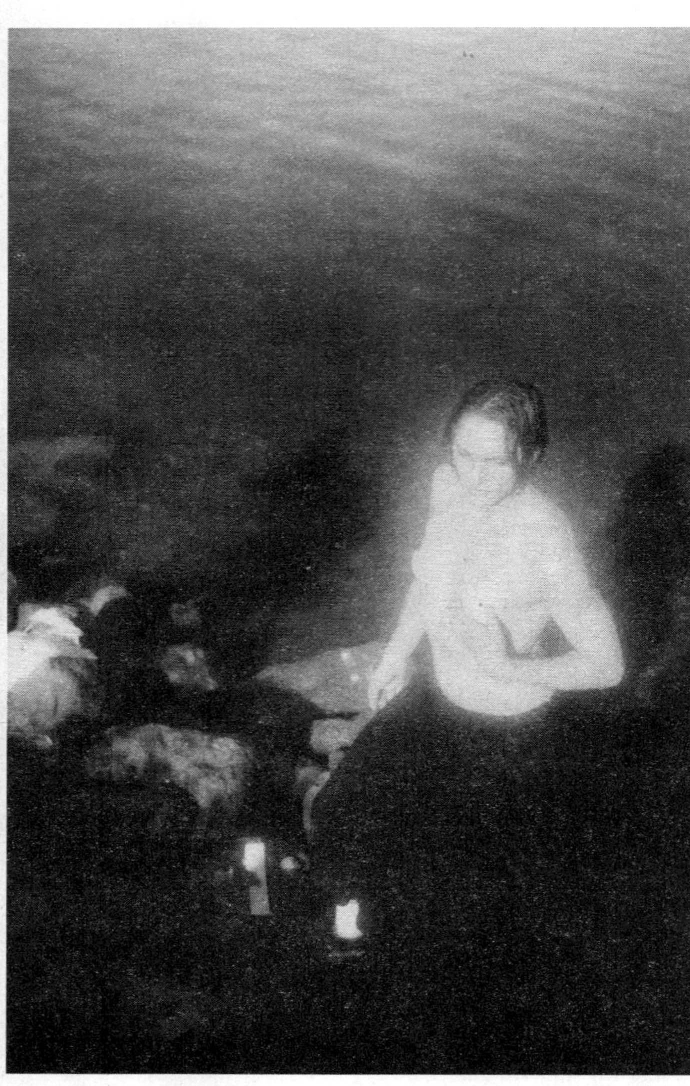

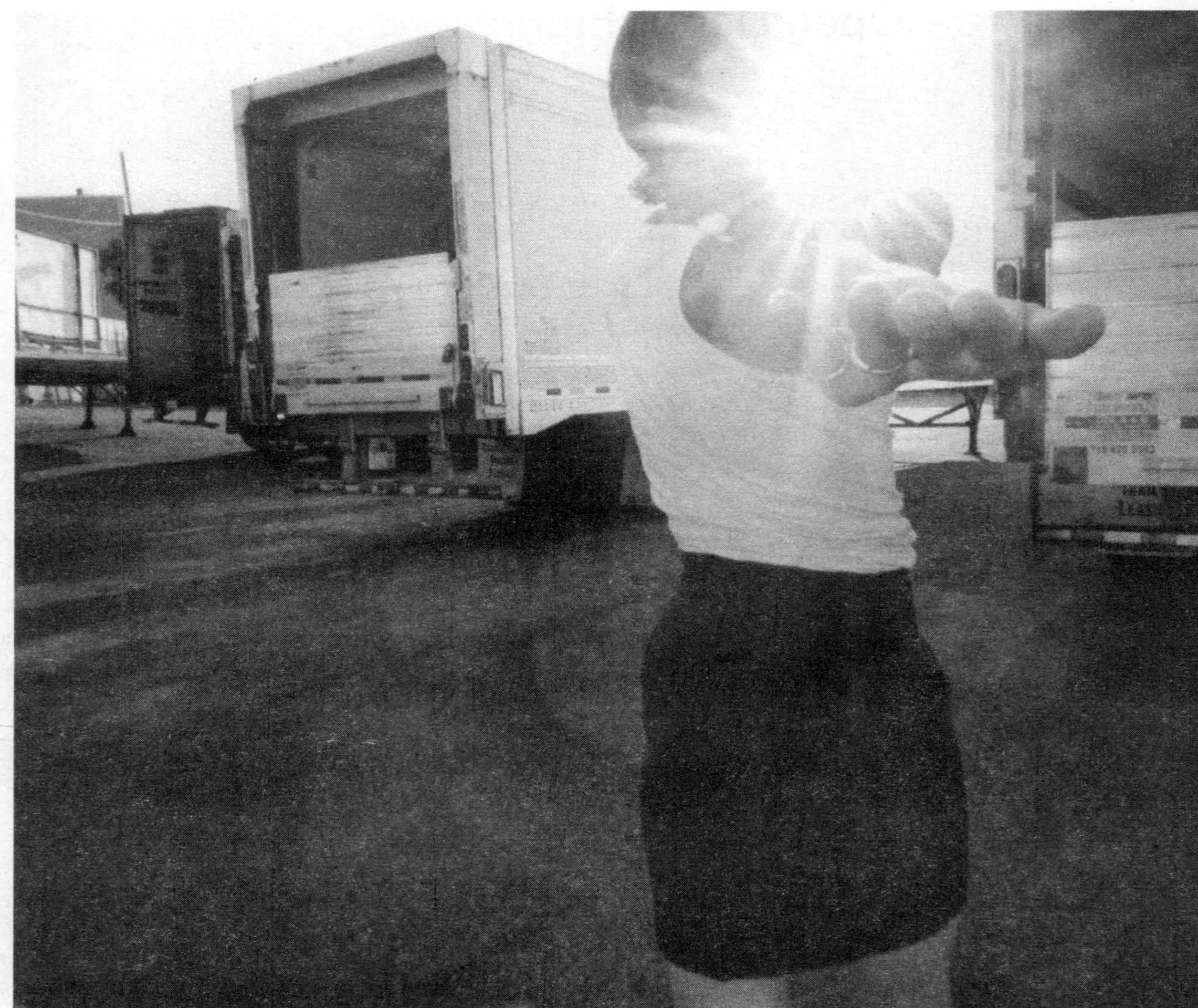

2. Is a nightclub a theater?
For a while I was convinced that a nightclub could be a kind of theater. I had to go to the edge of this claim in order to test it, ending up further away from the theater than when I had set out looking.

In the music video for her 2007 song *EVERYTIME,* Britney Spears runs, slow motion, down a glowing hospital corridor, her cracked psyche leaking through seductive popstar glam, eyes magnetizing the camera to witness the irresistible spectacle of her suffering.

Britney's choreography became the source for my own solo in an ensemble performance titled *GROUP WORK.*

enter performer
throw coat
arm right arm extended overhead, palm flexed
pace downstage 2345678
"yeah" dopplering under a hazy horizon
"yeah" echo chamber conducting memory through synapses into steps
elbow carving 90 degrees into waist
tilt, up up tilt, down down
tears, dance steps grasping into the darkness in front of your face
a bolt of white light flashing through vision
conduit facing out to the east
memory clouds an arcade of limbs
echoing into the domestic container
steps channel down, bubble up from the floorboards

1.
count one ladies incline hip left
arcing path inclining back counts 1 through 4
quarter turn to face partner
four hands forearms clasp, lift frame overhead, toned
couple drags right heel back, left, 1-2-3
couple cross to front of hall, replace couples front
couples turn to face back,
advance and retire
repeat

Partner dancing maybe is the most beautiful choreography, a script of undone edges and classical dramatic formations. Improvised encounters can follow a rigorous structure, yet still scrape with a risky unknown; each dance a point on a vast chart of permutating steps, partners, combinations. Risking love, dancers put their bodies on the line, joining hands, crossing with one another, stepping into unison. The love dancers meet each other by giving themselves to the edge, dancing for hours without stopping, without regard for their own wellbeing. The routine of their sacrifice is aestheticized, but the dancers themselves don't matter, they're disposable; interchangeable with the kids waiting in line outside.

A false equivalency forms between love dancing and all that is bad, dirty, and toxic about the nightclubs, but who even trusted the clubs with title to this choreography in the first place? Their agenda of louche consumerism meets an overcorrecting counterpart in overzealous self-preservationism, but perhaps a murky continuity joins this terrain of toxicity and absolutes, a way to conserve the potential energy held in the promise of finding each other by going to the edge together.

Can we have love dancing? The extent of our sacredness — transmitted body to body — exceeds any one context. Love dancing belongs to the dancers.

For so long I used to make solos and then I died three times, but I'm here talking about it, so who cares? I'm solo again — I can't help but need the other dancers. I'll take it.

everytime
Britney runs in slow motion down a hospital corridor
wearing an oversized men's white shirt, covered just barely past the tops of her thighs
She stands in front of a gurney where her own lifeless body lies,
crossing the partition to show us a newborn baby cradled in its mother's arms
Britney on the gurney being wheeled into the ambulance, her head lolled to one side
The baby again
Britney surfaces in the bathtub where her death scene played out moments before; radiant, glistening, grinning into the camera, having faked her own death and returned from the brink — it was all just an act,
She's loving it

JOSIE BETTMAN

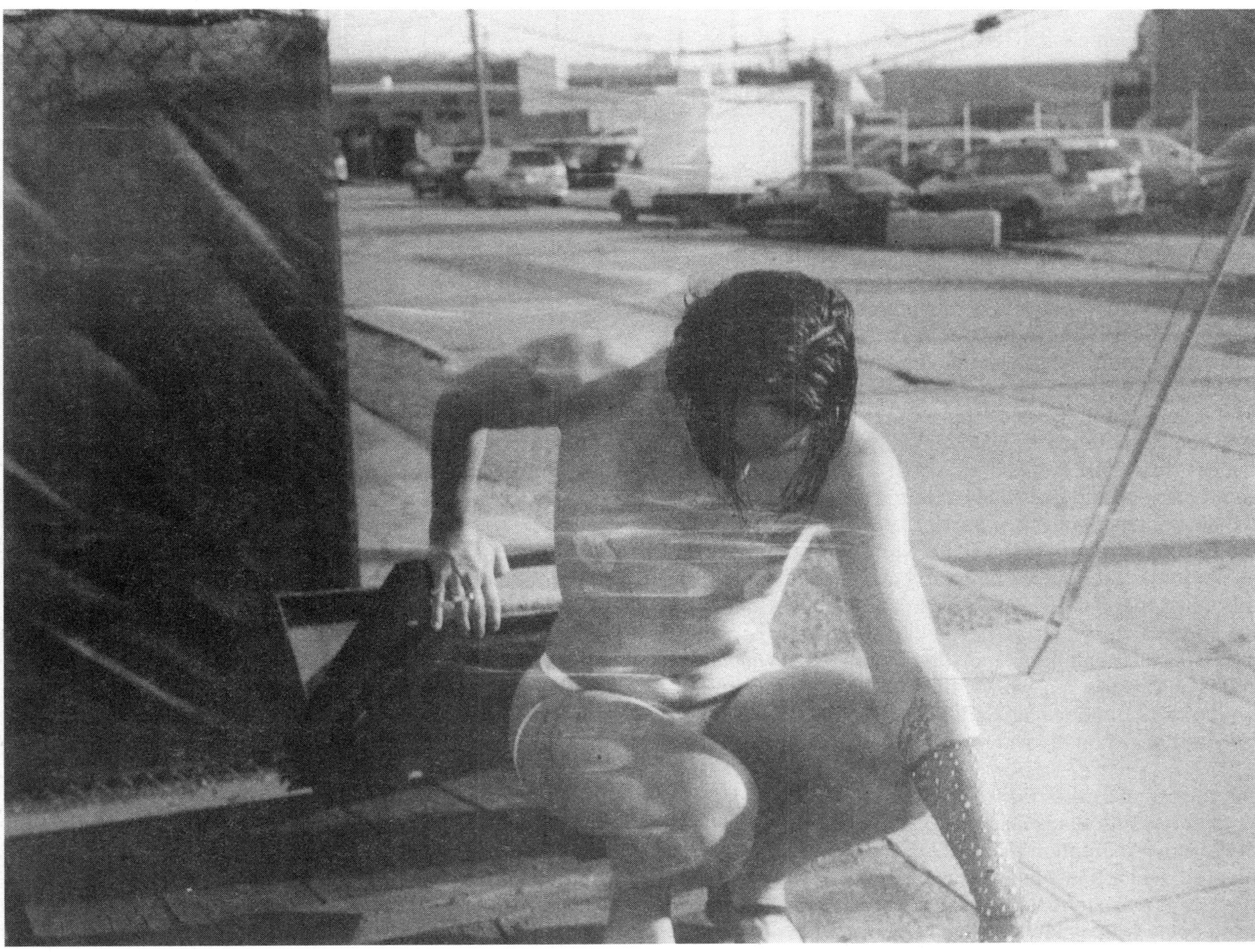

Photos by Zhi Wei Hiu

Questionnaire For Legacy

Authors
GARRETT ALLEN
AREWÀ BASIT
KYLE CARRERO LOPEZ

Contributing Editor
KAY GABRIEL

LEGACY is a New York-based collective of Black queer artists working across a pretty spectacular range of media — music, dance, film, performance, comedy, poetry. Can you talk a little about how you all met and how you decided to work together?

Arewà Basit The founding members of LEGACY met through the serendipitous cosmic pull of the NYC art, theater, and nightlife scenes. Our acute awareness of each other and our respective disciplines and practices grew as we did, and inevitably, we began collaborating on works together. In 2019, our founding members, Kyle and Garrett, collaborated on *BLK MLK*, a live performance piece which explored and challenged themes related to the Black queer male body and Black masculinity, inspired by *TONGUES UNTIED*. I was one of the featured artists. Each of us gravitated to each other through mutual respect and artistic interest, which inevitably led to the development of our collaborations. In 2020, in the aftermath of the public lynching of George Floyd, we found it imperative that we collectivize with the intention of seeing our dreams realized with the support of our peers, and we set up a crowdfunding effort to start the collective and launch our first project. We chose to form an LLC to establish equity and carve out a resource built for and by the community. We hope to make our dream of a world where we can create out of abundance, and not out of scarcity, a reality.

Why did you all feel that a production collective specifically would change the landscape for Black queer artists working in New York? What considerations do you bring to producing each other's work and the work of the artists you collaborate with?

Garrett Allen It is integral that our stories, experiences, and artistry be told for us, by us. Extraction, exploitation, and undervaluing have long been rampant in all artistic disciplines, and we found a deep need for space for Black queer and trans artists to be able to produce and share without the limitations that are created in a white supremacist and capitalistic system. Our first project, a music video for Arewà Basit's debut single "Fluid," was made with an entirely Black queer team. After wrapping this project, we received an immense amount of feedback that this intentionality of space and process was not only fulfilling artistically but also healing. Our hope is that we can not only support artists in realizing their visions but also highlight ways of making that are ethical and equitable and spread beyond our collective. Many relationships and collaborations that we have spawned have continued beyond us, which impacts the wider landscape of Black queer artists. Our consideration for each part of production is deeply rooted in maintaining the integrity of our collaborators' dreams. Though we may not be able to meet every part of this dream, that space to live in the expansiveness and possibility allows for us to offer support in the ways each individual project needs. As we continue to build our infrastructure and network, we are creating our own urgently necessary avenue to battle these systems and structures that aim to silence us. In this fight, we aim to use this infrastructure that we have built as artists in community to answer the need to diversify the industries in which we all desire to work. Yes, we want to fill a void in mainstream production, but above all, we want our community to be seen and heard on its own terms.

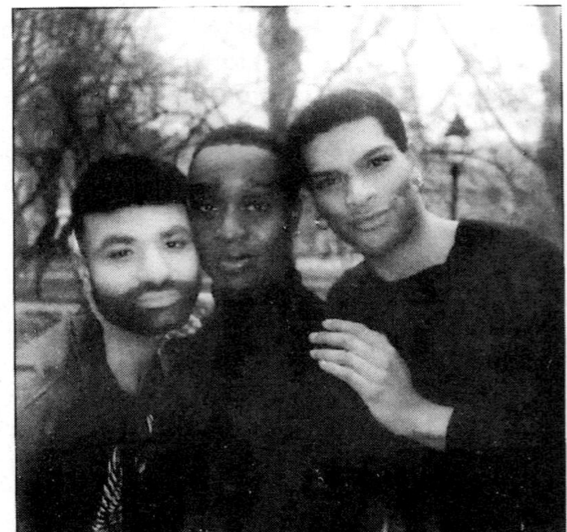

Photos by John Arthur Peetz

One thing that strikes me going through the videos from last spring's The Black Beginning is the breadth of sheer formal experimentation that LEGACY supports: you featured Junior Mintt taking the audience to drag church, Nile Harris's existential gingerbread man, Paris Alexander doing comedy in a club kid's blowup suit. What aesthetics and styles are you all drawn to, and what do you hope people take away from the collaborations you work on?

Legacy Each of us approaches questions of style and aesthetic differently in our individual work, which is part of what makes working together so exciting and unpredictable. From LEGACY's early days onward, one thing we've consistently agreed on is a commitment to supporting Afrofuturistic art, especially work that expands on what exactly that can look like; work that is formalistically forward, typically non-traditional, non-linear, and centered on world- building/atmosphere, though we aren't opposed to more standard storytelling or meaning- making structures. We aim to embrace Black queer expression in all of its multitudes, so the projects we take on cover an array of forms that is as vast as our experiences and voices. Serious and unserious, joyful and visceral, cerebral and intuitive: we want it all. Hopefully, any artist we collaborate with will come away with an expanded sense of their capacity to create within a distinctly Black queer dreamscape, as well as a sense of assuredness that their work deserves all of the support we can offer plus support that goes beyond our bandwidth. In an ideal world, it shouldn't ever be usual for Black queer and trans artists to feel as though our artistic ambitions might only be possible with the help of pockets that may or may not best serve us, and these collaborations are our way of striving for that ideal. As for spectators, we hope that the quality and character of our work speaks for itself and exemplifies what can happen when artists from our communities come together. On a technical level, there's an emphasis we naturally place on multi- and cross-disciplinarity; it's definitely a goal to leave audiences with a greater sense of connectedness between seemingly disparate forms of artmaking, like poetry and movement or drag and installation — or any other combination, really.

Arewa, Garrett, and Kyle, you all showed work in *THE BLACK BEGINNING* as well as helping to produce it. What feels different to you about working together as LEGACY from working on your own art practices?

GA Producing with LEGACY has deeply informed my individual art practice and vice versa. Though there is definitely a difference between being in the producing chair vs. being in the lead artist chair, I believe I have been able to learn how to support myself and others in oscillating between the two. My work with LEGACY has strengthened my artistic voice and deepened my connection to why I do what I do, especially as it relates to radical empathy, collective liberation, and building a better, brighter (and Blacker and queerer) future. Being supported by my peers and community in making my piece for *THE BLACK BEGINNING* was unlike anything I have experienced before. And feeling that fulfillment, healing, support, and integrity of my vision has made it so I never, ever want to have to compromise myself to fit something that has no intention of serving me.

AB The difference between my personal art practice and our work as producers and co-founders of LEGACY is rooted in determining the intention of the artists whose ideas and visions are being uplifted and supported, while honoring the integrity and sincerity of the work created. When we shot the "Fluid" music video, I remember feeling so held throughout the experience, especially as we were working with music that is so personal to me. The vulnerability of creating the music is mirrored in the production process, but I draw a certain strength from the teamwork of having a collective goal.

Kyle Carrero Lopez My solo practice is grounded in writing, which is usually a solo act (not counting the many conversations a writer has in their head with the work of the authors who influence them). LEGACY pushes me not to be solipsistic, since it's based in group work! Though the producer hat makes up most of what we do together, working with LEGACY on our live performance projects—like *WOMB! THERE IT IS*, which we developed as part of our 2022 Ars Nova Vision Residency, and performed excerpts of as part of BOFFO's Sunday Sounds programming on Fire Island—also gives me chances to work in ways that I don't usually, like in backup singing or dance, which are necessary forms of support for highlighting the rest of LEGACY's skill sets. It's a lot of fun, reminds me not to limit myself in what kind of artist I can be, and inspires me not to have a one-track mind in how I approach my writing.

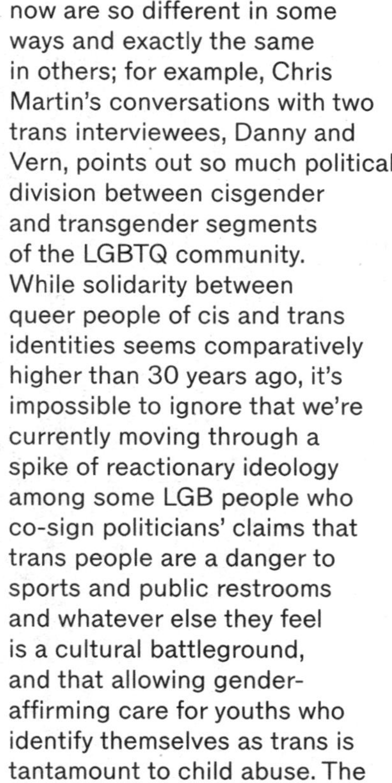

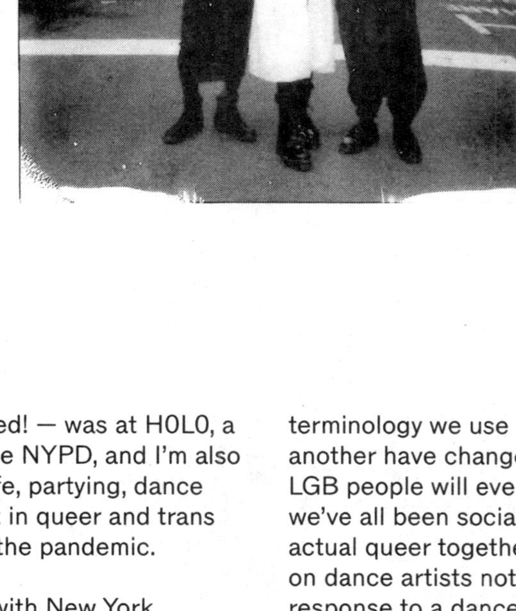

Can you talk a little about the relationship LEGACY has to nightlife? I'm thinking here of how your fundraiser this past spring — which I'm sorry to have missed! — was at HOLO, a club in Bushwick recently raided by the NYPD, and I'm also thinking about how it feels like nightlife, partying, dance music is so much more thickly present in queer and trans culture in NYC right now than before the pandemic.

L All three of us have been involved with New York nightlife for some time. It has been very fascinating to see how it has evolved and changed while remaining an important haven for our community. And this is far from new. From ballroom and voguing, to house and techno music scenes, to chosen club family, we have seen how important nightlife has been to Black queer people over time. And we have also seen how frequently our spaces have been co-opted by white, cis, het folks chasing what is "cool" or "in." However, communing through dance parties is not something that is just cool or fun; it's also a way of learning, growing, and building new modes of being. We care for one another in ways that we aren't cared for in the outside world. We create spaces that are safe for us to express ourselves in ways that make us feel most whole. And we celebrate living, being, and existing in the moment together. Being in lockdown, unable to commune in these ways, put into perspective how crucial these intentional spaces are for our community. Our hope for our latest event was both to fundraise to be able to keep building LEGACY and supporting artists as well as celebrate our existence and resistance to the forces of white supremacy, bigotry, and capitalism. The murder of O'Shae Sibley, killed for voguing outside a gas station in Brooklyn this past July, reiterated the fact that our joy, expression, and simple living is seen as a threat to a lot of society. We honor him and the countless Black queer and trans folks who have been unjustly taken from us because of hate. Nightlife, at its best, provides an opportunity to effectively counter daytime power dynamics. Most clubs don't want to be flooded with straight men, the demographic which controls the overwhelming majority of capital, industry, and cultural power worldwide; in Brooklyn, it's not uncommon for trans femmes, especially Black trans femmes, to be granted free admission and other perks at many parties, which is one way to offset the social transmisogyny and discrimination in fundamental needs like employment and housing that they face in day-to-day life. In the same way that LEGACY seeks to upend established norms that hinder artists in our communities, the best parts of nightlife work toward enacting more equitable worlds and outcomes than the ones we have now.

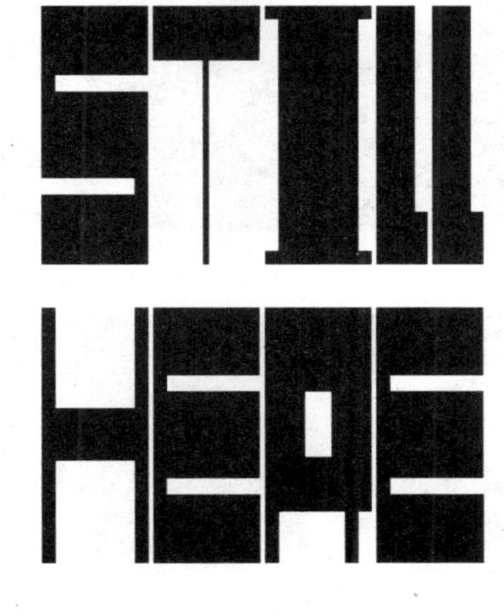

This issue of the *MOVEMENT RESEARCH PERFORMANCE JOURNAL* is, in a sense, supposed to reflect on and update the "gender" issue that the PJ published in 1993. That issue is *VERY* of its moment. Based on things you've read and watched and conversations you've had, what do you think is different about queer performance and artmaking in New York now as compared to 10, 15, or 30 years ago?

KCL It's fascinating to read through the "gender" issue and see how the conversations happening on gender right now are so different in some ways and exactly the same in others; for example, Chris Martin's conversations with two trans interviewees, Danny and Vern, points out so much political division between cisgender and transgender segments of the LGBTQ community. While solidarity between queer people of cis and trans identities seems comparatively higher than 30 years ago, it's impossible to ignore that we're currently moving through a spike of reactionary ideology among some LGB people who co-sign politicians' claims that trans people are a danger to sports and public restrooms and whatever else they feel is a cultural battleground, and that allowing gender-affirming care for youths who identify themselves as trans is tantamount to child abuse. The terminology we use and the ways we interact with one another have changed, but it remains to be seen whether LGB people will ever fully step away from the transphobia we've all been socialized into and toward a practice of actual queer togetherness. Jill Johnston's piece in the issue on dance artists notes a reviewer's casual homophobia in response to a dance performance on marriage by Jim Self, and one way I think queer performance and artmaking is different these days is that it's a bit harder for that kind of criticism to get a green light since there are more of us—queer and trans people—on editorial mastheads and scoring big bylines than there ever used to be. I think of how a critic once described Bill T. Jones's multidisciplinary dance piece *STILL/HERE* (1994) as "victim art" because of its focus on people living with HIV/AIDS; she refused to even go and watch it for herself. We're able to better advocate for the work of queer and trans artists through traditional channels and through social media, that great equalizer which has simultaneously platformed no shortage of fascist content, and yet has also fostered greater ease of access to archival footage and other materials, which has been paramount to LEGACY's practice of research and remembrance of what's come before us — and how many brilliant artists have been lost to HIV/AIDS, anti-Blackness, and homo/transphobia — that has allowed us to do what we do now. Artists like Tiona Nekkia McClodden are engaging in similar practices that trace and honor Black queer lineages, and that sense of reaching for severed connections feels key to a lot of contemporary queer artmaking.

GARRETT ALLEN
AREWÀ BASIT
KYLE CARRERO LOPEZ

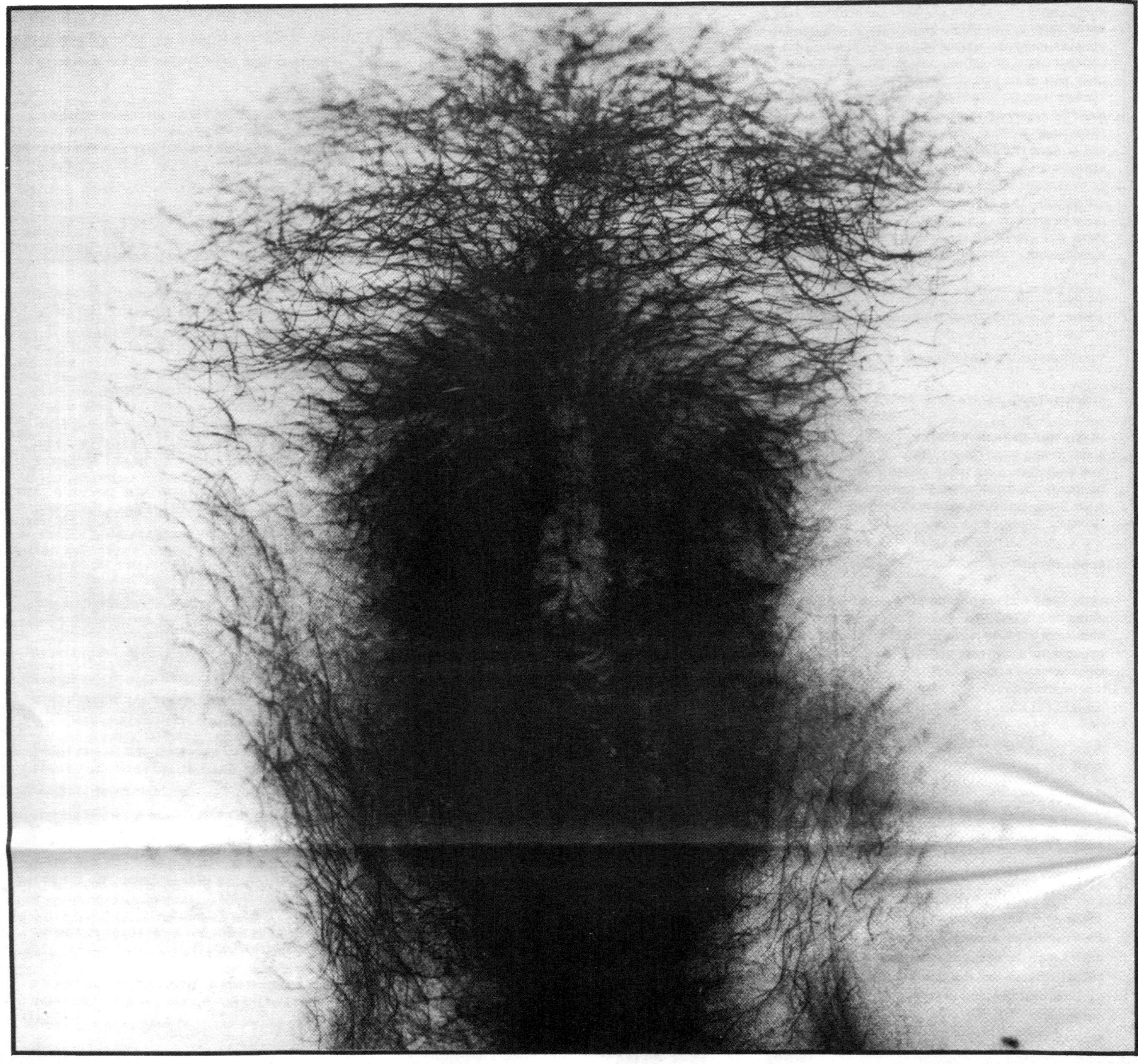

READ MY LIPS BEFORE THEY'RE SEALED

On May 23, the Supreme Court upheld the Federal Government's right to deny funds to clinics or doctors that provide information about abortion. At stake here is the fate of 4500 clinics and the lives of millions of us who use them.

The Supreme Court has ruled that those of us dependent on health clinics for obstetric and gynecological care--young women, women of color, low-income women--cannot be allowed to make choices regarding our own bodies. By banning doctors from saying the word 'abortion', the government deliberately increases the silence and terror that surround open discussion of sexual activity. The repressive atmosphere created by the gag order will only make it harder for us to talk about safer sex and what we want to do with our cocks and tits, asses and pussies. In the AIDS crisis, our lives depend on speaking openly and honestly about our sexual desires and practices.

"Disgusted" by our drawings of two men fucking, the Senate passed the Helms Amendment in 1987 prohibiting funds for AIDS education materials that "encourage or promote homosexuality". Legislating heterosexuality, the Federal government refuses us the images of ourselves that could save our lives.

Law after law, the State narrows our rights to make choices, our freedom to follow the choices our desires demand.

We fight for information about contraception and abortion because we are women, not just mothers. We come out as gay men and lesbians, rejecting a sexuality we don't feel. We put on tits and strap on dicks, slipping out of genders that restrain us. Our heroism is daring to imagine our bodies not as the machinery of reproduction, but as our theaters of pleasure.

Our bodies should be playgrounds, not just battlefields.

REVERSE THE SUPREME COURT'S BAN ON ABORTION INFORMATION. CALL SENATOR MOYNIHAN AT 661-5150, SENATOR D'AMATO AT 947-7390.

GANG

Authors
ZOE LEONARD
WELLINGTON LOVE
LORING MCALPIN
ADAM ROLSTON
DANIEL WOLFE
SUZANNE WRIGHT

Issue #3 of the *MOVEMENT RESEARCH PERFORMANCE JOURNAL* is most often remembered for the ensuing scandal caused by a one-page contribution from GANG, an artist collective that grew out of ACT UP (the AIDS Coalition to Unleash Power) as much as friendships forged around networks of activism in the late-1980s and early-1990s. "Read My Lips" featured a closely cropped image of a vulva with the statement "Read My Lips...Before They're Sealed," referring to the so-called "domestic gag rule," a policy originating in the Reagan-era that banned any federally funded health care providers from distributing information on abortion. Response to the printing of GANG's poster played out nationally, as the National Endowment for the Arts threatened to withdraw its funding from Movement Research and Senator Jesse Helms took to the senate floor flashing pages of Issue #3 in front of his colleagues. Less often recalled is the response that played out locally, as members of the dance and performance community took to a town hall divided over inclusion over the inclusion of such an explicit body politic in the *MRPJ* (see Tom Kalin's contribution to this issue for further reflection).

When we began to revisit Issue #3 for Issue #60, I knew I wanted to research GANG further. I reached out to Zoe Leonard, the only member of GANG I knew of at the time, and inquired about developing a work as much in response to "Read My Lips" as it might be a reflection on how such sensationalized moments pull focus from other aspects of the historical record. With some clarity, I wrote that I was "less interested in an historical reflection on the GANG piece and more interested in some way of responding to that work across the 30+ years since it was printed." Zoe was clear that a GANG project would only be possible if we could re-assemble the collective. Cold emails to GANG members, one after the other, yielded new names of potential participants, some who excitedly joined back up, others who never responded, some who are no longer living. The resulting conversation gestures to the breadth of GANG's work which has hardly been documented elsewhere. It speaks a crucial moment in activism where shifting priorities met with a desire to stave off the exhaustion of militancy by reintroducing form of joy and pleasure. It serves as a reminder of that movements are never tightly bound to history, ebbing and flowing into one another.

—Joshua Lubin-Levy

Suzanne Wright Gosh it's so nice to see everyone. But I do want to start by acknowledging Michael Perelman, a central member of GANG, who passed away a few years ago.

Daniel Wolfe One of the great things about Michael, and it's related to my experience of GANG in general, is that he was simultaneously very serious and also somewhat aware of his own absurdity. Similarly, GANG wasn't as serious as Gran Fury, at least in many moments it had an awareness of a sense of humor about itself and its limits that was paradoxically freeing, so that we could do a performance or do the piece in the *PERFORMANCE JOURNAL*, or whatever. There was something light and comic about it compared to some of the other forms of activism.

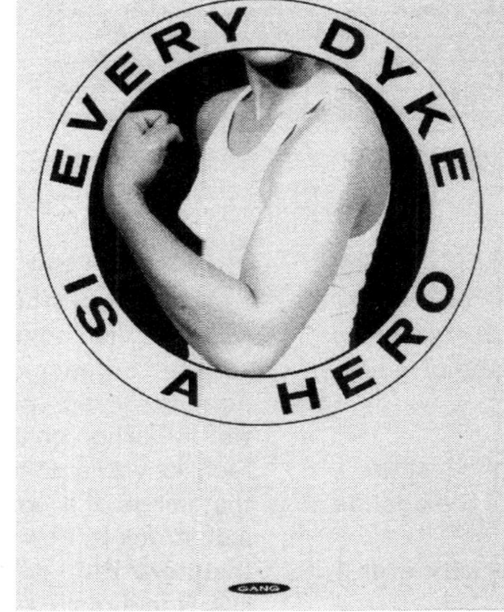

GANG, *EVERY DYKE IS A HERO*, 1990, Print lithograph, 11 × 8 1/2 in. Courtesy International Center of Photography.

Adam Rolston It was out of ACT UP, 100%, but I was also drawn to in GANG because there's the Venn diagram of the women's rights, gay rights and AIDS activism—and while AIDS activism was getting tackled in a lot of the collectives coming out of ACT UP, the other two weren't as much. We wanted to focus on a broader agenda, and to me that's also what made GANG special.

ZL And I really love that about GANG and wonder if some of that playfulness had to do with when we started. We'd already all clocked several years of activism. I think my attraction to GANG was to be part of a collective driven by being artists, and collaborating in a way that didn't use the same strategies that had become part of a recognizable activist style, the set strategies of taking commercial iconography or design tropes and playing with them. We gave ourselves a freer rein. And I don't remember what year we started, but I know it was at a point when a lot of us were starting to feel really burnt out from the amount of tragedy, the amount of loss, but also from going to so many meetings and so many protests and getting arrested so many times and wanting a different comradeship with each other. I felt like we also wanted friendship, and wanted sustenance inside this really overwhelming task of trying to change the world.

AR I agree so much with that. There was a churn. You would join an affinity group, you would work on something, and then you'd go on to the next one. There was a churn that happened. At the point GANG started, I know I was looking to find a slightly smaller cell to identify with and belong to,. But it's also interesting, Zoe, what you just said about the strategies of appropriation and advertising, because the topic here is "Read My Lips," which does borrow from commercial advertising, but it also borrowed from Grand Fury's "Read My Lips." So, the piece of the *PERFORMANCE JOURNAL* is sort an appropriation of an appropriation.

Loring McAlpin Just going back to our origin, GANG came at a time when Queer Nation had started, so there was already activist energy that was siphoning off from ACT UP into queer politics. And it was a moment when there was a division within ACT UP and there was some uncertainty about where it was going to go. There was burnout, we'd all been doing it for a couple of years. We formed really through affinity, through friendship networks rather than coming from the floor of a larger organization. And that really meant that the tenor was different. The other thing about appropriation, the one thing that we did do that was different was that we did a couple projects where we tried to appropriate the voice of governmental authority. We created a poster that was something you would see in an immigration hall with a picture of Bush and the statement, "Undoing the restrictions of not allowing foreigners with HIV into the country." And we did another thing that was related to the police department. Remember the yellow and blue sticker?

DW Yeah, it was like a sticker for the subway that said that gay bashing would be punishable under a certain statute, even though there was no such statute. The idea, as rendered by our colleague Peter Bowen was to do things that were ob-scene, behind the scenes and bringing that forward. But in addition to that...I mean we did performance, we did those stickers, we did a video, and it was experimental in the sense of, "Okay, well let's just try this mode or that mode." And one of the greatest things for me about the power of groups is that they enable you to do something you wouldn't have the courage to do on your own. I never performed before or sincebut there were a lot of things that we did together that I wouldn't have been able to do by myself. That, and the fact that we were men and women together was something that was parallel to healing some of the tensions within ACT UP. One of our first things was just a very simple graphic that said, "EVERY DYKE IS A HERO," and it's relevant to the subject of "Read My Lips" Obviously those are not my labia, and I don't even know whose they were. I was like, "I can't remember. Whose were they?" And I don't even know if I ever knew.

AR Yeah, no, it was never disclosed.

SW No one will ever know.

ZL I don't want to digress too much, but we know that a lot of women were working on issues related to women and at the same time because of the amount of homophobia and gay bashing, and the horrific response from the mainstream of this country and the government, one of ACT UP's biggest charges was to celebrate gay male sexuality. And speaking for myself, I felt like I was missing my own sense of pleasure and the sense of my body—and something about my body and my life that wasn't only about illness or fear or transmission of disease. fierce pussy formed explicitly to create more lesbian visibility and to celebrate lesbian desire in the face of all of that homophobia, and as a space for us women to connect. And then I think Suzanne joined GANG and I was like, "Oh, I want to do that too, that sounds really fun." Because it just seemed like there was an energy and sense of friendship a smaller group where everyone seemed to enjoy each other's company. And GANG was not organizing protests, but was making creative work that would sustain us and give us a sense of pleasure as we made it.

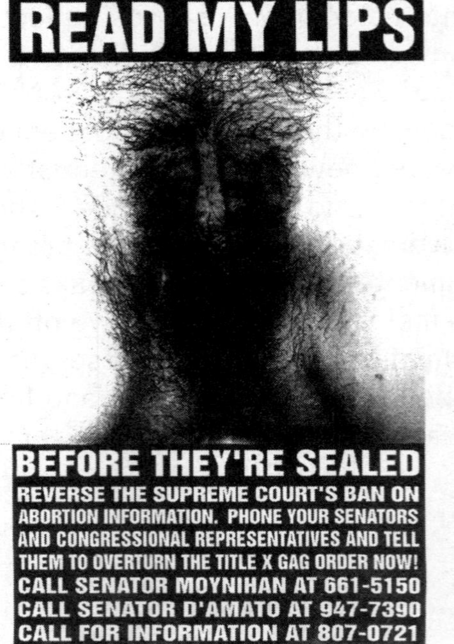

GANG, *READ MY LIPS*, 1991, Print lithograph, 17 × 11 in. Courtesy International Center of Photography.

AR Our little group embraced looking beyond just the politics of AIDS activism and a broadening of the agenda.

ZL I think we were interested in intersectionality, even before that term was being used.

SW Also, what about Holly Hughes? She was in GANG for a little bit, remember? Is she on the list?

AR Is there a list?

DW In the BAM performance that you referenced with you and Michael, remember she was supposed to get an award and she too was totally burned down by all of the NEA scrutiny and she was like, "I'm sick of being myself. Could you guys be me instead?"

DW And you guys went up and performed as her. But in terms of people who aren't present, there's Martin. There was Peter Bowen, who was on the cover of *OUT WEEK* as the new clone or that was just my idea that he should have been...

LM He was.

DW And then there was Heidi Durrow, Maria Perez...

WL And Bob, formerly Bob Beck was in, and wasn't Jessie Folstein in as well?

AR Yes. Yes.

ZL Also, somebody brought up that first poster, "EVERY DYKE IS A HERO," and although she wasn't in GANG, it was [Nancy Brooks-] Brody's arm in that photograph.

SW That's right. Oh my god.

ZL So that's another serious moment of rest in power for one of our people that's not with us anymore. Rest in Power.

Wellington Love Picking up on Zoe's comment about intersectionality, the conversations around diversity, equity, inclusion, and I'm sure there are precursors that you guys could point to even before GANG and thinking about House of Color and Gang of Four and Grand Fury and all those groups. Those were sort of precursors to contemporary discussions around DEI. Obviously it's advanced, but it is interesting to think about the generation that has come after us, what they maybe don't know, or that there was always somebody who was fighting, there was always somebody who was pushing, and these conversations aren't exactly new.

AR Well, it's a good thing to point out, particularly because this is targeted towards an audience that is looking back. And Wellington, one of the things that I was struck by in your film was that term transcestors, that there is this consciousness that there is this generation that came before that actually did set the stage. And I have to say, when you said that Zoe, about intersectionality, I felt proud because in GANG we were having fun but we were also trying to connect across differences.

ZL When the COVID-19 pandemic happened and every article in the *TIMES* and every post on Instagram was like, "Oh my god, what the pandemic has revealed!" I was like, are you fucking for real? That drove me so bananas, because I was like, no, thirty years ago, when we had a totally different pandemic, we were all like, "Look how this reveals the inequity" And the activists that had come before us in the feminist health movement and the civil rights movement...

AR That was the sense of humor Suzanne was talking about, just to point that out.

SW When I look back at Issue #3 now, as a professor and somebody who is still an activist in not only my life but my work, I felt so dumbfounded by the fact that there's no sense of urgency, that we have gone back in time, that I was fighting for reproductive rights. Now we're finally saying the word abortion on a daily basis, but that's about it. I really feel like we've gone into a time capsule and gone back. And that image of a woman's pussy with "Read My Lips," I was just struck by how freaking kick-ass that is, and where is that now? But I don't know, it got my feathers up. I was just like, "I feel really angry." And I'm like, "All right, well, I got to start another movement. That's it." But I'm a little long in the tooth to be doing this. I want other people to do it as well and find where that is, locate in themselves where that is to then actually do something , and that's one of them, reproductive rights.

DW I can't remember who, if any, of you guys were with me when the Movement Research community had a tribunal after Issue #3 was published, but these were all people who were dancers, contact improvisors, about liberating the body from constraint , and their objection was really that our piece was too on the nose, too crudely political. They were super upset that somehow this crude activism had infiltrated the province of the artistic. And it was Bill T. Jones who stood up for us. So I will say that one of the things about GANG, for me, I never considered myself an artist, but the artists who were there, Adam and Suzanne and Zoe and Loring and Wellington, et cetera, were all willing to go there to the more direct activist confrontational place in addition to making art that was not only that. And that was an incredibly valuable contribution, but it felt out of sync with the Movement Research community.

LM How did it come to the group? Was it through Richard [Elovich] who made the offer?

DW Yeah, because Richard had funding from Philip Morris to do that *PERFORMANCE JOURNAL*, and so he offered it to Tom. I don't know if it was whether Tom or Richard gave us a page, but we just had a page in the journal.

WL My thought about this is that everything is escalated. Yes, we have much more visibility, much more exposure. We're not just in these marginalized queer film festivals or these exhibitions at PS 100 . We have many more access points, but at the same time, the people who come after us , they also have more access, they have towers for the war. Even if I think about my mornings with MSNBC, it's already evolved from "abortion care" to "abortion healthcare." Even in recent weeks you can hear the language has changed, and I think it's interesting because they're planting seeds, which I think are great because it's not just abortion, it's healthcare.

ZL It occurs to me in relation to this thing about explicit language and specifically this poster, the "read my lips before they're sealed" poster, that there was this moment when we made that poster and it could be on a journal that was sold on newsstands, that it could actually circulate through the world. And right now, I wonder if you even tried to show that in a museum there would be...

AR It would be a problem.

SW: Oh yeah. Signs everywhere warning "Don't let your children in here."

DW Trigger warning.

ZL Talking about the relationship to art and iconography, and what kind of iconography can be used, maybe I can trace the genesis of the photograph in that poster. We really wanted to respond to the legislation that was not going to allow healthcare providers to even say the word "abortion." But the poster came out of a conversation that Suzanne and I were having when we were in San Francisco on a trip, and something clicked where one day we were just like, "Yes, that's it, put a pussy there, and then those words 'read my lips before they're sealed.'" Make a pun on this already existing activist thing. So we were literally responding to censorship with an explicit image.

SW It was shock and awe.

ZL Later, in my own work, I ended up making an artwork where I used a lot of pussy shots and recently I had the occasion to revisit that work and gather a lot of the documentation, which I made for Documenta in 1992. That project was definitely, in some ways, inspired by the piece that we made in GANG. But looking back, it occurred to me I don't know if I would have the guts to do that work now, but I also wonder what museum, what publication, what kind of platform — no matter how progressive — would even allow that to be published no matter how progressive? We're seeing how the conversation is being so shut down about Gaza and institutions firing people and refusing to allow their students to protest. I think there's a real shutdown around explicit imagery — although there's massively sexualized imagery obviously all the time in advertising.

AR More than ever

ZL But in this particular instance, I think either we wouldn't be allowed to show it or we would have warnings

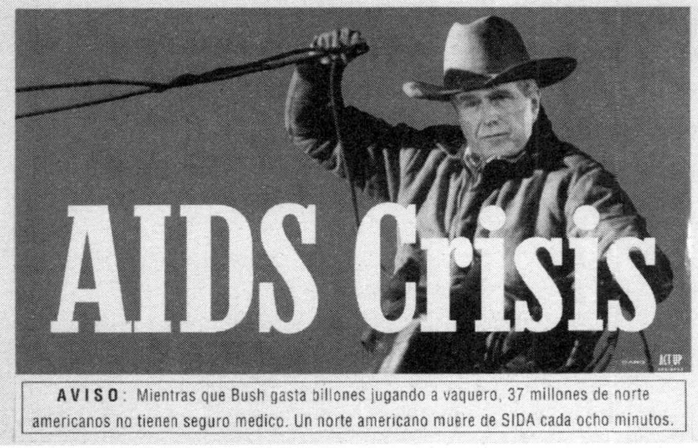

GANG, *AIDS CRISIS*, 1991, Print lithograph, 13 1/2 × 20 1/2 in. Courtesy International Center of Photography.

all over the galleries. But for me, it's the directness of our language, and our ability to actually depict our bodies and match our bodies with language that has to do with government legislation and say, "You know what? It is that direct. It actually is this: get out of my pussy."

SW And a hairy pussy.

AR Not beautifully groomed.

ZL That would be the thing. People being like, "Oh my god, she didn't wax."

SW How ungroomed!

AR But there is a platform that the internet was invented for where everybody is looking at things like that, and that's porn.

DW I actually think funding was pulled after the issue because the real infraction was the inclusion of legislation — because the poster violated the divide between not-for-profit foundation dollars where you're not allowed to legislate for particular pieces of legislation. I mean, I'm sure it was the pussy plus the legislation, but just to say that those constraints vis-a-vis politics are already built into the foundation, not-for-profit institutional establishment — which is you can make art but don't connect it to political actions so explicitly or you're in violation of the terms of the funding.

DW But I would also say that, for me, there's something about time travel or moving back and forth in time, about GANG. That poster seems, of course, totally relevant now, except of course the lips are sealed, the repeal of Roe vs. Wade has happened. But even beyond this poster, Suzanne mentioned Michael Perelman, I always associated Michael Perelman's involvement in GANG with my sense that his gay education had happened in a different era of gayness — he was very familiar with Christopher Street Queen tropes and Betty Davis imitations.

AR It's like he teleported out of the 1950s or something.

DW And he had made a conscious effort to be an emissary between the 50s and the 90s. And then, I mentioned Peter Bowen who was so terminally 90s...there was a lot we did about contemporary performances of gayness or straightness, performances that were about performing moments in time or representation. There was always a time travel piece for me, more in the people maybe than in the products. Even that video about movies that were important to us when we came out, that was all about past period in time.

AR "Read My Lips," to take it back to that, is about putting our bodies forward and using our bodies and in a way that does connect to performance, but it's also where we came out of. We were literally putting our bodies in the street. There was something physical about the attack on our bodies, disease, but also just that we were putting our bodies on the line. And so that makes sense that it would appear in the work.

LM but I'm struck today by how little there is on the street that's oppositional or political. There's practically nothing.

AR Zero

LM In that era, there were people wheat pasting all over downtown and you just don't see that anymore. Of course, there's the internet, but I don't even know whether that's happening on the internet. So it's harder, in some sense, to reach a broad range of people than if you physically encountered it walking around the street in the city.

AR Okay, I've got an idea. Let's redo "Read My Lips" on the street.

SW Do you remember at BAM when we had everybody stand up? That to me was the most memorable part of our performance. We all did these little things. We basically appropriated this idea of standing up if you are Jewish or gay...

DW It was the King of Denmark's expression of solidarity to get all Danish citizens to put on a Jewish star so that no one would be able to identify the Jews. So we asked everyone to stand up as if to be identified with Holly, who was being targeted for the defunding in the NEA controversy.

SW That's right. And we had everybody stand up to say they were gay.

AR This is becoming a GANG meeting. We're spit balling ideas. I love it.

ZL I really remain deeply interested and committed and excited by the idea of affinity and by how energizing this conversation was, how good it is to see all your faces and to feel like we can talk about things and get each other riled up and excited and want to make something new. But I'm not always sure about what public space is right now and where you reach people that aren't already, preaching to the choir. What does that mean when you're not speaking to people who are already absolutely going to agree with you? SW: I wonder though, a little bit, Zoe, I totally hear what you're saying and I agree with it and I think that we are in a very vulnerable space. You just don't know where people are coming from, what their filter, history has been in regards to how they view you. But I wonder how much we're preaching to the choir because I'm rethinking the choir, I've been really shocked about the choir lately. If we came up with something that was as shocking I don't know if it would be preaching to the choir. I suspect it might be refreshing,

ZOE LEONARD, WELLINGTON LOVE,
LORING MCALPIN, ADAM ROLSTON,
DANIEL WOLFE, AND SUZANNE WRIGHT

Movement Research
Performance Journal

Author
DAHLIA DAMOISELLE

Contributing Editor
ANH VO

Psalm for Single Mothers

Every client I take to bed makes a mother of me eventually
teenage madonna and child with no clue how to care
for grown men suckling at milkless breasts
what it is about my androgyne slimness / clit too large / ovaries on the outside
aching to make life from an ersatz womb (can they smell her?)
every john who's rich in money is a pauper in tenderness & touch
so why do I still struggle to make ends meet when
no matter how hard mommy spanks them/they always beg for more

Listen, I learned from the best
made a saint of my mother
who had a master's degree & taught me to be too proud
to collect unemployment & too sad to leave the dance floor
til morning turned the new boyfriend into a pumpkin & her sobs shook
the paper-thin drywall on finding the pantry as empty as our stomachs
& the electricity went out anyway

I ask the morning star why god has to be such a cunt
why *TEEN MOM* is just another word for
oldest girl in the orphanage
& why he made me wish for a body that could make life
& why he thought an army of orphans would console my unbloodied sex

I, girl surrounded by sharp objects for the things
I'm too weak to o p e n / if I cut you
an entrance would you notice the struggle
to ache alive a fertile cradle into my sex?
Listen, if there's one thing the army taught me it's
YOU GO TO WAR WITH THE BODY YOU HAVE NOT THE BODY YOU MIGHT WANT
OR WISH TO HAVE AT A LATER TIME
but like so many single mothers mowing the lawn while daddy's away
my petals never open no matter how many bayonets I bury in my skin

If you ever want soldier sons, a piece of advice:
raise a small, warm-blooded thing
with all your love & a lifespan of one or two years
so when they die, you will mourn them longer than they had ever lived
I'm doing you a favor / these sons you send to battle
will never call / drink too much & leave their toys around the house
round in the chamber just in case their memories overrun the gates
& the last evac out is what soldiers' mothers fear most

I'm sick of telling war stories because people don't listen
so to paraphrase: my brother lost himself in Kandahar
to an army of fathers he thought could give him
a better home than the one I made for him
in summary: these days, when I listen
to him speak his voice becomes the bedroom we shared as children
& just as vacant & distant & irretrievable

My sister is a veteran of the wars fought in our living room
PTSD from daddy's night raids littering
trails of civilian casualties across the kitchen floor
I wonder if she believes me when I say I walk the streets alone at night
as exposure therapy but never tell her
I'm seeking penance in a man with daddy's hands
to punish me for every night I fled father and left her defenseless

I wish my maternal instincts ended with my siblings' silence
I made a rule to give every ending I wrote a small measure of grace
a token of love to give my grieving lines because everyone dies
& at least I'll have left a fragment of me
yet I falter; I wish I had faith that nothing ever ends
& nothing ever dies but how I could live with such fetters?

In the photo of bà nội on my altar she does not smile
saint resting bitch face: I pray this body of spiro this blood of estradiol
hail grandma serving cunt make me in your scowling image
so at least I'll know I'm just as beautiful
& I wonder how someone so beautiful could've made a son so ugly
& how someone so ugly could've made a woman who makes herself
the sort of mother who knows what sons who lose their mothers
do to daughters who look just like them

If I was my father's mother I'd see
how he just wanted to make someone else feel
the way he felt / April 1975 / sixteen on a distant shore
liberation razing all he loved
a strange new home a world without: daily beatings
/ sons returning to mothers draped in the flag
/ & mothers who die too soon
I'll see how he failed at everything he did anyway

& remember when I hated the girl on the bus
in the floral dress her stubble stood proud
her tracheal bulge rasping from too much laughter—
how she just wanted to make someone else feel
desire intense enough to be mistaken for hate
& make a girl who forced a boy onto herself
be a mother to / her son / her daughter / herself

If my mother was right; & *THERE WILL BE NO ONE TO CARE FOR YOU*
WHEN I'M GONE & if I'm anything like her
I'll sew gold into the seams of your clothes &
wait among the torchflies & I'll rub your back
while we watch for the boat that spirits you away
to a new country where I'll teach you
to see the illusion of plenty on store shelves &
to never talk to the police & how home feels
just like a half-remembered song played on an untuned string

I'll always have my boy / my girl / you children inside me
I'll go gray worrying whether my fear of
coups by motherless juntas has made me
forget to teach you how to find your joy outside me
I'll still buy my girl her chibi dolls & animal stuffies
& all manner of sweet things long after you've outgrown them
how I'll still remind my boy he can have dolls & wear pink &
kiss boys if he wants / long after you've learned to love them

& if I love these children I can never carry nor birth
I can love every student & john & friend & mother & sibling
& enemy & father / & make this motherless mass
my dark-haired mistress for blessed art thou among women
who takes my prayer-clasped hands her lips
promise to break the beads chaining child to cross
Listen carefully when her words abolish
worship for fathers who are never there
and the paradise promised that will never come

DAHLIA DAMOISELLE

Movement Research
Performance Journal

Author
PHUONG PHAN

Contributing Editor
ANH VO

Can The Body Remember? Propaganda Images in Performance Art in Vietnam

Can the body remember? aims to be an open question and invites discussion about the impacts of propaganda images in the practice of contemporary performance artists in Vietnam. This question emerged from decades-long conversations I have had with the artists about their works. Examining the strategies leveraged by Lại Diệu Hà, Nguyễn Xuân Bắc, and Trần Lương, I show how these artists have turned government propaganda into a tool for criticism and reflection on their own collective memories in relation to state-sanctioned imagery. Thereby, I show how the artists have turned propaganda images into a tool for criticism and reflection on their own collective memories with propaganda images. Published below is a portion of this longer project, focusing specifically on the third section on the work of Lại Diệu Hà. Not included in this excerpt is an extended discussion of the performance work Lập Loè by the artist Trần Lương, in which the artist uses the symbolism of a red scarf to think generationally about the imprint of communist ideology on the body; as well as a section on the visual artworks of Ngô Xuân Bắc, whose artistic works are deeply engaged with the many facets of propaganda and its visuality in urban landscape.

THE INTERVENTION BY AND ON HER OWN BODY WAS A VISUAL ACT TO DESTROY THIS LONG-LASTING UNDERSTANDING OF WOMEN'S EXISTENCE BEING RESERVED FOR MEN

<u>Lai Dieu Ha – The body remembers</u>

As one of the few female performance artists of her generation, Lại Diệu Hà, born in 1976, is known for her works that raise questions about gender and the role of women that is still shaped by patriarchy and Confucian concepts of virtue that overshadow how women are perceived in Vietnamese society. Often exposing her own body in her performance, she plays with aspects of taboos, shame and discrimination that are associated with the female body, thereby also reflecting on her experience. The naked body became essential for the artist to radicalize the female body, to break the Confucian framework of virtue and the Western dogma of beauty. It took her ten years to truly remove herself from the prescription of a female body in Vietnamese society. She, too, experienced the pressure of fulfilling beauty ideals of white smooth skin, black ebony hair and a curvaceous body that was perceived as ideal and feminine. The gaze of men had turned her to an object of desire — "Geisha like," as she recalled — so much so that it was important for her to get rid of these features (rũ bỏ), to throw away this "gift" which for her was also poison. Seeing the body as a tool (cơ thể là dụng cụ), Hà instrumentalized her own body parts, translating them into equipments for performance (đạo cụ trình diễn), which also meant to step out of her comfort zone of being adored and admired by many counterparts. Hà developed a series of "cut off performances" (cắt xẻo) in which she was naked on stage, and used knives and scissors to hurt her own body in front of the audience. According to Hà, at that time, a woman being naked on stage was something that shocked the people. The performance caused her to be perceived as being hysterical and mad (con dở hơi). Paradoxically, the moment when she was on stage with this performance was also the moment when Hà "did not feel any pain." To her, it was some sort of resistance against the Confucianist notions of a woman within worship engaging in feminine chastity as part of domestic virtue — of being the gentle sex responding to male obsession. The intervention by and on her own body was a visual act to destroy this long-lasting understanding of women's existence being reserved for men. Being aware of the risk of turning her body and herself as and into an object under the male gaze, after the performance series "cut off" Hà took a break from the arts for a couple of years. According to her, she wanted to open doors, challenging the audience's understanding of what performance was, but also be able to claim the body still belonged to her.

THE GENTLE SEX

Hà is one of a few female performance artists who continuously works with her own definition of what performance is in the context of Vietnam — a medium that was first introduced in late 1990s by artists such as Trương Tân, Nguyễn Minh Thành and by Trần Lương in the early 2000s; that has been and remains primarily dominated by male artists. In the context of Vietnam, a country that has been shaped by communist propaganda arts for decades, Hà strongly believes that in Northern Vietnam, performance embodies propagandistic characters. Since the American war in Vietnam, propaganda culture has been constantly and rigidly produced by the Party's cadre. In literature, music, and dance, certain propaganda images penetrated the body, and propagandistic images are reproduced through gesture. Hà retrospectively spoke about how she'd often use her hand to gesticulate, raising her right hand in the air (vung lên). Later on, she realized that this particular gesture is an image that is familiar to the people in Vietnam, and has been used frequently in propaganda posters. As a daughter of a propaganda poster artist, Hà grew up with these images. They were everywhere in their family house, as her father used to create the posters at home. Hà recalled watching him draw as she (sometimes) helped him color the motifs and assisted him and his colleagues with distributing the posters in their district. His only child to become an artist, Hà strongly believes that her choice for the arts was deeply influenced by her father. At the same time — and this is the most complex and interesting part of their relationship — she neglected him, and he abandoned his artistic career until he passed away in 2010. It was her father's death that prompted Hà to deeply engage with his work for the first time. It was Hà approaching propaganda arts that gave rise to propaganda arts that gave rise to Đọc về một tiểu sử (Reading A Person's Life), a performance resulting from her study with the complex and contradictory relationship she had with her father, propaganda poster artist Lại Văn Thành.

In Đọc về một tiểu sử (2022), Hà stood on stage and read out loud to the audience a text that she wrote about her father. She also invited the audience to read with her lines she had composed based on fragments of his diary. Reading with her, the voices of the audience overlapped with hers, and they created a dissonance in rhythm and sound, constantly disrupted and intervened by words stuck in throats. During the reading, the audience learned about the poster artist Lại Văn Thành, a story of a man who dedicated his entire life to propaganda arts — an occupation and a commitment to a genre that is largely understood as problematic amongst contemporary artists today. In the text, Hà weaved her own post-humous thoughts about her father with his self-reflection about how he started his career, the challenges he faced, and the shame he developed over the years for not being acknowledged as a true artist by his contemporaries. There were moments of humiliation that he went through as he was working for a communist apparatus that was definitely not solely constructed on the common narrative of equality, solidarity and brotherhood. Reading these lines, the audience become part of the performance, and they became complicit in his life path, within and throughout all the obstacles and shame.

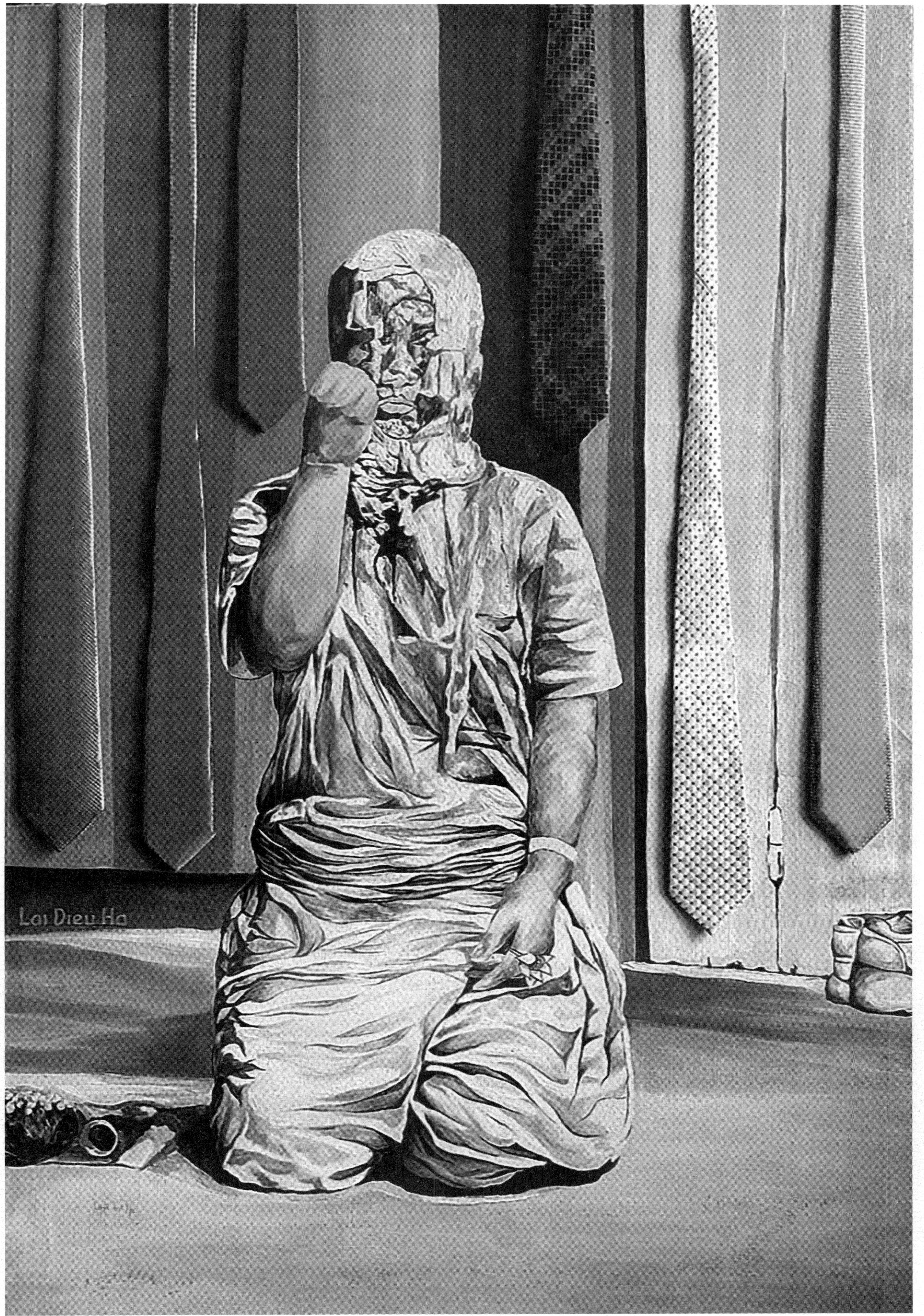

Lại D ệu Hà, *HIỆN THỰC CHẬM LẠI*, 2021, oil on canvas. Image courtesy the artist

Hà's father belonged to a generation of Vietnamese artists who served as soldiers at the front and later, when the American war officially ended in 1975, continued to work as cadres in the production of the state's propaganda arts. His entire artistic life was built from the persistence of state propaganda art which were and still are, despised and disdained by dissident artists. Work by propaganda artists working in the state's apparatus have not been acknowledged as works of art. Often, they are understood as being conformed, and lacking artistic creativity and intellectuality. It is precisely this common perception, or perhaps this prejudice, about the production of art and culture under communism that makes it impossible for propaganda to be regarded as something that deserves serious consideration.

Vietnam's history is shaped by wars, ideologies, and political mischief between 1945 and 1975, and followed by an isolation from the global world until the late 1990s. Vietnamese art history is crucially shaped by socialist realism, and propaganda art is a genre that, due to its complexities, has been largely ignored by scholars. The agony and disdain for propaganda intensified in the 1990s when foreign actors entered Vietnam for the first time, claiming an authority of having "introduced" Western contemporary arts to Vietnamese artists at that time. This is not the place to discuss any further their Janus-faced contribution, but with their arrival, pre-existing socialist realisms and persistent propaganda arts were placed on the scales and compared to Western contemporary art that was, at that time, considered modern, progressive and "civilized" (văn minh) by Vietnamese artists.

For a long time, Hà shared in this climate of anti-propaganda arts. Although — or perhaps precisely because — she grew up with propaganda arts by her father, she ignored and neglected the political, cultural, and aesthetic values of propaganda posters which are, as she now understands, something quite significant in Vietnam. In the last few years, Hà has been interested in the question of how propaganda and performance are conceptually intertwined, and where they diverge from one another. Propaganda and performance share the aim of communication: condensed messages in a limited temporal and spatial framework. At the same time, the notion of time and space is also the aspect that tears them apart. Performance works mostly appear ephemeral: each time they're different, and never repeatable. The performers react and interact with the environment, sometimes actively affected by their audience. The nature of propaganda arts is the persistence of repetition and frequent endurance. Images created by the artist are made to be multiplied, to be copied by other people (which makes the claim for authorship ridiculous) and finally, to be circulated as far as they can go. At the same time, they function temporally, and the quantity of their being does not guarantee their currency and value. To some propaganda poster artists, propaganda posters need to be on point and on time. This dimension might bring propaganda posters once again closer to performance art.

In our conversation, Hà mostly emphasized the fact that engaging with her father's propaganda work shaped the way she now practices performance. She defines performance art as the spirit of being combative, precise, temporal, and on point, which not entirely different from the language of propaganda posters. Hà recalled that as the only girl in the family she often raised her fist to argue with her parents and brother. The fist, also a symbol of socialism and communism, appears again and again in her works. Hà often spans an arc between propaganda images and performance. She works with symbols and the aspects of performativity that can shape social interactions. Hà is interested in the density of symbols in propaganda posters that manifest and shape people's visual world, leading them to concrete action.

Now, using propaganda art in her performance, she has turned propaganda art into her medium, using the power of propaganda to re-shape and to re-define the common notion of propaganda art. While this may be interpreted as a proposal to critically rethink propaganda arts in Vietnam in general. Perhaps, one should have the courage to admit that propaganda art has played its part in what contemporary art in Northern Vietnam has become today.

PHUONG PHAN

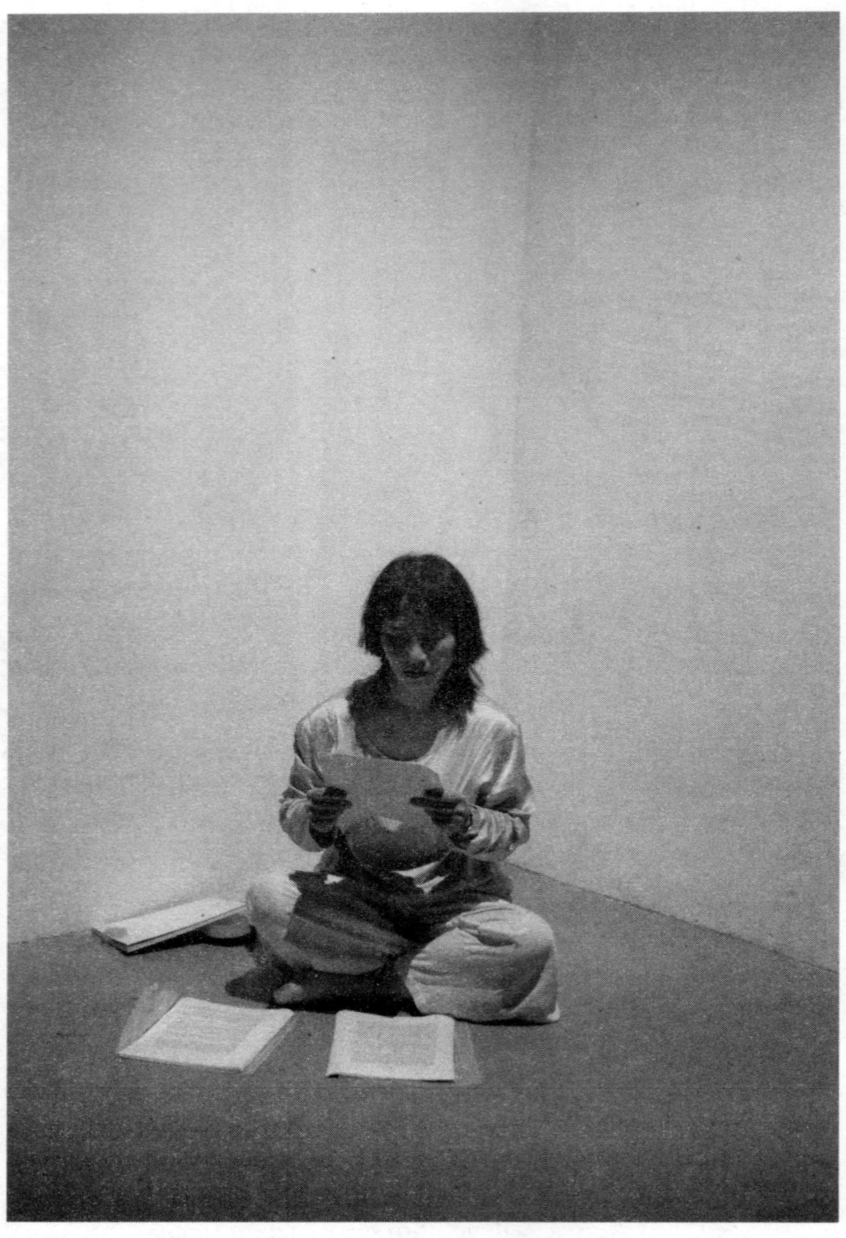

Lại Diệu Hà, *ĐỌC VỀ MỘT TIỂU SỬ* (2022), performed as part of "Sáng Trưa Chiều Tối" ["Morning – Noon – Afternoon – Evening"] at Á Space, March 26, 2022.
Image courtesy the artist.

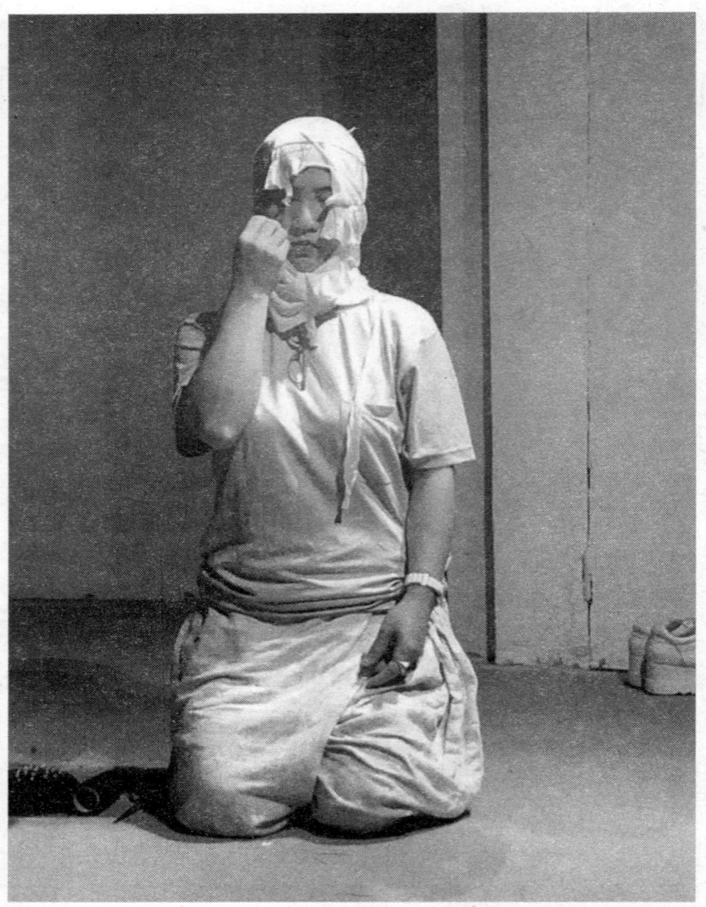

Image courtesy Lại Diệu Hà.

Issue 60
Spring/Summer 2024

MAGMA & PEARLS is an origin story for *THE CREATION OF THE DOLLS*. The current chapter of work follows the journey of the dolls—a word that loosely means a trans woman so flawless she can no longer be considered real, underscoring how camouflage and metamorphosis serve as strategies for survival, and, ultimately transcendence. My project aims to bring different communities together to lean into the healing power of sharing our stories and cultivating worlds in our names. We all become stars building our own galaxy, universe of glory.

— Keioui Keijaun Thomas

Author and
Contributing Editor
KEIOUI KEIJAUN THOMAS

"Touch This Skin, Honey"

What is it
about the closeness of
familiar skin that
drives
people
crazy? No Beyoncé

They touched my skin
and my entire body shivered.

Their hands following the
journey of my spine.

Touching skin to skin to understand
every single bone concealed by my flesh

Touching to understand the
history of our skin tattooed
by every sunrise marked by
our ancestors' DNA and
melanin.

Against every attempt to hold us down. Our
eyes open, again in the morning light

And Still We Rise. Black and Luminous like
the other side of the moon.
They wiped away the accumulated dust that
had held me, together,
hardened my exterior illusion.

This body, this skin, this orgy of bones
I call home. This vessel, rough and soft at the
same damn time.

Sometimes, I wonder
what they see when they look at me. I
wonder if they see me inside of me
If they see the tenderness behind my
eyelids? Protected by every lash

With my eyes closed, my heart is wide open.
Stop and imagine that

"Heaven Bound Dolls"

For Saint/Motha Cecilia Gentili
in our sister/ her daughter Rio Sofia's words: "A Trans Titan"

May these words hold us as we grieve and celebrate her life <3

Who knows more about the wind than the sea

Ocean breeze on the banks of white sand in
the Florida keys

Sometimes I feel like I'm heaven bound

The ocean swallows me whole Covered in
gold a new mold

transness as a full bodied spectrum of
existence. The way we show up in the world,

Brave and beautiful in all of our nuances
with so much grace while changing the world
and exceeding expectations

A rapture of undoing
An anointment by the universe saying Bloom
Bloom
Bloom

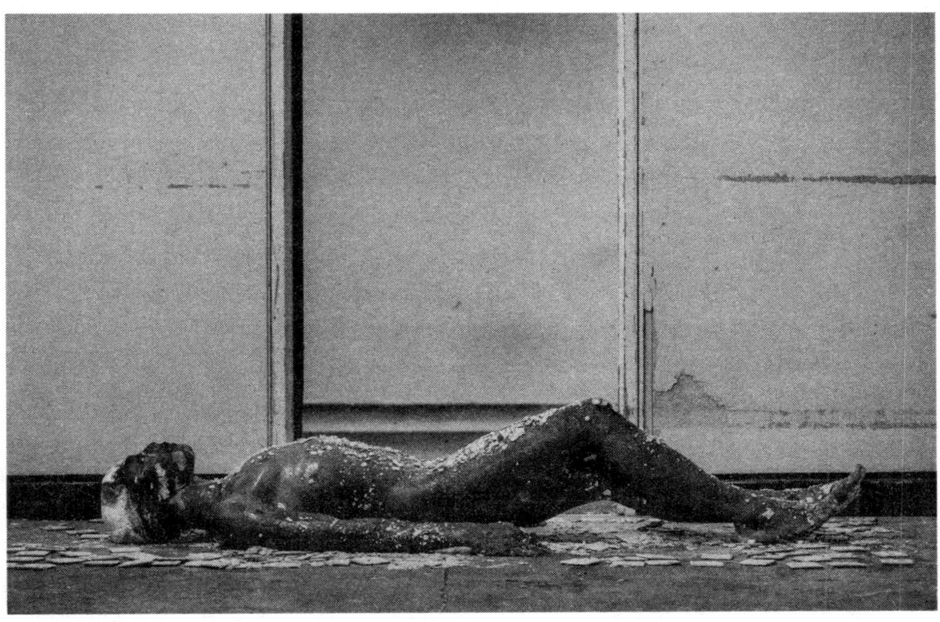

Keioui Keijaun Thomas, *THE POETICS OF TRESPASSING: PART 1. ABSENT WHITENESS, PART 2. LOOKING WHILE SEEING THROUGH, PART 3. SWEET LIKE HONEY, BLACK LIKE SYRUP* (Ipswich, UK: SPILL Festival of Performance, 2014). Photo by Guido Mencari.

"Black Aunties"

Sometimes I feel like the
ocean is the closest living
relative I know.

Like a black auntie that's
really yo cousin but old
enough to be
respected like yo mama's sista.

Ya know, the kinda auntie cousin
that managed to wade thru
the small town troubles.
Found ha a nice house
outside the hood y'all call home.

Wading in the wada just across
the riva. She been holding life
forces, souls and secrets never
to be told.

"Black Like The Bottom Of The Ocean"

She is called Dark and Lovely. Relaxed
so deep her light goes undetected while
rocking our world.

Black like an entire galaxy at the edges of
milky way. Hair laid
down by time.
Black holes even envy her shine

Braided and weaved together like old church
rhymes. Gleaming in her blackness, an
abyss never to be fully known by mankind.
Undefined

Black like obsidian, baby
her soul catches fire. Lava wakes in her stride

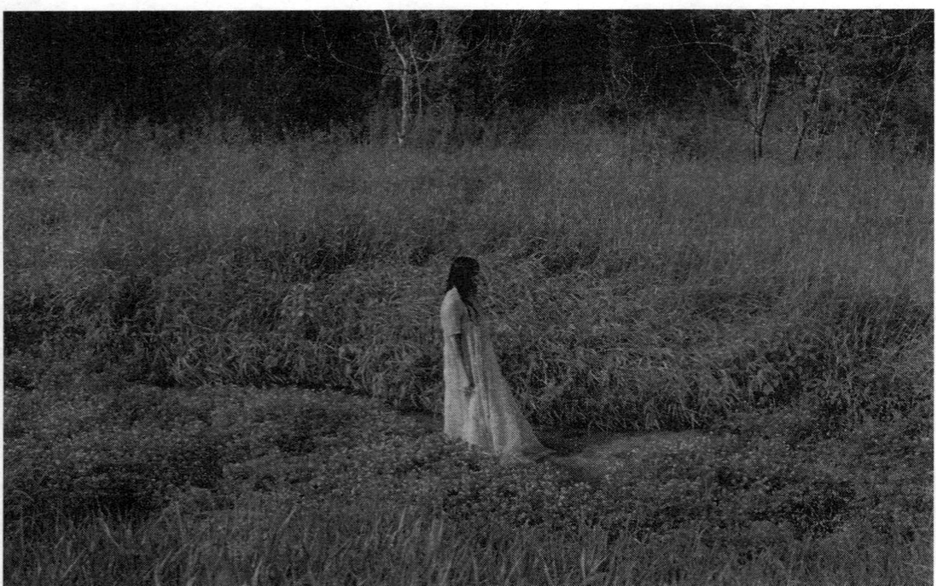

Keioui Keijaun Thomas, *COME HELL OR HIGH FEMMES: ACT 2. THE LAST TRANS FEMMES ON EARTH: DRIPPING DOLL ENERGY*, 2021. Photo by Hannah Patterson.

"Jade Daggers Buried in the Garden"

Hold me
like we've just finished fucking
under a waterfall.
Wet and hard diamond pressure

Kissed by a star
the same star sign you see
when you make love inside of me.

You say, it makes you hold me harder than
your cock pressed against
the inner walls of my spectrum.
A thousand whimpers in the moonlight,
tucked in between my thighs.
Rise, soft and gentle.

Like a jade dagger, ready to open you up. Cutting
through the bullshit to find the truth. No more code
switching in order to survive.
My camouflaged armor dropped down by my ankles. I say,
get on your knees, if you want to greet me.
Like a black femme queen. You can kiss my feet
not my ass cuz that would bring too much pleasure to your lips.
Make you pray for moments like this
in the rose garden where Black Femmes reign supreme.

"Napping in 2020 (or a Pandemic)"

and my ego said
but you've traveled the world

and my body said
but you still hungry hoe

and my spirit said
you got more work to do

and my body said
you still got pain and trust issues that
trauma sit deep in you

and my ego said
but you can get dick anytime
you want

and my body said
you like your belly rubbed and
your neck kissed

And my tongue said
you like your water sparkling

And my heart said
what do you really need

and my body said
say what you want

and my ego said do
you boo

and my spirit said
you are Marva's grandchild
and Bridget's baby— it's in your blood,
sweat and tears mama

and my ego said
don't post that
maintain their fake ass perception of you

and my body said
take a nap

"Meteorites (Fall On Deaf Ears)"

and I've watched the ocean rise
and fall like meteorites and I've
kissed your neck and stroked
your skin
and rested in your eardrums and
laughed in your belly and
believed in your glory and
maybe listening
to your spirit
delivers you from your ego and
sometimes you arrive
at the heart of it all
bodied and content.

"Washed Up by the Tide"

I once was sharp like
a stone dagger

but I've learned to be
softer

over time,

washed up
and rinsed
by the tide.

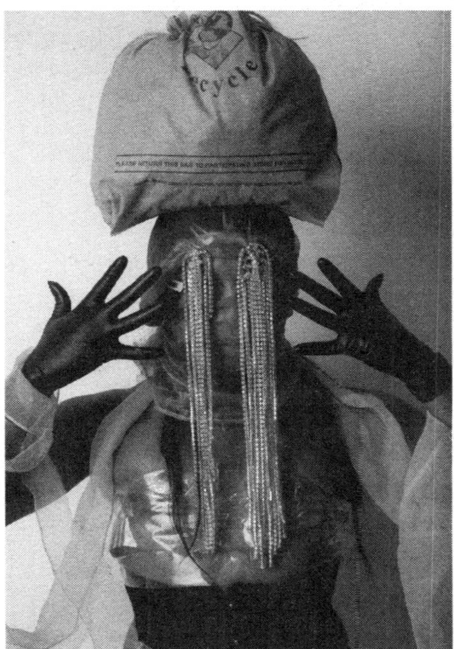

Keioui Keijaun Thomas, *COME HELL OR HIGH FEMMES: JOURNEY OF THE DOLLS* (New York, NY: Perrotin Gallery, 2022). Photo by Guillaume Ziccarel i.

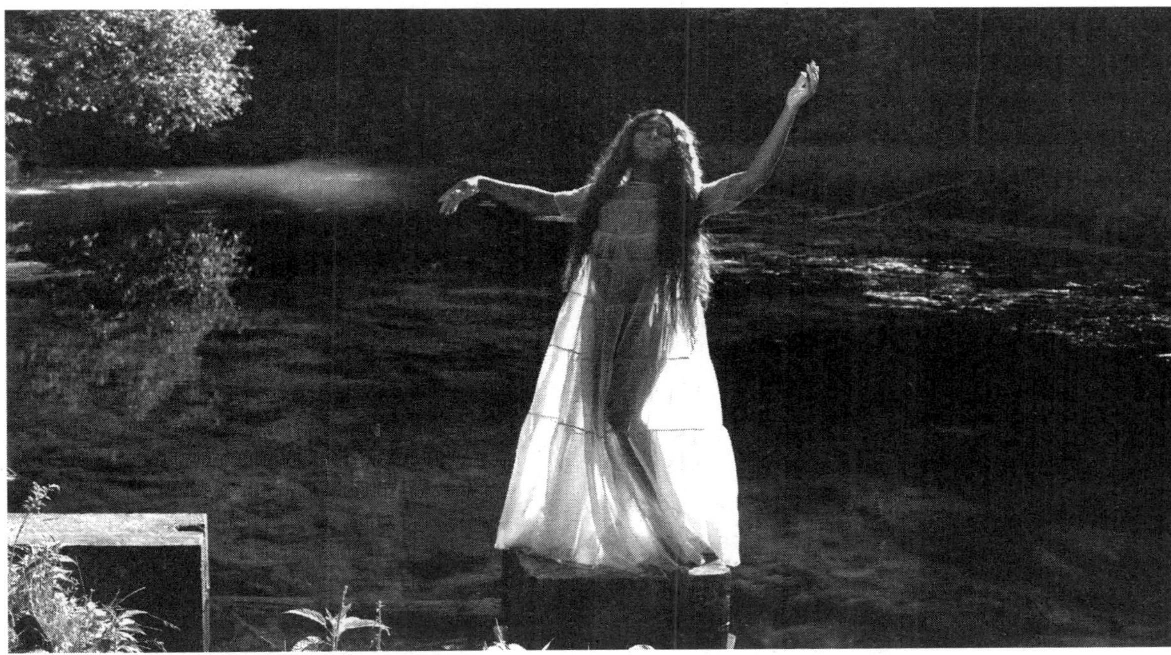

Keioui Keijaun Thomas, *COME HELL OR HIGH FEMMES: ACT 2. THE LAST TRANS FEMMES ON EARTH: DRIPPING DOLL ENERGY* (film still), 2021. Filmed & Edited by/with Christopher Sonny Martinez.

"Immaculate Marbles"

perhaps, it is in my spirit
or my grandmother's, mother's red
blood cells or kidney disease.

perhaps, it is somewhere
in the dust of my shedding skin cells collected on
my imagined lovers' bedsheets, drenched from
summer heat.

perhaps, it is in my faggot sweat left
behind on the dance floor,
collecting puddles of runoff doll energy.

perhaps, it is so vague, so nuanced
i will never have the words to describe it, but i do
feel it, sometimes.

immaculately marbled feelings of
dolls transcending.

Keioui Keijaun Thomas, *COME HELL OR HIGH FEMMES*
(New York, NY: Performance Space New York, 2021). Photo by Maria Baranova.

"7 o'clock on the Dot (circa 2008)"

I use to know this boy
named

We would fuck
on his water mattress

He dated a girl named but

he always wanted me

I would suck his dick
and he would play with my hole.

I used to know this boy named

We use to ride the slide together

before cock fighting.
He use to like my ass

pressed against his dick.

Down we'd go.

I used to know this boy named

He was my first time.
I lost my virginity to him when I was 16. I

cried. I felt him.

I used to know this boy named

Same name but separate escapade. We
would play in the woods together.

Dick to throat, ass to dirt. Dick to
pillow, ass up.

I used to know this boy named

He had a French last name.
We would fuck
in the back of his pick up truck.

Nasty and raw
in the middle of the country.

I used to know these boys from the block.

"They Call Us the Gurls (or Doll Headquarters)"

They call me a star because I listen to their
wishes and birth dreams

They call me dat girl because I let my spirit
reign supreme

They call me a hoe because I know how to
make a nigga wanna believe in serving
hospitality

They call me a saint because I never let the
church faze me

They call me a slut because I've spent days
on my knees not praying to a god that never
could see me

They call me a bad bitch because I speak
with mountains and earthquakes between my
eyes

They call us nasty because we can touch our
toes and still make a bitch feel our souls

They call us ghetto because our tongues
know how to untwist harm and open oceans
in the middle of projects and concrete
jungles

They call us ratchet because our words are
innovation sparking revolutions

"Never Forget 1861 (or Negro Truths)"

How can you say forget the past (nigga)
and in the same breath praise the confederacy as
your history — marked in the pages of fallacy

40 acres and a mule wiped clean
of your brutality— buried in misery.

Your granddaddy say reparations
aren't warranted after centuries of slavery — enslaved
memories on cotton and sugar cane receipts

Picked and plucked as plantation goods not
even the crows could speak
even in the blood of descendants hanging in your galleries

Gospel hymns murmured in fear
after so much blood, sweat and tears— stained stories in gods
ears

Not even soap can wash away the treachery
under the Spanish moss and in-between your molar teeth
Your tongue can't regurgitate any truth— with so much blood at
the roots

How can you say
we don't deserve to be paid for centuries
swept under
willow tree graves.

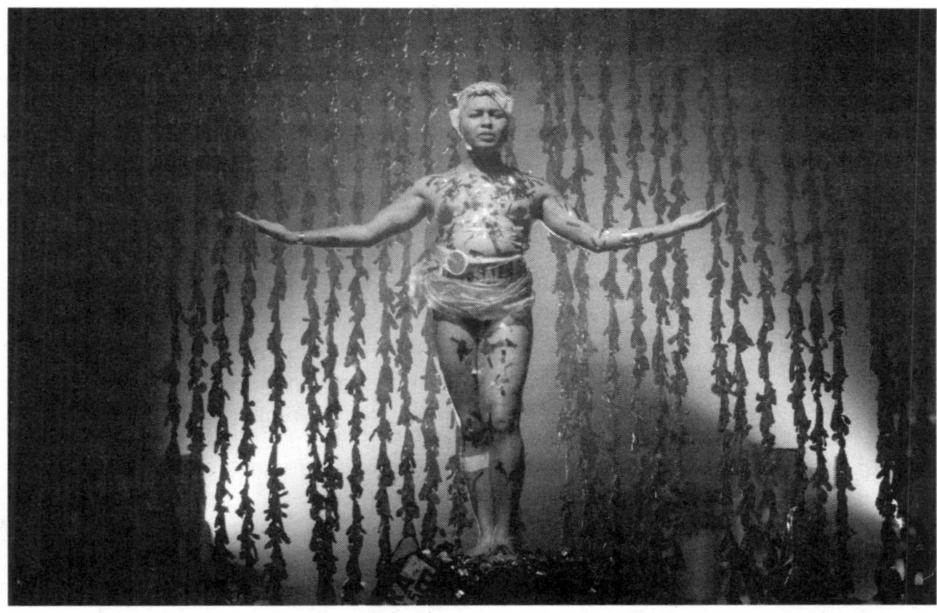

Keioui Keijaun Thomas, *COME HELL OR HIGH FEMMES: THE ERA OF THE DOLLS* (New York, NY: Abrons Art Center, 2023). Photo by Christopher Sonny Martinez.

"The World Shall Shake"

When an alien meets a goddess the
world shall shake.

Language will greet her tongue to ask
for grace. Oceans will lap
at her thighs sharing stories of light years in
time.

Even black stoicism shall reside. Tongues
will untwist ancient lies to be alive.

Even gender shall rise, beyond our eyes.
Hypnotized in glory. Angels will sing
melodies of our loves embrace. Deep love to
us everyday.

KEIOUI KEIJAUN THOMAS

Language analog for trans

Author
ZOEY LUBITZ

Contributing Editor
AMALLE DUBLON

I'm 15, running through the sheets of rain falling in downtown Portland. Through the moiré of my wet lashes, I make out puddles reflecting the electric sign of a neon cowboy. My full bladder impels me through traffic in desperation, hoping that a place to pee might materialize on the other side of SW Third Ave. A car's horn is held in caesura. Brakes squeal as they clench in anguish against their metal contact zone. The driver's voice cracks out of the window through the water, "get out of the street lady." Warm, slowly soaking, then heavy and sodden, the denim quickly turns to cold sandpaper. I peed in my jeans.

The feeling of the inverted (mis)gendering was the hot red wire, not euphoric — raw and alien. A short circuit arching to the black ground that was the misperception of my age; the driver calling me, an acned 15-year-old boy, "lady" instead of "girl" meant I had been completely misapprehended in a way that added to my cold and wet confusion. Maybe the misgendering was merely one aspect of a gross error, and it meant nothing more than through the weather someone thought a 15-year-old boy was a full-grown woman. Wires crossed for a minute in that near collision of car and kid, woman and girl and pavement...

At 23, I moved to New York because I didn't really know where to go after a big breakup. I was reading *DHALGREN* and obsessed with the way it eroticized everything chaotic. The breakdown was rhythmic, miscommunication and confusion were poetry, fear and suspense were rich with possibility. As I followed Delany's bisexual poet through a crumbling urban environment, the cracks in the city around me threatened to split like the ones in the book, the precarity in focus sharp and anticipatory. Lots of older people would see the big book in my lap and say I remember loving reading that. He writes, "You meet a new person, you go with him and suddenly you get a whole new city...you go down new streets, you see houses you never saw before, pass places you didn't even know were there. Everything changes."[1] In fracture there is openness. Sociality alters the environment. I loved the J train, because you could stand outside on this scaffold — the potential to become unlatched, bend, and collapse — and smell Broadway. The light came through the smeared windows, catching on their etched and abraded glass, which fogged up with condensation like the windows of my childhood classrooms. On the J you weren't underground. It was a pleasure to be able to see just over the buildings and into the apartments, and the sky — whether it was heavy or light that day, drying out the wet trash and paper, or making wet paper, then mulch.

In another Delany book, another poet protagonist, Rydra Wong, bestselling author in the galaxy, is less flâneuse, and more of a cryptographer-on-a-mission — though in characteristic Delany style, sexually liberated and surrounded by characters with beautiful custom body mods. Her curiosity inspires her to reluctantly accept a military assignment: decode a series of garbled, undecipherable transmissions, each intercepted only seconds before enemy terrorist attacks on military installations. *BABEL-17* is the codename for the transmissions, and, she discovers, actually an entirely new language, as well as the title of the novel. Rydra maps the mystery of this alien language using her training as a linguist and cryptographer, augmented by certain neurodivergent intellectual proclivities resulting from a childhood brain infection. Like her childhood illness, learning to use the language quite literally transforms her consciousness. At one point she wakes up captive, after being incapacitated when her ship is sabotaged and nearly destroyed. Her first thoughts are thrown into a language that is somewhere in translation, in English, but also outside of it:

> Abstract thoughts in a blue room: Nominative, genitive, elative, accusative one, accusative two, ablative, partitive, illative, instructive, abessive, adessive, inessive, essive, allative, translative, comitative. Sixteen cases to the Finnish noun. Odd, some languages get by with only singular and plural. The North American Indian languages even failed to distinguish number. Except Sioux, in which there was a plural only for animate objects. The blue room was round and warm and smooth. No way to say warm in French. There was only hot and tepid.[2]

Rydra is transformed by a language that affects her senses, her spatial orientation, her linguistic capacity, and her awareness of time, space, and bounds of self. She can anticipate others' actions so coherently and with such speed to the degree that she can read minds, and, to her annoyance, the world slows down around her. This happens performatively in Delany's writing: his writing style changes as she does. And I think so does the reader; she also changes in the reading.

Language and gender are bound up with one another.

In her book *HISTORIES OF THE TRANSGENDER CHILD*, Jules Gill-Peterson puts language acquisition at the heart of the normative conceptualization of gender. She writes about John Money, the infamous John Hopkins sexologist,

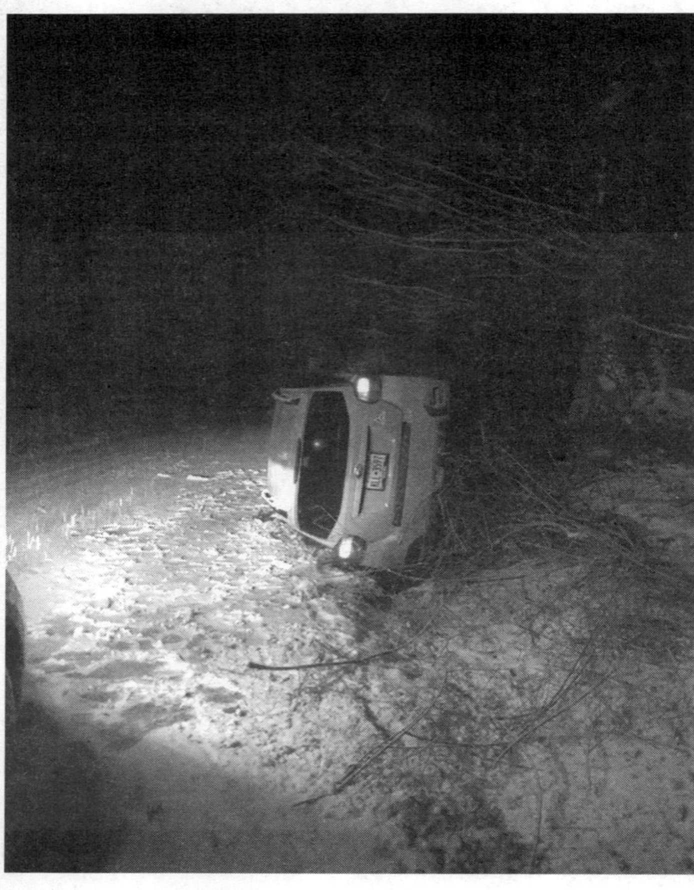

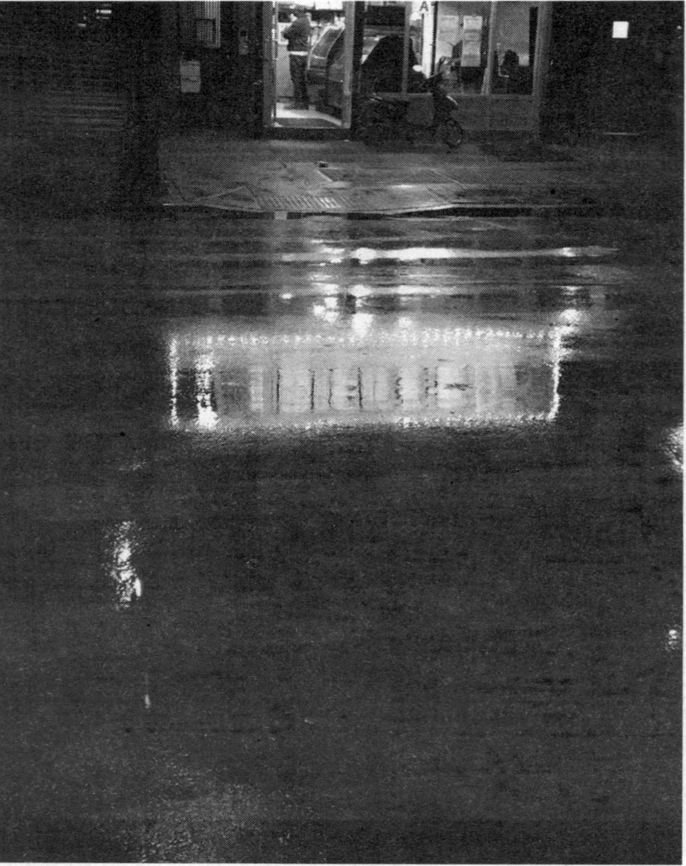

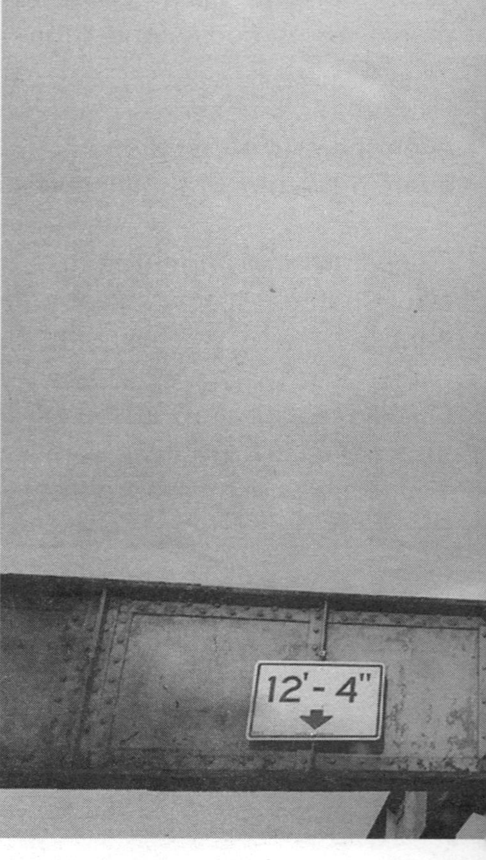

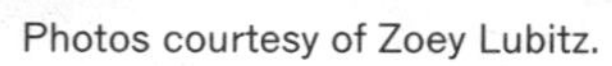
Photos courtesy of Zoey Lubitz.

1 Samuel R. Delany, *DHALGREN* (1974; reis. New York: Vintage Books, 2001), 318.
2 Samuel R. Delany, *BABEL-17 / EMPIRE STAR* (*BABEL-17* 1966; reis. New York: Vintage Books, 2001), 111.
3 Jules Gill-Peterson, *HISTORIES OF THE TRANSGENDER CHILD* (Minneapolis: University of Minnesota Press, 2018), 118.

who, in collaboration with psychiatrists Joan and John Hampton "deployed an analogy to language acquisition as a form of developmental plasticity to secure their argument about how gender was formed."[3]

The analogy goes that when an baby is born, they do come pre-programmed with a native language. Infants have only the capacity for language. Therefore "gender role may be likened to a native language."[4] Like language, a "gender role" is a culturally specific social phenomenon, and is acquired. Sound familiar? Gill-Peterson shows how their work in the 1950s rested on a notion of childhood sexual "plasticity," in which the infant's sex is briefly open and mutable, and later shaped and habituated into a specific gender role. They went further: the more native in that language – that gender role – the patient becomes, the more solidified and less plastic the patient's sex becomes, and so, quite horrifically and in accordance with their program, intersex infants and children were assigned a sex surgically, prior to their acquisition and solidification of a "gender role" as defined at Hopkins. Quite radically, and to terrible effect, Money believed that a child could be sculpted — as long as they were still early enough in their development, and therefore plastic enough — to be made into either a boy or a girl.

SEXUAL PLASTICITY ECHOES

Gill-Peterson's account of American sexology, and her archaeology of the gender/sex complex, strikes me in its correction of the idea that liberatory feminist politics invented gender: rather, the concept of gender and its likeness to language was first conceived and deployed as part of a conservative medical project — ironic, given the current vulgar and repressive discourse on "gender ideology." In her words, "[a]lthough gender has come to be associated with cultural malleability and feminist political projects, as far as its conditions of emergence are concerned it is better described as a medical device mobilized to face the potential conceptual collapse of binary sex."[5] The more these scientists and clinicians studied the variously sexed aspects of the body — gonads, genitals, secondary sex characteristics, hormones, chromosomes, behaviors, psychologies, and on — the more wonky the idea of binary sex was becoming. So, while their theory of sexual plasticity echoes (or anticipates) the liberatory aspects of a queered gender fluidity (connoting performance, experimentation, and non-normativity), in its inception, gender arrives on the scene to regulate the material instability of sex under scrutiny and re-installs the arbitration of binarized sex as the distinct territory of medicine. Plasticity and the figure of the child were key to this project. As Gill-Peterson argues, "[c]hild development as a temporal form restricts plasticity to a profoundly conservative narrative, domesticating it in the service of a newly rigid sex binary."[6]

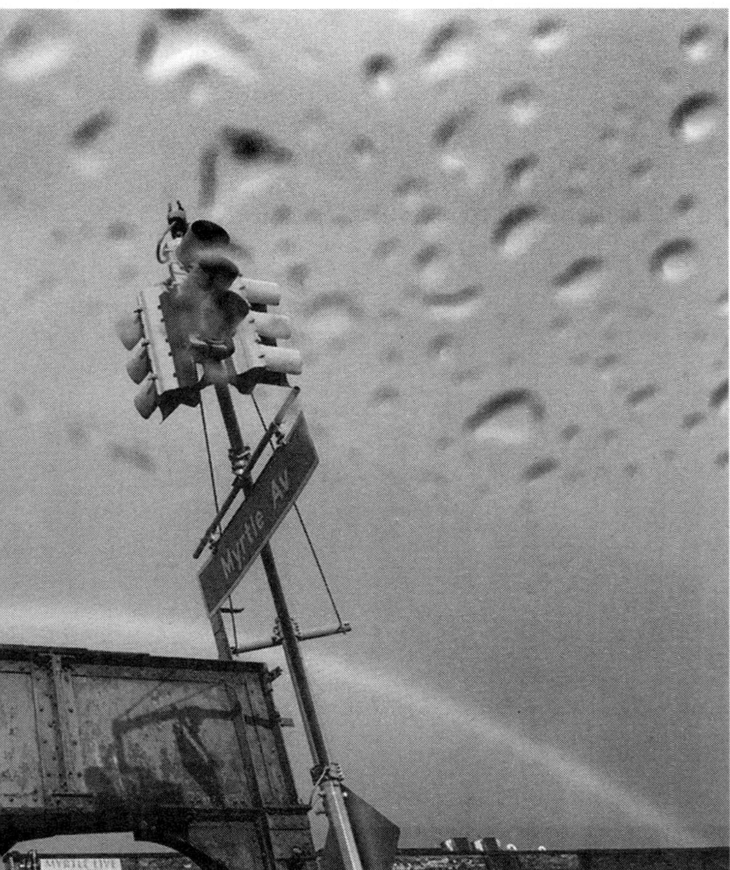

That "rigid sex binary" had me thinking about the 1991 "Gender Disarray" issue of *MOVEMENT RESEARCH PERFORMANCE JOURNAL*, and how in some weird, hard-to-stomach way, it also reveals a kind of loosening of gender that may have since become more constricted. Some of the writing, from today's outlook, evinces a cringe: provocative and probing interview questions, many exoticisms, essentialisms, transvestites and hermaphrodites in drag. The writers search for terminology not yet arbitrated. I am enthralled by the drastic difference from what I perceive as the more consolidated language for talking about gender, sex, and sexuality today. Anxiety around disarray breeds the need for bureaucratic stabilization: infographics and diagrams; trainings and workshops. "Well first of all, gender and sex are separate," rings a chorus of thousands of explainers, to the old and uninitiated, in my memory of the 2000s and 2010s. In this moment, when "Gender Disarray" might appear as a transphobic TV news headline, there is clear motive for the interest in medical and therapeutic validation of trans identity, although this tendency is hardly new. In the introduction to his book *MOBILE SUBJECTS*, Aren Z. Aizura describes his experience of seeking gender-affirming medical interventions in a highly medicalized and gate-kept context, writing, "[s]ome trans people seemed to echo or internalize the gender dysphoria clinic's logic of true transsexuality,"[7] where "true transsexuality" excludes forms of identification that exceed or confound binary gender and the standards set by clinical and medical definitions of transsexuality.

The restoration of the binary in such scenes is not only just about genderqueer and non-binary forms of identification but is also always and already a product of a medical discourse structured by white supremacy. Gill-Peterson's work also shows how Money's theory of plasticity is also fundamentally racist. According to articulated and concealed aspects of the model, whites are both more plastic as infants and more gender-differentiated as adults. In practice, this meant the exclusion of children of color from the clinic,[8] and the broader exclusion of trans people of color from medical contexts writ large.[9]

Teaching *GENDER TROUBLE* this year for the first time to my class of trans students — reading it for the first time in a long time — I think I got Jay Prosser's critique of Butler in an experiential way: Butler's semiotics leaves something out, a felt reality of gender that exceeds theory's interest in it. Jack Halberstam quotes Prosser's intervention that "there are transsexuals who seek very pointedly to be nonperformative, to be constative, quite simply to be," adding that "many transsexuals do not want to represent gender artifice; they actually aspire to the real, the natural indeed the very condition that has been rejected by the queer theory of gender performance."[10] In Gender Trouble the only mention of Johns Hopkins is, tellingly, not a reference to Money's clinic, but to "Structure, Sign, and Play," the lecture given there by Jacques Derrida in 1966 that brought poststructuralism to the American academy. I am, however, still enthralled by Butler's moves, their dialectical inversion of common sense: gender is not the social superstructure to the base of sex, rather sex is as constructed as — or even constructed by — gender. In Butler's critical reversal I also read an echo (or appropriation?) of Gill-Peterson's Money, namely that gender precedes binary sex, as the map precedes the territory. Of course, collapsing the two only makes sense in explicating the antinomy. Not in terms of their aim. Butler's work on gender is a critical account of biopolitical and

HIS WRITING STYLE CHANGES AS SHE DOES. AND I THINK SO DOES THE READER; SHE ALSO CHANGES IN THE READING. LANGUAGE AND GENDER ARE BOUND UP WITH ONE ANOTHER

4 Gill-Peterson, 98.
5 Ibid, 119.
6 Ibid.
7 Aren Z. Aizura, "Provincializing Trans" in *MOBILE SUBJECTS: TRANSNATIONAL IMAGINARIES OF GENDER REASSIGNMENT* (Durham: Duke University Press, 2018), 7.
8 Gill-Peterson, 80, 159-60, 197.
9 "The frequent absence of black trans and trans of color children in the clinic's archive, in particular, is not only a product of medical gatekeeping or the whiteness of transsexuality. It is also a product of a distance practiced by black trans and trans of color people from institutional medicine, which was well understood to be a dangerous and frequently violent apparatus." Gill-Peterson, 31.
10 Jack Halberstam, *IN A QUEER TIME AND PLACE: TRANSGENDER BODIES, SUBCULTURAL LIVES* (New York: New York University Press, 2005), 50.

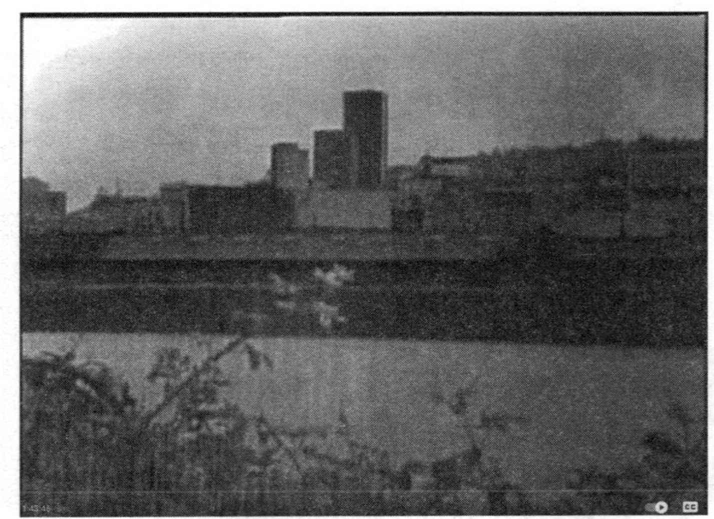

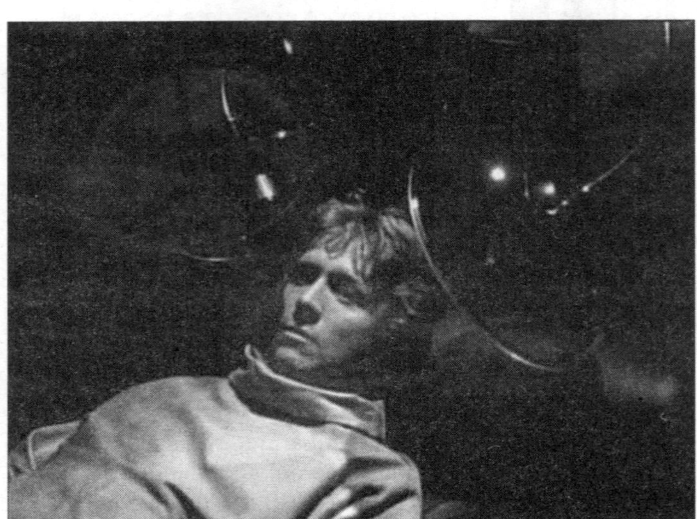

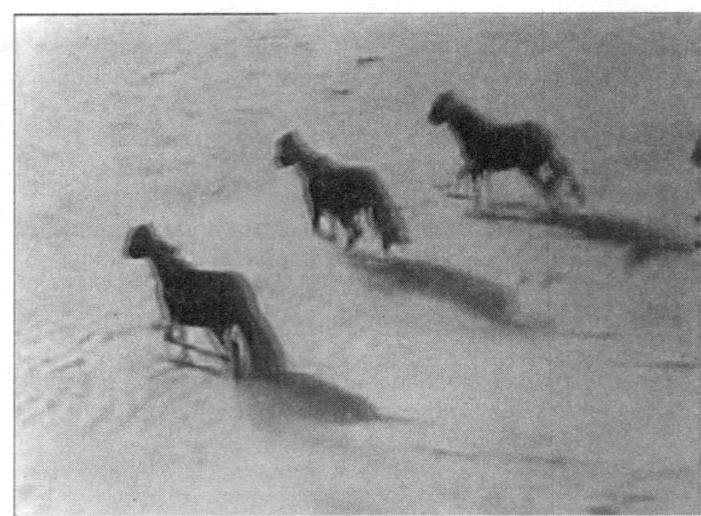

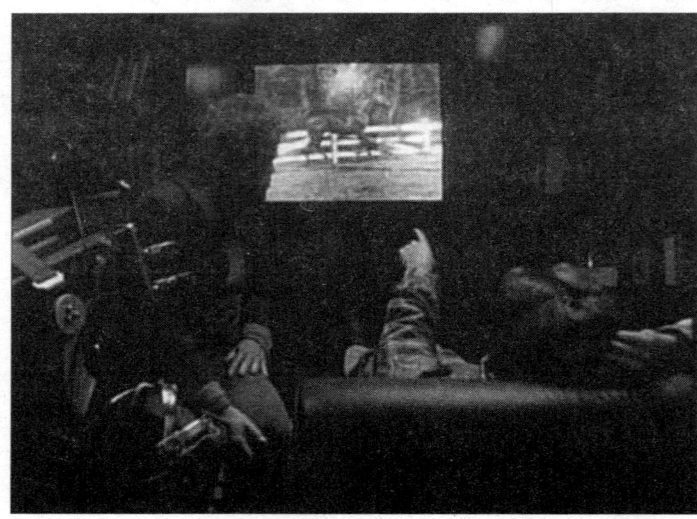

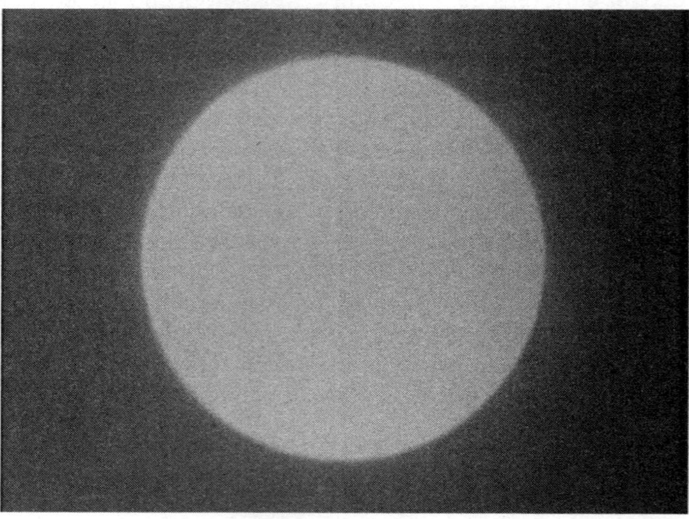

discursive structures, distributed and historical processes of subjectification; where Money's output is clinical practice that sought to capture and instrumentalize the specific normative possibilities of plasticity. As my editor Amalle Dublon wrote in a comment on a draft of this essay, "Butler's argument [...] is that the power to performatively produce a person's gender/sex is distributed widely, not located in any one person or institution. The scope, frequency, and variety of performative acts that produce gender makes gender easy to intervene in, but hard to decisively determine."

The impulse to re-naturalize sex appears in the many permutations and infights that postdate the Issue #3 of the *MOVEMENT RESEARCH PERFORMANCE JOURNAL*, the Sodom (of a previous culture war) on which this issue looks back: medical vs. political transness, truscum vs. theyfab, wrong body vs. gender as performance. I don't mean to simplify these oppositions and contradictions, and especially not to conflate Butler's work with a conservative, medicalized account of transness. Of course, for Butler, gender, sex, and sexuality are not analogous to language, but constructed through language. Where "analogy" implies the comparison of discrete things, Butler insists on a performativity that is caught up with language.

The language analogy relies on an unquestioned idea of the native language, discounting bilingualism, aphasia, indeed the arbitrariness of language understood through multilingual experience, through learning a new language, through translation. What makes a language native? The unquestioned performance of mastery in a language? Or the way one feels about the shape of language, not needing to know the rules and conventions, but feeling them? And then what becomes of this analogy if the primacy of a native language is really an affective structure, both a product of, and displaced by, historical and political exigencies or dalliance? If surgical and endocrinological intervention is occasioned by the imperative that various aspects of sex must be (or can be) made to match up with — or prior to — this acquisition of a gender role, what happens to the analogy in reverse? If gender's analog is language, what is the analog of sex?

So perhaps one thing the old language analogy does is displace the material interventions on people's bodies, conveniently excluding them from the frame for the purpose of the comparison. The scientific model of plasticity that the analogy supports also makes a set of universal and transhistorical assertions. Money's "gender roles" are sophisticated devices. As a sexological model that accounts for the arbitrariness of this language or that gender as contingent and impermanent aspects of culture, the concept of plasticity and the gender/sex binary are posited as transhistorical facts, as the new science. Imagine the Money's Hopkins lab as a space station in North America, producing strange new products to populate the recently emptied frontier and remake the territory according to a consolidated, gendered map cooked up in Baltimore.

Science fiction is defined by a kind of conceptual simple machine: something about the setting, or a technology, or some kind of other conceit or literary device makes the reality of the fictional world different from our own. Ursula Le Guin wrote that it is not predictive, but descriptive, that "you can read it, and a lot of other science fiction, as a thought-experiment. [...] let's say this or that is such and so, and see what happens [...] thought and intuition can move freely within bounds set only by the terms of the experiment, which may be very large indeed."[11] In *BABEL-17*, the thought-experiment is often understood to be the Whorf hypothesis, an application of a kind of linguistic relativism. First, Rydra determines the alien transmissions are not a simple code to be deciphered, but an entire language. As she begins internalizing and assimilating it, we learn how it feels: "Babel-17; she had felt it before with other languages, the opening, the widening, the mind forced to sudden growth. But this, this was like the sudden focusing of a lens blurry for years."[12]

I've felt something like that, the past reorganized in an instant, and then again over time: the crossover into thinking in another language, and not just realizing I was trans. Metaphors and analogies are getting mixed now. I'm thinking of when I was on a U.S. State Department-funded language education program in Himeiji, speaking very little English. I suddenly had access to an understanding, difficult to put into words; a sensitivity to cultural differences in the smallest aspects of sociality, and the untranslatability of that specificity.

11 Ursula K. Le Guin, Author's Introduction to *THE LEFT HAND OF DARKNESS* (1969; Author's Note 1976; New York: Ace Books, 2019), 15.
12 Delany, *BABEL-17*, 113.

The thought experiment driving *BABEL-17*, however, is not so much the linguistic relativism thesis — the idea that all aspects of perception, understanding, and meaning differ, potentially vastly, depending on one's native language. Rather, it might be the fact of change. If Money's analogy of gender to language was used to articulate a scarcity of time, an expiration date beyond which the child's gender, like their native language, is sedimented, *BABEL-17* offers a different version of plasticity. Where the former reduces transition and transformation to a logic of re-assignment of intersex patients, (its treatments and interventions not available to trans people,) in the latter we see a model of re-orientation defined through the transmissibility, reception, ingestion, expression, and uncertainty of that which is non-native. Like hormones and surgeries, in Delany's novel Babel-17 was developed in a lab. The analogicity of mutation, of mutilation, cannot account for the digitality of this language virus: the body is left behind. It's a model of language originating, but not ending, in the disembodied transmission. What seemed to be some magical thing, some unknown element, turns out to be a sophisticated military technology. Language is imagined as a biological weapon, a kind of virus that enhances the people who learn it, contorting them into super soldiers. It's taken me a while to arrive, but I want to make an argument for contagion, and for mutilation. I remember the slow battleground of the culture wars centered on Clinton-era theories of influence and contagion. Video games make you violent. Weed is a gateway drug. Broken Windows. Rap music. Elves and witches. Exposure and interest beget deviant behavior. Cooked books from the culture wars and the war on drugs.

Rather than say that transition is a process of uncovering something deeper that was always there, let's say we understand transition as the capacity for change as a question of form, as a gamble or risk, as something unknown rather than known, not an epistemic question at all — am I really trans? In Delany, this happens at the level of form. It's not merely a surrealist exercise: the book performs by modulating its style, changing its voice. Le Guin's "let's say" is the "let's say" of a speech act, not merely a turn of phrase. It reminds me of what Deleuze and Guattari said about Kafka, that his works are a literary machine,

> that breaks the symbolic structure, no less than it breaks hermeneutic interpretation, the ordinary association of ideas, and the imaginary archetype [...]). We believe only in a Kafka that is neither imaginary nor symbolic. We believe only in one or more Kafka machines that are neither structure nor phantasm. We believe only in a Kafka experimentation that is without interpretation or significance and rests only on tests of experience.[13]

The reading is entering into the machine, which outputs a break in the realm of experience. It isn't symbolic or imaginary. It's not just Rydra changing, it's you, thrust into an unexpected, previously foreclosed desiring-body. Subjected to mechanical alteration, mutilated by a contagious new form. Be careful what you read.

It's kind of awkward, reading *BABEL-17* alongside *HISTORIES OF THE TRANSGENDER CHILD*. It's not necessarily an obvious pairing. I listen to an audiobook of the Delany in the car on commutes on the Taconic to my teaching job. I listen to it again when I'm driving back down to the city on 22, lost in the story, not remembering the last twenty minutes of driving, the sun setting. And then a deer. I forgot my heart until it hits as the high beams illuminate two dots at the corner of my right eye; and in the same instant, at the edge of the strange shape flooded with halogen light, its body frailed by winter, gray in the night. The neck extends down, holding its skull and teeth, covered in flesh and quills of hair, touching the grass delicately. Each green blade has its own shadow. I see the crumpled side panel of my car. A handful of hairs plucked by converging metal sheets, years ago, where the deer hit headlong, eyes closed, sending the Chevette into full rotation across three lanes of traffic just outside Cleveland, Ohio. Another thought: I remember my surrender. I remember the first snow last year, covering the back road. The disembodied crash. My car without traction, no way to turn or slow, mounting the snowy berm, small twigs sticking up, almost making it to some white fence before turning over. I'm okay. I'm going seventy miles an hour.

ZOEY LUBITZ

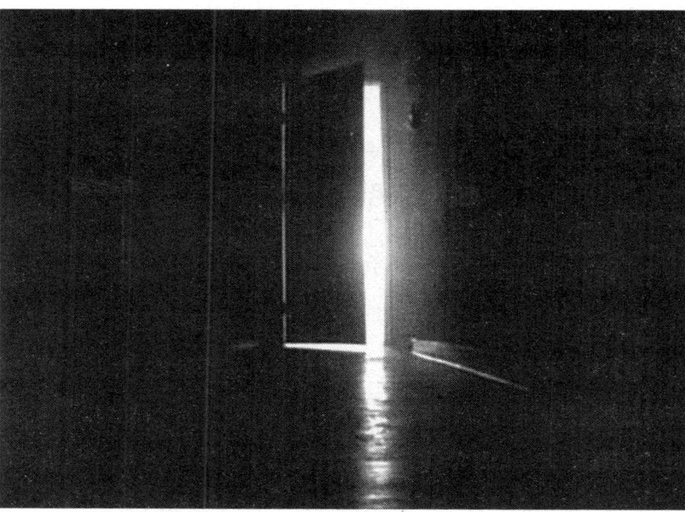

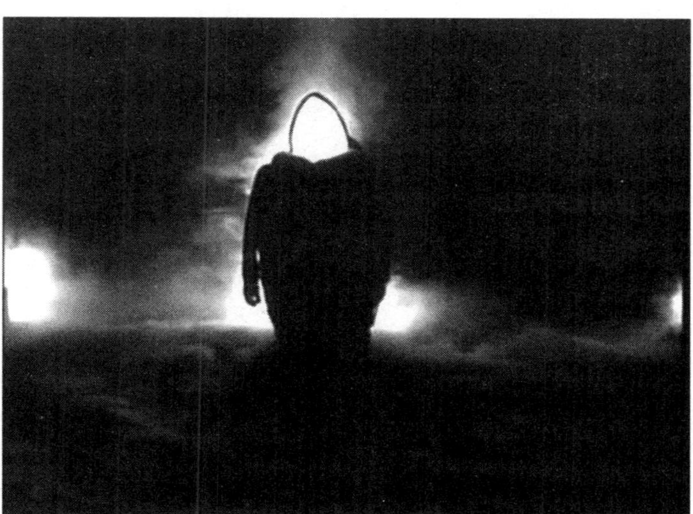

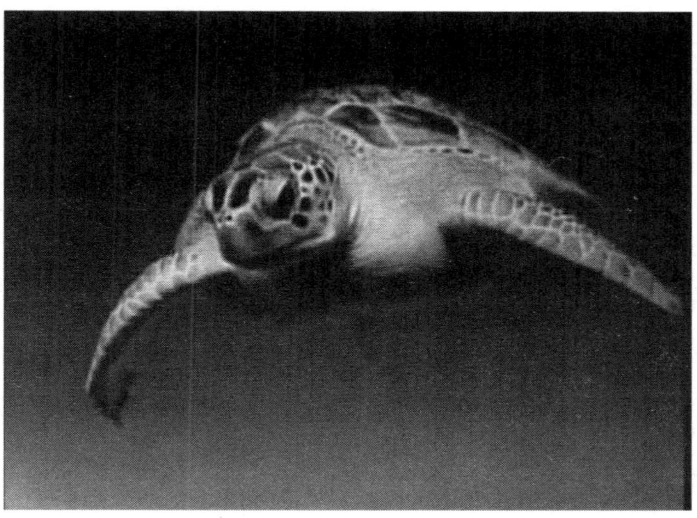

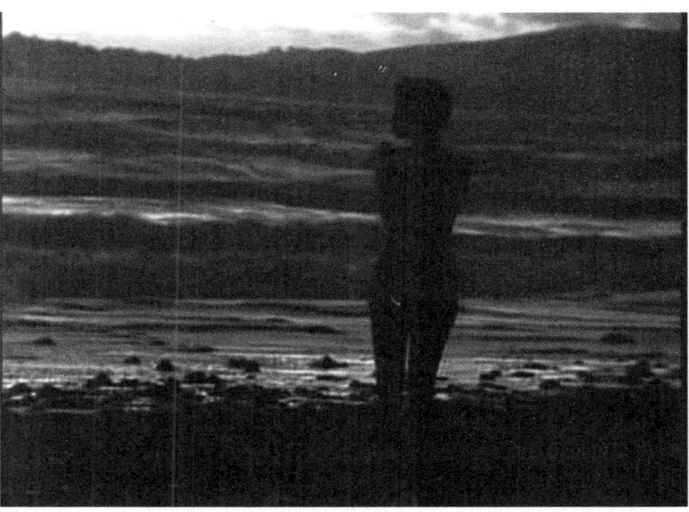

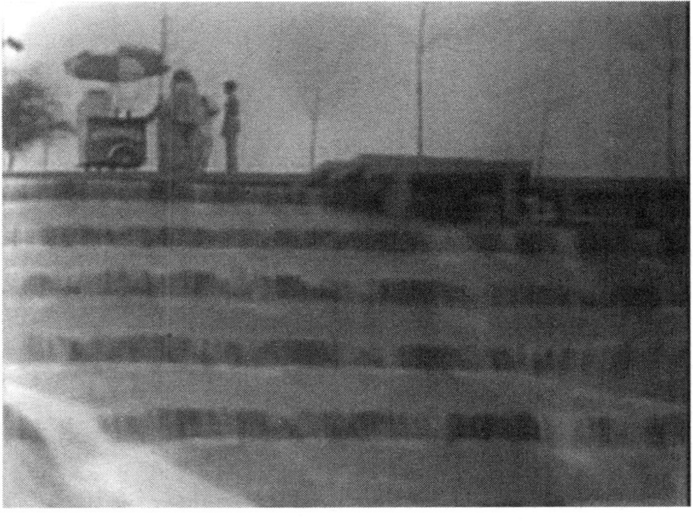

David Loxton and Fred Barzyk, *LATHE OF HEAVEN* (film stills), WNET, 1980.

13 Gilles Deleuze and Félix Guattari, *KAFKA: TOWARD A MINOR LITERATURE*, trans. Dana Polan (1975; Minneapolis: University of Minnesota Press, 1986), 7.

Movement Research
Performance Journal

Author
KAI SUNDERMANN

Contributing Editor
KEIOUI KEIJAUN THOMAS

Siren's Womb

"Is it really so sad and dangerous to be fed up with seeing with your eyes, breathing with your lungs, swallowing with your mouth, talking with your tongue, thinking with your brain, having an anus and larynx, head and legs? Why not walk on your head, sing with your sinuses, see through your skin, breathe with your belly[?]"

—Gilles Deleuze and Felix Guattari, "How Do You Make Yourself a Body Without Organs"

"Six divisions ago, on a white-sun water world, we lived in great shallow oceans [...] we were many-bodied and spoke with body lights and color patterns among ourself and among ourselves."

—Octavia Butler, Dawn (Xenogenesis Triology Vol. 1)

the room's been flirting with the three of them casting
nitrous dreamspace halfway across
the ship dreamworking
a most distant and familiar nonlocal warmth
saffron hazy between slumber and wake
a pine, ache, throb without object

her architecture is blurring ground softening
into a six-inch bed of muddy topsoil sealed with epidermis her roof a lopsided dome
sporting two large openings two gas-ferrying vents
two vocal tracts

two candescent apertures

any past trace of the perpendicular shed away pillars melted into unruly stalagmites
more meadow-like than cave the feeling of a wild soft outdoors
nestled deep in folds of flesh

the trio enter the neighbouring canal lost
with more of an inclination to drift than navigate the wet heat
indicating an exothermic locale

no one is sober enough to remember exactly where the afters is

motions of light pulsing through the flesh of her walls quicken
in anticipation of her treasured crowd, illuminative trails
guiding them toward her opening they enter crawling
sweat breaking within several out-breaths air thick like yolk
saturated

not by humidity, scent, color, or other biochemical envoy but by the unbearable:
to become different together an overspilt yearning not a lack to satiate
but the gestation of a common wealth of needs unaccountable in
pregnant becoming more than one less than two
more and less than one more and less than three

the floor sweats profusely

beads of moisture pool on its glossy skin through indiscernible curvature
a basin forms

their mass perspirations slipping toward center growing in volume and momentum
like quicksilver sperm nosediving
into boundlessness

a low rumble

the same resonant frequency as the tissues
starts to grow a total vibration of everything
through the pulse of interlocking hands hearts felt
beating in iambic syncopation with a near-audible intensity out of sync
but in time

the rumble snowballs into a rolling bassline rising sonic spiral
setting in unstoppable motion frictionless caress shimmering notes
in an arpeggiated dance of tangled limbs craned necks
greeted by twin pillars of golden light face basking in
cracks of crepuscular dawn thin columns
strobing in halftime with cardiac kick

she spits
iridescent silk relational history history of differentiation translated
into a single thread's titanic length wrapping
suturing binding implanting
this opaline cocoon in her topsoil lining

(sub)merged weightless
dance of darkness beyond articulation
unprecedented communicative ease writhing, rocking, spasming
in this soft knit where do i end and you begin
no cinematography more blissful than lover's eyes the eye a patch of skin that fell in love with light
sobbing drips of ecstasy
lapping licking lambent

KAI SUNDERMANN

Gender Performance Reconsidered

Issue 60
Spring/Summer 2024

Author
TOM KALIN

Contributing Editor
MRPJ

Soon after I met Richard Elovich in the late 1980s, we became friends and collaborators within the AIDS activist groups ACT UP and Gran Fury. In 1991, I designed a card for Richard's Bessie Award winning one-man show, *SOMEONE ELSE FROM QUEENS IS QUEER*, and he memorably embodied Doctor Hulbert (a psychiatric trial witness that examined murderers Leopold and Loeb) in my first feature, *SWOON* (1992), which was filmed during this same time. In the summer of 1991, Richard invited me to guest edit and design the *MOVEMENT RESEARCH PERFORMANCE JOURNAL,* Issue #3. He had been the Executive Director of Movement Research and stepped down to serve as Chair of the Board. Cathy Edwards and Guy Yarden became MR's Co-Directors. Guy was also a wizard in the (then) rare, dark arts of desktop publishing and was a key player in the issue's production.

I'm amazed, now, by those crowded months of summer and autumn 1991, at how many things seemed to happen at once. After three decades in NYC, I now live in a tiny Catskills hamlet, and I wonder at the thousands of acres of meadow cleared by hand, or the miles of stone walls laid in the 18th and 19th centuries. People paradoxically seemed to have more time in an era of simpler technologies. The same now appears to be true, looking back at 1991. Without cell phones, social media, or email, we lived analog, not digital, lives. We used phone trees, or fax and copy machines to get the word out; we found information on fliers posted in the street, or by word of mouth. Lo-fi, old school turned out to be remarkably effective.

ACT UP protests were becoming ever more corporeal, with a massive die-in staged at Bush's Kennebunkport summer home that Labor Day weekend. (A year later, on October 11, 1992, ACT UP staged a political funeral in Washington D.C., culminating in activists dumping the ashes of loved ones, dead from AIDS, on the White House lawn.) And exactly a year before *that*, on October 11, 1991, Anita Hill began her testimony against Clarence Thomas before the Senate Judiciary Committee, chaired by Senator Joseph Biden. The world had only recently been swallowed by the 24-hour news cycle. I finished *SWOON* in my sixth-floor Attorney Street walk-up with the TV constantly on, leaning against the outrage I felt while I edited.

If memory serves, we moved very quickly on Issue #3, gathering texts and images over a month or two, and putting the issue together in an intense stretch of about a week. Richard, Cathy, and Guys' collaborations made it possible for me to connect with people I admired but didn't know, including Jill Johnston, John Kelly, Kate Bornstein, Peggy Shaw, and Lois Weaver. I decided to title the issue "Gender Performance," inspired by the recent writing of Judith Butler, who asserted

> If gender is drag, and if it is an imitation that regularly produces the ideal it attempts to approximate, then gender is a performance that *PRODUCES* the illusion of an inner sex or essence or psychic gender core; it *PRODUCES* on the skin, through the gesture, the move, the gait (that array of corporeal theatrics understood as gender presentation) the illusion of an inner depth.[1]

Butler's visionary writing mirrored what surrounded me already in my daily life or at night in the Pyramid Club, BoyBar, the Clit Club, or Meat: the inventive theatrics of dazzling friends like Mona Foot, Trash, or Ryan Landry. To me, these friends were *so* dazzling, I put them in a movie: superstars, all. The dance and performance world also seemed remarkably...queer to me, and I naively imagined

1 Judith Butler, "Imitation and Gender Insubortination," ed. Diana Fuss, *INSIDE/OUT: LESBIAN THEORIES, GAY THEORIES* (New York: Routledge, 1991), 28.

Engagements

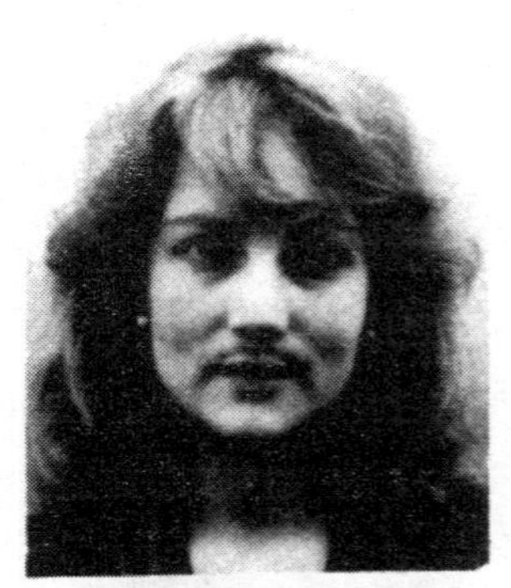

Engaged
Dr. and of Onamia, N.Y., announce the engagement of their son, , and , a daughter of and , of New York.

The future bridegroom, a graduate of Old Dominion University, is the public relations manager for MXP Business Systems, Twin Falls, Md.

His mother is a dentist. His father is dental hygenist with his wife's practice.

A graduate of the Unviersity of Wisconsin, the future bride is a vice president and area manager of Expert Electronics, Groveton, overseeing state and local government accounts.

Her mother is a cardiologist at New York Hospital Cornell Medical Center. Her father is a recreational therapist.

The couple plan an April wedding in Danville, N.Y.

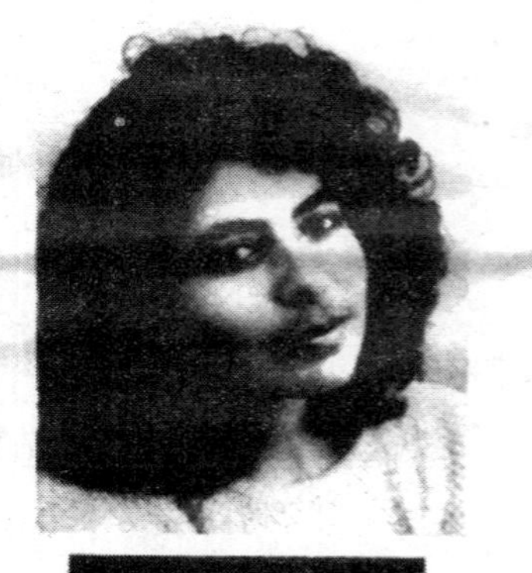

Engaged
will marry in May, the future groom's parents, and both of Preston, have announced.

The bridegroom, who is called is a graduate of Georgetown University. He is an elementary school teacher in teh Windsor public school system.

His mother is vice president of the 3rd National Bank. His father is a nurse.

The bride, who is known as is a Northwestern Unviersity graduate. She is executive director of planning for Merrill Finance Corporation.

Her parents are and of Mount Prospect. Her mother is a traffic engineer for International Research Technology in Winchester. Her father is an executive secretary for Chicago Pride Industries, Foxboro.

Jeanne Dunning, untitled, 1991.
Originally printed in Issue #3, Movement Research Performance Journal (Fall 1991).
Courtesy the artist.

a receptive reaction to what I also understood was a very provocative publication. I think about 15,000 copies of the journal were printed and mailed.

And then a bomb dropped. Twenty days after the Anita Hill hearings began, on October 31, 1991, the notorious bigot, homophobic Senator Jesse Helms, waved a copy of Issue #3 on the Senate floor, declaiming, "I'm gonna hold it up briefly...and it is a blown-up picture of a vagina with some of the crudest language I ever saw...I was in the Navy for four years during World War II and I've heard it all and I've seen most of it, but I've never seen such rottenness as is being supported by the National Endowment for the Arts."[2]

I'm describing this moment as if I witnessed it in person, or saw it live on television, but no. I have, finally, watched dear, despicable, dead Jesse, now in 2024, through the miracle of C-Span. Without a readily accessible archive, citizens back then had a challenging time seeing exactly what their government was doing. Helms was having a hissy fit since the NEA had granted Movement Research $4400 and some of that money had been spent on Issue #3. He complained bitterly about "NEA-funded porn star Annie Sprinkle—remember her?" And then he hauled out his censorious laundry list:

> Pictures of surgically created hermaphrodites, that is to say, people with both male and female organs. It features nude photographs and articles featuring a variety of so-called gender-confused people including transvestites, transsexuals, crossdressers – and a new one on me: transgenderist, whatever that is. And then there's a fictional story written in the first person by Lazarus describing his homosexual liaisons with Jesus Christ both before and after the crucifixion. And there's a full-page devoted to what I briefly held up at the outset of my remarks, that says, "Read My Lips Before They're Sealed." And then there's another ad urging readers to join a Washington, D.C. protest against President Bush's 'murderous inaction on AIDS,' quote unquote.[3]

Helms was enraged on multiple levels by the collective GANG's piece *READ MY LIPS* (1991). Shocked by its cheeky escalation of Gustave Courbet's *THE ORIGIN OF THE WORLD* (1866), Helms lashed out, freshly sulking from criticisms of his Helms Amendment and defensive about the recent Rust v. Sullivan Supreme Court decision.[4] GANG's pleasure-centered, affirmative outlook in the face of the Supreme Court's legislation was too much for Jesse to bear: "Our bodies should be playgrounds, not just battlefields." Helms failed to tack his amendment that restricted NEA funding onto a bill when the Senate voted 73-25 against him.

The second bomb dropped soon after, in a public town hall at Judson, called in the wake of the NEA funding scandal and the pushback from Philip Morris, who was also a Movement Research funder. I remember my pulse racing, sitting next to Richard, facing an angry room. I don't remember much objectively about that day, honestly. I was nervous as hell and felt like an interloper who had accepted a dinner invitation and then puked all over the sofa. Many in the audience challenged Richard and me. I do remember Bill T. Jones's generosity and open reaction. Beyond my nerves, I was also disappointed, and angry, that what I thought was an amazing, even visionary, publication had been treated like inconvenient porn, best left stashed under the bed.

With no traditional editor's letter in Issue #3, some of the individual and collective contributions were more visible, or legible, than others. The project about Lazarus and Jesus that Helms scorned was created by Powers of Desire, a collective formed by artists John DiStefano, Renee Edington, and her husband Mat Francis.[5] When I recently wrote John about this issue, he told me Renee and Mat had died, two of the people who contributed that aren't still with us. John Lindell provided a whisper-thin column of text on the left margin, in counterpoint to a Kate Bornstein interview.[6] John's work frequently reconfigured porn texts in the découpé or cut-up style pioneered by William

Weddings

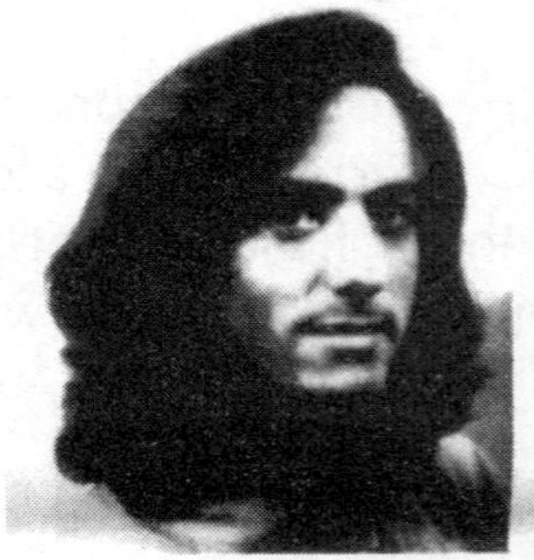

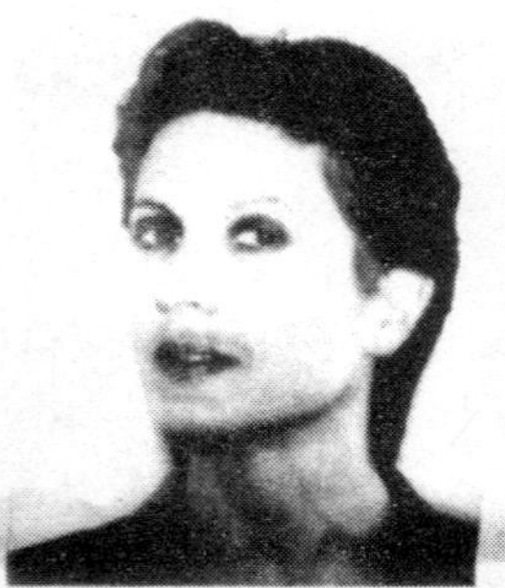

Married
and were married recently in the Chapel of the Holy Souls.

officiated at the Jan. 14 ceremony.

The groom is the son of and the late

His wife is a partner of Cumberland Chapels, Norridge. Her parents are of Hinsdale. Her mother is a retired funeral director.

Guests at a wedding breakfast in the Fairmont Hotel following the ceremony included State's Attorney the groom's sister.

Following a honeymoon trip to Hawaii, the couple are at home in Minneapolis.

Burroughs with surreal and sexy results. Five members of Gran Fury contributed to Issue #3. Artist Jeanne Dunning, who I knew from Chicago, contributed a series derived from her untitled project, here presented as "Engagements" and masquerading as a series of matrimonial announcements.[7] Dunning's potential brides all sport ghostly mustaches, applied by the artist herself, and an uncanny touch that echoes Duchamp, while remaining distinctly Dunning's own.

It's exciting to revisit this vital time capsule. Jill Johnston describes how she became a dancer because she fell in love with her college teacher who later introduced her to choreographer José Limón.[8] Johnston describes how she didn't fit in with Limón's company, "stranded between the sexes," and "sure I wanted to be one of his boys." My own essay considering criminal Ed Gein connects to a piece by Peggy Shaw and Lois Weaver considering their work-in-progress *LESBIANS WHO KILL* (1992).[9] Intrigued by "female serial killer" Aileen Wuornos, Deb Margolin (the third member of Split Britches along with Peggy and Lois) wrote the script. A lesbian couple in the South, May and June are suspected of Wuornos's crimes. June explains, "[w]e look to where our own images and histories intersect with the issue and find our own impulses in that intersection. In other words, looking for our own desire and impulse to kill that comes from our own image of abuse in our daily lives." Chris Martin's interviews and Annie Sprinkle's photographs "shake up these categories, opening up new spaces for identity" and articulate a vision of a world we would later call nonbinary.[10]

In October 2010, there was a panel that considered *MRPJ* @ 20, held at the Judson Memorial gymnasium. This time, instead of outrage, there was celebration. Again at the 30th Anniversary of Movement Research, celebration and reflection reigned. And here we are, generation to generation, still considering the complexities and implications of Issue #3. What an honor it is to be part of this conversation.

One of my favorite contributions in Issue #3 comes from writer Donald Woods, who captures the encroaching frailty of age, seen and experienced across gender. At very nearly 62 years old, these observations carry new weight:

> I am aging fast in the sixth-floor window. Travelling with the woman instead of windswept on the motorbike with my arms circling his waist. I am with her on the stairs stopping for air and hearing sounds in the night that I used to doze through and sleepwalking to the toilet to pee. ...I walk slowly like a dignified old man and see my self as this woman struck by young vital endless traffic, snap flash movements and jolting taxicabs.[11]

TOM KALIN

2 "Funding for National Endowment for the Arts," October 31, 1991. https://www.c-span.org/video/?22442-1/funding-national-endowment-arts.
3 Ibid.
4 Rust v. Sullivan, 500 U.S. 173, was a case in the United States Supreme Court that upheld Department of Health and Human Services regulations prohibiting employees in federally funded family-planning facilities from counseling a patient on abortion.
5 Powers of Desire, "The Dawns We Shanghied In each Other's Arms, Exhausted," *MOVEMENT RESEARCH PERFORMANCE JOURNAL*, Issue #3 (Fall 1991), 13.
6 John Lindell, untitled, 16.
7 Jeanne Dunning, untitled, 18–19.
8 Jill Johnston, "How Dance Artists and Critics Define Dance As Political," 2–3.
9 Peggy Shaw and Lois Weaver, "May Interviews June," 4–5. Tom Kalin, "Gender Performance," 5.
10 Chris Martin, "World's Greatest Cocksucker," 6–7. Photographs by Annie Sprinkle, 6–7, 14–15.
11 Donald Woods, untitled, 15.

Thinking Back, 2020

Issue 60
Spring/Summer 2024

Author
ISIS AWAD

Contributing Editor
KEIOUI KEIJAUN THOMAS

I keep saying I want intimacy
I want love
but I don't know if I am capable of either to be honest
I just have an intense desire
to want to be wanted
Like I really miss that
I still have to remind myself
to relax and breathe a few times a day
I still have to remind myself
to stop clenching my jaws
to shake myself into the present
catch my posture slumping
my shoulder muscles tensing
Catch me forgetting to suck my tummy in
Dissociate compulsively into a twirl of hair
My hair is the longest it's ever been
Most days I cannot stand looking at it
I start to regret the day I went and fetched my mirror from my storage
unit and hung it up in my friend's guest room that I've been living out of
too long
I hate my body
I hate my body
I hate my body
But it's also mine

I try to think back to when
I wanted my body so much
When I turned myself on
When I would take all my clothes off
Lay naked on my back on the warm, yellowed, porcelain of my tub
In the bathroom my siblings and I shared in Kuwait
At the apartment I lived in until the age of 17
When I would bend my knees close to my chest
Shortening the distance between my hole and my center
Position myself so that when my toes slowly turned the bathtub faucet open
Eyes closed, it would drip thick drops right on the tip of my puckered hole

How I would close my eyes
Curl my knees even closer to my chest using the edge of the tub as leverage
To lift my waist up and my head forward to meet my center
As far as I could
Feel my tailbone groan from the tub's hard surface
Then forget all about that and only feel my bits get hard as I finally reach its tip
with my tongue
My poor, strained tongue sticking so far out it's cramping Hear my breath scour
my compressed lungs for air
Feel the closeness to myself
Lick the underside of my bits and it starts to taste deliciously salty preemptively
me
Heavy, controlled drops on my hole

I moan so quietly with each tap
And whine my hips
Make the water lick my bootyhole all around
Every millimeter of my hole
And around my hole
And just at the very edge of my hole
Right on my hole
Fully connected to my hole
Centered with my hole
Activating every nerve ending, and pleasure beginning
My toe slowly pushing down on the faucet tap turn that drip into drizzle
Let it rain
Tapping my hole making a lake
Slithering down the Valley of Inner Thigh
Collecting in the Reservoir of Sternum
I push my face and my hips even closer together
Curled up into my own chest

Pulling my dick closer to my mouth with my hand
Worrying I am causing permanent damage to my spine
As my lips finally reach close enough to circle around
And I lick the underside of its head and taste my cum about to come out from the base

Wet with water and drool
The smell of my own raw spit
Then
I cum, I cum,
I taste the cum as it suddenly fills my mouth
It's warmth shocks me even though I knew it was coming
I can't even breathe and I want to gasp for air
But my lips holding on to the tip of my dick won't let me
Struggling whether to let it out and watch the cum spurt out of my dick so close to my face
Or keep swallowing like it's not my own
I decide that I want to
I want to see a dick that just happens to be mine cumming right on my face
All over my fucking lips
Dripping down my chin and I try so hard not to moan
And I hope no one at home can hear me moan
And I swallow my sweetest cum straight from the slit
Farm to table
And when the waves of orgasm are done sweeping through my curled body
I slowly unfurl my waist back down like the new growth of a fern on a timeless, humid forest floor
And my lower back cracks
A single loud crack
Every single time

Closing, 2021–2023

My practice
My methodology
My politics
My reactions
My opinions
My reactions
Stem from a deep desire to unlearn and transcend
The oppression that has seeped its way into my fibers
As a result of circumstances and lived realities
That were and continue to be Beyond my control
For now

My journey is about
Understanding the circumstances that hold me back in this white supremacist, hetero-patriarchal society
As my strengths
Technicalities
There is power in owning all the things they think about you but won't say to your face
If they mad, then chances are you're doing it right
But lead with love
There is unique strength, and exhaustion
In holding outsiderness and uncomfortable in-between-ness

My trans-femininity
My HIV's undetectability My he/she-ness
My hair texture's 3C-ness My brownness
An Egyptian
Who is African
No, North African Just Arab
Or Caucasian
According to the US Census
Whose mother always yelled at to get out of the sun
Before their skin got too dark
Until she couldn't yell no more

Whose father shouted at to go to the barber

Every three weeks like clockwork
Before the hair got too nappy

Everyday
I work to know, accept, and cherish myself and all my realities
Specifically because of the qualities I am discriminated against for
Which I hold deep inside
And on the surface of my skin
Like beauty spots
On the face of exalted poet, Assotto Saint
Who I learned about from Pamela Sneed
Who taught me how to weave my words and thoughts
And who's book, *FUNERAL DIVA*
Showed me that I had been writing poetry my whole life
But never knew it, because the genre never felt accessible to me
Who taught me that poetry is not only for the aristocracy
That it is how we and our ancestors tell our stories
That need to be heard
It is how Nawal El Saadawi
Pioneering Egyptian feminist, teacher, and writer
Scribbled her memoirs on a roll of toilet paper with a smuggled eyeliner pencil
While locked up in a women's prison in Egypt that could not silence her

In *FUNERAL DIVA*, Pamela Sneed describes Assotto Saint Striding willfully up the church aisle
Heels held high
Proclaiming to the church what no one there would acknowledge
That his friend, Donald Wood, had died a proud gay man
Not of unknown causes, but of AIDS That image is forever branded on my soul
Reinforcing my gait
Affirming my cunt

I unlearn by questioning
By listening
By reminding myself
That there are no facts, but that everything is real
That nothing is inherent
Especially not trauma

Lived experiences can be shared, but not translated
Nonlinearity, fragmented memories, semi-3ctional story-telling
Dreams and nightmares
Are all legitimate sources of history-keeping

Thank you, melanin
Thank you, language
Thank you, perspective
Thank you, cute shoes (but also fuck you)
Thank you, forgiveness
Thank you, HIV
Thank you, ability to apologize and forgive
But never forget
Thank you, laughter
Thank you, estrogen
Thank you, testosterone
Thank you, lovers
And thank you, haters
Thank you, Assotto Saint
Thank you, Pamela Sneed
Thank you, Saeed Jones
Whose memoir as a black gay man in America,
Taught me that my story is worth scribbling down
HOW WE FIGHT FOR OUR LIVES
Thank you, Audre Lorde
For reminding me that "I am not free
while any woman is unfree
even when her shackles
are very different from my own"
Healing is falling back in love with everything you were made to hate about yourself

ISIS AWAD

Bios

Aaina Amin is a writer and organizer based in NYC. She is currently studying to be a psychotherapist.

Isis Awad is a curator, writer, and poet from Cairo, Egypt. She is Founding Director of the curatorial practice Executive Care*, and at the time of writing this bio, Conference Manager at Point Source Youth.

Josie Bettman is a choreographer and performing artist who practices dance-making as a mode of both self-generation and interpersonal relation. Since 2019, she has developed a series of solo performances in an 8×10ft room that visualize transformation through extremes of scale, repetition, and effort, performing these solos at venues such as Bronx Academy of Art and Dance; Movement Research at the Judson Church; Junior High, Los Angeles; and Galerie Les Filles Du Calvaire, Paris. She also works jointly with Lavinia E. Bruce as SECT, inc., and has collaborated as a performer in works by Anna-Thérèse Witenberg, Phoebe Berglund, Milka Djordevich, and Amelia Heintzelman/Leah Fournier.

kaijo caggins (they/he) is a Black trans neurodivergent performance artist and educator. kaijo received their BFA in Dance from University of the Arts, under the direction of Donna Faye Burchfield. kaijo created multiple works that were presented virtually in "The Big Share: Wild Constellations", UArts School of Dance, under the facilitation of Meredith Glisson, Fana Fraser and Katie Swords Thurman. he recently performed in a work curated by Niall Jones and Sara Procopio at Camping 2022 in Pantin, France. kaijo observes experimental paths of possibility and radical defiance through pleasure in their performance practices. he works alongside objects, textures, sculpture, sound and atmosphere; with an emphasis on land histories, genealogy, and displacement.

Nhung Dinh is an independent artist, curator and filmmaker working with queer communities in several countries. Most of her projects are collective works that are rooted in her approach to participatory and relational aesthetics in which her roles as facilitator, artist, curator, and organizer are overlapping. She is the founder of Bàn L4n-Vagina Talks — a public art and education project in Hanoi, Vietnam, that consists of performances, workshops, and exhibitions.

Dahlia Damoiselle is a queer, transgender writer of Vietnamese heritage. A child of war refugees, her work centers on legacies of violence in times of conflict. She has published in *BLUNDERBUSS MAGAZINE, MCSWEENY'S, SLICE MAGAZINE, FOREIGN POLICY, TIME MAGAZINE, THE DAILY BEAST*, and *COLUMBIA JOURNAL*, among others. She lives with her two cats in Brooklyn, NY, and she serves as an adjunct English lecturer at CUNY Brooklyn College.

Amalle Dublon's writing about dependency, sexuality, art, and music has appeared in *GLQ, ARTPAPERS,* and *TDR: THE DRAMA REVIEW*, among other publications. They help to organize I Wanna Be With You Everywhere, a serial gathering of disabled artists and writers. Their artwork, made with friends and loved ones, has been exhibited at Artists Space (New York), Museum MMK für Moderne Kunst (Frankfurt), ARGOS Arts (Brussels), and Dazibao (Montreal). Amalle received a PhD in Literature from Duke University, and teaches at the New School.

Kay Gabriel is a writer and organizer. She's the author of *A QUEEN IN BUCKS COUNTY* (2022) and *KISSING OTHER PEOPLE OR THE HOUSE OF FAME* (2023), and the co-editor of *WE WANT IT ALL: AN ANTHOLOGY OF RADICAL TRANS POETICS* (2020), all from Nightboat. She's the Editorial Director at The Poetry Project, where she edits the *POETRY PROJECT NEWSLETTER.*

GANG

Wellington Love is a filmmaker and producer as well as founder and director of *W/ LOVE PRODUCTIONS*. From 1993–1999, he was the Executive Director of NewFest, and a founding member of the video collective House of Color.

Zoe Leonard lives and works in New York and operates across photography, sculpture, and installation. During the 1980s and 1990s she was an activist with ACT UP (AIDS Coalition To Unleash Power) and the queer activist art collectives GANG and fierce pussy.

Loring McAlpin is currently working on an oral history project, an offshoot of work in documentary film for the past decade. He's heartened to see the current interest of a younger generation in the collective work springing from ACT UP and Queer Nation.

Adam Rolston has been engaged in the practice of architecture since 1985, studied both in Syracuse and in Italy under the influence of the northern Italian Rationalists, and is a Founding Partner of INC Architecture and Design. An artist closely associated with ACT Up and in 1990 he co-published (with Douglas Crimp) *AIDS DEMO GRAPHICS* exploring the role of graphic design during the AIDS Crisis.

Suzanne Wright is an artist whose work has been shown internationally and across the US. She is a founding member of fierce pussy, and during her undergraduate became an active member of ACT UP and D.I.V.A TV (Damned Interfering Video Activists). She is currently a professor in the school of art and art history at the University of Iowa.

Daniel Wolfe is executive director of the UCSF-UC Berkeley Joint Program in Computational Precision Health, building a new discipline at the intersection of artificial intelligence and machine learning, clinical and public health practice, and equity.

Amelia Groom is an art writer whose work has often been concerned with time; its undercurrents, its blockages and trickling detours, and the possibilities for its re-routing. Her book *BEVERLY BUCHANAN: MARSH RUINS* was published by Afterall, and she has recently written essays on Scheherazade and "oblique parrhesia"; Mariah Carey's refusal to acknowledge time; and the importance of cats in the art and antifascist activism of Claude Cahun and Marcel Moore.

Hongzheng Han (they/them) is a faculty member and Academic Content Manager at Sotheby's Institute of Art. They are also an associate curator at the Modern Art Museum Shanghai. Focusing on queer and racial identities, Han has been invited as a guest speaker at the Asia Society and Museum, the Central Academy of Fine Arts, the University of Edinburgh, the University of Pittsburgh, the University of Michigan, New York University, the Brooklyn Rail, Christie's Education, the Asian Creative Foundation, among others. Han's recent curatorial works include Within Global Isolation: Asian Artists in America; Runaway World 2020: Ten Chinese Artists Group Show, Beyond Borders: Art in the Post COVID Era, Standing Out, the Outstandings, Deformation and Reformation: A Modern Taste of Asian Identities, Mirror Image: A Transformation of Chinese Identity, among others. Han's curatorial works have been reviewed by *ARTFORUM, ARTSY, VOICE OF PHOTOGRAPHY*, and the *NEW YORKER MAGAZINE*, among others.

S*an D. Henry-Smith is a collaborative practitioner working primarily in poetry and photography, and by extension, sound/performance and publishing. Recent solo exhibitions include "tremor low" at ROZENSTRAAT in Amsterdam (2023) and "in awe of geometry & mornings" at White Columns in New York (2021). Henry-Smith has read and performed previously at The Poetry Project, Basilica Soundscape, 47 Canal, Solomon R. Guggenheim Museum, The Studio Museum in Harlem, Stedelijk Museum, Metro54, and elsewhere. Their book *WILD PEACH* (2020), was published by Futurepoem, and shortlisted for the PEN Open Book Award, and they are the author of two chapbooks: *BODY TEXT* (2016) and *FLOTSAM SUITE: A STRANGE & PRECARIOUS LIFE, OR HOW WE CHRONICLED THE LITTLE DISASTERS & I WON'T LEAVE THE DANCE FLOOR TIL IT'S OUT OF MY SYSTEM* (2019), the co-author (alongside Imani Elizabeth Jackson) of *CONSIDER THE TONGUE* (2019), and the director of *LUNAR NEW YEAR* (2021). Henry-Smith regularly collaborates in sound, poetry, performance, and education with Dweller Electronics, Imani Elizabeth Jackson as mouthfeel, Ryan C. Clarke, Danny Sadiel Peña, Gabrielle Octavia Rucker, and Derica Shields, among others.

Tom Kalin's work focuses on the portrayal of gay sexuality both in the age of AIDS and historically, as in his acclaimed New Queer Cinema feature *SWOON* (1992). Informed by his work with two AIDS activist collectives, ACT UP and Gran Fury, Kalin's video work is characterized by beautifully murky appropriated images and vibrant original portraits and performances. Kalin co-produced the feature films *GO FISH* (Rose Troché, 1994) and *I SHOT ANDY WARHOL* (Mary Harron, 1996) and is on the film faculty at Columbia University.

LEGACY (Garrett Allen, Arewà Basit, Kyle Carrero Lopez) Founded in 2020, LEGACY: A Black Queer Production Collective promotes collaborative, cross-disciplinary craft while pushing forward a mission of equitable compensation for Black queer and trans artists. Recent projects include Poetry in Motion, a collaborative dance and poetry piece included in the HOT! Festival programming at Dixon Place; THE BLACK BEGINNING, a video series highlighting Black queer artists of varied artistic practices (now fiscally sponsored by the New York Foundation for the Arts); *WOMB! THERE IT IS!* and *BBL:* Black Beginning Live, both presented as part of LEGACY's 2022 Vision Residency at Ars Nova; and excerpts of *WOMB!* performed for Juneteenth in partnership with BOFFO and the Black and Brown Equity Coalition of Fire Island.

moss lovejoy (they/he, performer/choreographer/ educator/scholar) makes dance to feel community, control catharsis...sometimes these things are at odds with each other, and moss expects to be working through that for quite some time. Meanwhile, they earned a BFA in Dance from the University of the Arts ('17) and an MFA in Dance from Sarah Lawrence College ('23). He has performed at The Joyce Theater, Triskelion Arts, Brooklyn Arts Exchange, and Spoke the Hub, and shown work at Dixon Place, Arts On Site, Under St. Mark's, and Brooklyn Music School among others.

Zoey Lubitz is a curator and arts worker in New York. She co-directs the Center for Experimental Lectures with Gordon Hall, teaches art history at Bard College at Simon's Rock, and works in the archives of Felix Gonzalez-Torres.

Amber Jamilla Musser has published widely on race and critical theory, queer femininities and race, race and sexuality, and queer of color critique. She teaches at the CUNY Graduate Center and is the author of *SENSATIONAL FLESH: RACE, POWER, AND MASOCHISM* (NYU Press, 2014), *SENSUAL EXCESS: QUEER FEMININITY AND BROWN JOUISSANCE* (NYU Press, 2018), and *BETWEEN SHADOWS AND NOISE: SENSATION, SITUATEDNESS, AND THE UNDISCIPLINED* (Duke University Press, 2024).

Ann Pellegrini is Professor of Performance Studies & Social and Cultural Analysis at NYU, and a psychoanalyst in private practice in New York City. Their books include *PERFORMANCE ANXIETIES: STAGING PSYCHOANALYSIS, STAGING RACE*; *LOVE THE SIN: SEXUAL REGULATION AND THE LIMITS OF RELIGIOUS TOLERANCE* (co-authored with Janet R. Jakobsen); and *GENDER WITHOUT IDENTITY* (co-authored with Avgi Saketopoulou).

Phuong Phan (she/her) is a Vietnamese-German independent researcher and curator based in Berlin, Germany. Phuong is vested in the intricate interrelationship between art and social science. Her primary focus revolves around curating exhibitions rooted in anthropological research, exploring the domain of contemporary art emerging from Southeast Asia. She is interested in the complexities inherent in SEA contemporary art within the socio-historical and cultural landscape while juxtaposing this regional perspective within a broader global context Parallel to curatorial works she is writing on her PhD manuscript on socialist propaganda posters in Vietnam.

mik phillips (he/they) is a white, trans, queer, + fat multidisciplinary artist based on Lenni Lenape land (currently known as Philadelphia). their research deeply investigates how queerness inhabits performative structures and how in these spaces, vulgarities exist in simultaneity with notions of intimacy and care. he is committed to expanding on, continuing, remembering and moving inside and through queer futurity through the lens of movement based practices, text, sound/voice, collaboration and enactments. mik aims to distort time and go elsewhere while living inside a constant welling; a need for quivers, heaving, uncontrollable laughter, sobs, and indiscriminate violence guides them into creating temporary worlds that are maniacally unkempt and grotesquely forgiving.

Keioui Keijaun Thomas (she/her) is a Florida-born, New York City-based performance and multimedia artist. She received her Master of Fine Arts degree from the School of the Art Institute of Chicago and a Bachelor of Fine Arts degree with honors from the School of Visual Arts in New York. Thomas is a 2022 Recipient of the MAP Fund, the inaugural winner of the Queer | Art 2020 Illuminations Grant for Black Trans Women Visual Artists, and a Franklin Furnace Fund recipient in 2018.

Annie Sprinkle is an ecosexual multimedia artist who loves to collaborate with humans and other creatures and entities. Sprinkle began her career doing sex work and making adult films from 1973–95. She has documented her sexual evolution for over five decades, appearing in dozens of documentaries, arty films, and photographic works. Along the way, she met artists, activists and scholars who shaped her involvement in social justice, human rights, and freedom of expression, and she remains avidly committed to these ideals today. She has performed at the Museum of Modern Art (NY), the Venice Biennale, documenta 14 and received a Guggenheim Fellowship for filmmaking. She has authored six books, her last one being *ASSUMING THE ECOSEXUAL POSITION: THE EARTH AS LOVER* from University of Minnesota Press, which she co-authored with Beth Stephens, her beloved partner and collaborator of the last 21 years.

Gavilán Rayna Russom is a visionary artist, scholar and curator based in New York City. Over the past two decades she has produced a complex body of works oriented towards providing alternatives to binary thought and fixed modes of categorization. In addition to her recorded music, performance work, DJing practice, published writings and exhibitions, Rayna is the founding director of Voluminous Arts, a cultural organization that creates space for transgender artists to create expansively

Avgi Saketopoulou is a Cypriot and Greek psychoanalyst in private practice in NYC, and a member of the faculty at New York University's Postdoctoral Program in Psychotherapy and Psychoanalysis. She is the author of *SEXUALITY BEYOND CONSENT: RISK, RACE, TRAUMATOPHILIA* from the Sexual Cultures Series, NYU Press (2023), co-author, with Ann Pellegrini, of *GENDER WITHOUT IDENTITY,* from The Unconscious in Translation Press (2023), and in critical conversation with Dominique Scarfone in the volume *THE REALITY OF THE MESSAGE: PSYCHOANALYSIS IN THE WAKE OF JEAN LAPLANCHE* from The Unconscious in Translation Press (2023).

Kai Sundermann
Working as a rave illuminator under the alias WILDBLUR, Kai Sundermann plays with instruments of lambent dance and studies the w(e)aving of light, flesh, and sound. She is devoted to the sensuous conditions that nourish anti-colonial dissidence, seeking the renewal of our habits of assembly on dancefloors, streets, and shores earthwide.

Anh Vo is a Vietnamese choreographer, dancer, theorist, and activist. They create dances and produce texts about pornography and queer relations, about being and form, about identity and abstraction, about history and its colonial reality. Their critical writings focus on experimental practices and socio-economic relations in contemporary dance and pornography.

Geo Wyex (b. 1984, New York City) is an S.P.Y. artist and educator, based in Rotterdam, NL, working in music, performance, narrative sculpture, sound, and video. Their most recent record *ATM FM* (2020), was recorded in Rotterdam and released through Muck Studies Dept. - a constellational narrative framework, and an imaginary city agent surveying the bottom of low-lying water areas, "looking for stars out of what stinks." Muck Studies Dept. merges inherited black atlantic funk and folk poetics with techniques of investigative journalism. The project connects mud, water, metal gas, ass, rocks, coins, keys, extractive industry, and sensual expression of belonging to that flood. Research areas include New Orleans, New York, and the Netherlands.

Contributing Editors

Amalle Dublon

Kay Gabriel

Keioui Keijaun Thomas

Ahn Vo